WOMEN, ETHNICITY AND NATIONALISMS
IN LATIN AMERICA

Women, Ethnicity and Nationalisms in Latin America

Edited by

NATIVIDAD GUTIÉRREZ CHONG
Universidad Nacional Autónoma de México, Mexico

ASHGATE

Published by
Ashgate Publishing Limited
Gower House
Croft Road
Aldershot
Hampshire GU11 3HR
England

Ashgate Publishing Company
Suite 420
101 Cherry Street
Burlington, VT 05401-4405
USA

Ashgate website: http://www.ashgate.com

British Library Cataloguing in Publication Data
Women, ethnicity and nationalisms in Latin America
    1. Minority women - Latin America - History 2. Ethnicity -
    Latin America - History 3. Women - Latin America - Identity
    - History 4. Women in Politics - Latin America - History
    5. Nationalisms - Latin America
    I. Gutiérrez, Natividad, 1959-
    305.4'88'0098

Library of Congress Cataloging-in-Publication Data
Women, ethnicity and nationalisms in Latin America / edited by Natividad Gutiérrez Chong
    p. cm.
    Includes index.
    ISBN 978-0-7546-4925-0
    1. Women--Latin America--History. 2. Women in politics--Latin America--History. 3.
Nationalism--Latin America. I. Gutiérrez, Natividad, 1959-

    HQ1460.5.W626 2007
    305.48'80098--dc22

2007001515

ISBN 978-0-7546-4925-0

Printed and bound in Great Britain by Antony Rowe Ltd, Chippenham, Wiltshire.

Contents

PART 3   MULTICULTURALISM AND THE REVIVAL OF ETHNICITY

List of Figures

List of Tables

List of Contributors

Natividad Gutiérrez Chong received her PhD from the London School of Economics. She has researched and published extensively on indigenous peoples, women and nationalisms in Latin America. She was a founding member of the Association for the Study of Ethnicity and Nationalism (ASEN) and also of the newly funded Association for Research of Ethnicity and Nationalism in the Americas (ARENA). She is senior researcher and lecturer at the Social Sciences Institute of the National University of Mexico (UNAM). She is the current editor in chief of *Revista Mexicana de Sociología*.

Gabriela Bernal Carrera is an Anthropologist (UNAM). She has carried out research on ethnicity, gender and education. She is presently working on the indigenous movement of Ecuador and the transformation of the nation-state. She lectures in the School of Applied Anthropology at the Salesiana and Polytechnic University in Quito.

Elena Lazos Chavero is professor and researcher at the Institute of Social Sciences (UNAM) since 1992. He has a BSc in Biology (UNAM, Mexico), Master in Anthropology (ENAH, Mexico), Ph.D. in Anthropology and Socio-Economic Development (EHESS, France). His main topics of research are: conservation and management of natural resources, gender and natural resources, perceptions of risks and ecological deterioration, collective action, biotechnology and transgenics in rural societies. He is the author of three books, 22 book chapters and 15 scientific articles.

Arnd Schneider is Associate Professor of Social Anthropology, University of Oslo, and Reader in Anthropology, University of East London (on leave). He writes on contemporary art and anthropology, migration and ethnographic film and was co-organizer of Fieldworks: Dialogues between Art and Anthropology at Tate Modern, London (2003). His main publications include *Futures Lost: Identity and Nostalgia among Italian Immigrants in Argentina* (Peter Lang, 2000) and *Mafia for Beginners* (Ikon Books, 1994). He co-edited *Contemporary Art and Anthropology* (with Chris Wright, Berg Publishers, 2006), and his most recent monograph is *Appropriation as Practice: Art and Identity in Argentina* (Palgrave, 2006).

Irene Garcia is a PhD candidate of Cinema Studies at New York University. She previously earned a masters degree in Media Studies from the National University of Mexico. She is currently working on her dissertation regarding how Mexican immigrants in New York City use media to build transnational connections between their new place of residence and their hometowns in Mexico. She is also interested in Latino media produced in the United States and the current trends of the Latin American cinemas.

Ana Cristina Ramírez Barreto is lecturer in the Faculty of Philosophy at the Universidad Michoacana de San Nicolás de Hidalgo. She earned her B.A. in Philosophy at the same University (UMSNH), a Master's Degree in the Philosophy of Culture (also at the UMSNH), and her Ph.D. in Social Anthropology at the Centre for Anthropological Studies of El Colegio de Michoacán. Her Doctoral Thesis is entitled 'El juego del valor. Varones, mujeres y bestias en la charrería en Morelia 1923–2003' ('The Brave Game: Men, Women and Beasts in the Charrería, Morelia 1923–2003').

Leticia Janet Paredes Guerrero lectures and researches at the Centre of Regional Research Dr Hideyo Noguchi, Autonomous University of Yucatan. She has undertaken research on the political participation of Yucatecan women for her doctoral thesis. Some of her publications include: 'La mujer en la política' and 'La mujer en el ámbito municipal', Revista de la Universidad Autónoma de Yucatán, no. 201 (1997) and 'Mujeres y elecciones', *Origen, Gaceta de Mujeres en Lucha por la Democracia A.P.N.*, 2001.

Margarita Zárate obtained her PhD from University College, London. She is a senior researcher and lecturer in the Anthropology Department, Metropolitan Autonomous University (UAM), Iztapalapa, Mexico City. Her main research interests are: ethnic identities, gender and social movements. She is currently collaborating on a wider project on transnationalism. She has published on peasant and ethnic identities, gender, and subaltern movements.

María Eugenia Choque is an Aymara historian, former Director of the Oral History Andean Workshop in La Paz, Bolivia, and is a former grantee of The Rockefeller Foundation Indigenous Initiative housed at the Department of Native American Studies, University of California, Davis.

Guillermo Delgado-P. is an Andean anthropologist and obtained his PhD from the University of Texas, Austin. He lectures at the Latin American and Latino Studies Department, University of California, Santa Cruz. He is an active member of the Indigenous Research Centre, University of California, Davis. He is the current editor of Revista-*E* www.bolivianstudies.org at the Association of Bolivian Studies. Along with the musicologist John Schechter he edited the trilingual text *Quechua Expressive Art* from the Series Bonner Amerikanistische Studien (Bonn).

Maylei Blackwell is a lecturer at the Centre Cesar E. Chavez for Chicana Studies at the University of California, Los Angeles. Her present research looks at the different organizations undertaken by colour and indigenous women facing globalization. Her publications include: 'Contested Histories: las Hijas de Cuauhtémoc, Chicana Feminisms and Print Culture in the Chicano Movement, 1968-1973', Chicana Feminisms: A Critical Reader (Duke University Press), 'Encountering Latin American and Caribbean Feminisms', *Signs*, Journal of Women in Culture and Society (2002), and 'Time to Rise: US Women of Colour – Issues and Strategies' (available at www.coloredgirls.org).

Preface

The collapse of the Soviet Union and the re-emergence of ethnic conflict in Eastern Europe charged nationalism with renewed interest. In the academic field, the concept and meaning of nationalism became the centre of wide attention, as the implications of the break-up of once a powerful and culturally diverse nation-state could not be ignored. Nationalism re-emerging as the result of the disintegration of a unified nation-state posed, on the one hand, new problems of definition while on the other, prompted other areas of research. Nationalism, in general, became a prime focus of redefinition and rethinking.[1]

The reposition of nationalism was associated with unpredictable expressions of ethnic conflict and revival which seemed to have been suppressed during the process of nation-building and now were again flourishing. The revival of ethnicity was questioning the centrality of the nation-state. As the wave of nationalism was touching every corner of the globe, scholars working on Latin America,[2] were finding methodological avenues to connect their cases, and were interrogating the main approaches of nationalism addressed by leading scholars in a somehow inevitable Eurocentric framework.

What place was Latin America taking in the new current of thought? Why was it left as a different phenomenon not matching the overall concern of ethno-nationalist resurgence? Of course, the production of studies on Latin America is vast and diverse. As a case in point is the scholarly research on colonialism in the New World, or the pioneer ideologies of national liberation, resulting in a splendid historiography

---

1   One of the first expressions of academic concern made public was the organization of the first conference of the Association for the Study of Ethnicity and Nationalism (Asen) "Nationalism in a Post-Marxist World: Contemporary Reflections" (London School of Economics, 1991). This meeting reunited leading theoreticians on the field living at that time in Great Britain, Eric Hobsbawm, Anthony D. Smith, Ernst Gellner, Raymond Pearson, James Mayall, and Anthony Giddens, among others (See Gutiérrez N. and Smith, A.D., *Understanding Nationalism*, Montserrat Guibernau and John Hutchinson (eds), Polity Press, 2001, Preface). More international conferences have followed since then as well as academic projects, such as the journal *Nations and Nationalism*, together forming part of the multidisciplinary impulse of approaching the re-emergence of nationalism.

2   A similar experience was also extended to the USA and Canada. The foundation in 2005 of the Association for Research of Ethnicity and Nationalism in the Americas (ARENA) is a result of a group of scholars whose goal is to 'Promote research, knowledge, and understanding of nationalism, nation building, national identity, and ethnicity in the Americas and the larger world' http://www.cas.sc.edu/arena and H-Nationalism, an internet discussion group under the auspices of H-Net http://www.h-net.org/lists.

which paved the way for further studies on the new territorial nations.[3] But the scope of time of anticolonial struggles against European metropolis and empires which led to nation formation in Latin America (early eighteenth century) was difficult to connect with a revival of ethnicity within an independent and plurinational state in the late twentieth century. To put it in other words: the nations of Latin America were too old to match the new thinking. In addition to that, another vital factor was that ethnic conflict despite its historical prevalence in all regions of Latin America has not been itself manifested as a continuing threat to the existing nation-state. Ethnic conflict has so far not been a secessionist phenomenon in Latin America.[4] Another aspect which may help to explain the marginal side of Latin America in contemporary nationalist thinking is the debate between modernists and historical-culturalists (ethno symbolists) concerning the relevance of ethnic roots in the making of the modern nation.[5] The tension between the Pre-Colombian past and the indigenous peoples as emblematic carriers of ethnicity is a central theme of cultural history but not sufficiently framed in the dynamics of the debate of modern nationalism.[6]

The focus of nationalism in Latin America was mainly associated with political and economical features derived from the prevailing underdevelopment of the region. In which corporative politics, military and dictatorial regimes, overpowering parties, ideological discourses of official nationalism, among others,[7] took a forefront. The centralizing state in conducting strategies of unification and nationhood became a fruitful scholarly concern.[8] On the other hand, the multivariate role of the state in

---

3   Some examples: David Brading, *Los orígenes del nacionalismo Mexicano*, Sep Setentas, México, 1973; Gloria Grajales, *Nacionalismo incipiente en los historiadores coloniales*, Universidad Nacional Autonoma de Mexico, 1961, Antonello Gerbi, *Viejas polémicas sobre el nuevo mundo, en el umbral de una conciencia americana*, Banco de Crédito del Perú, Lima, 1946.

4   The presidency of the Aymaran Indian, Evo Morales, faces the proposals of autonomy from regional departments in the Eastern part of Bolivia. The Civic Committees of such proposal do not claim any Aymara or Quichua identity and regard themselves as a Hispanic group with Guarani ethno-cultural influence. They seek to constitute a federal asymmetric and plural state allowing the control of Bolivia's strategic and vast natural resources, that is oil and gas, in the territories of Santa Cruz, Beni and Pando (Juan Carlos Urenda Díaz, *Autonomías departamentales*, El país, Santa Cruz de la Sierra, 2003).

5   See The Warwick Debates on Nationalism (24 October 1995) http://members.tripod. com/GellnerPage/WarwickO.html. 'Do nations have navels?' *Nationalism*, Ernst Gellner, Weidenfeld & Nicolson Books, London, 1997.

6   See Gutiérrez, N. (2006) 'Ethnic Origins and Indigenous Peoples: An Approach from Latin America' in *Nationalism and Ethnosymbolism*. Athena Leoussi and Crosby, S. (eds.) (Edinburgh; University Press) (Forthcoming).

7   For a comprehensive overview of studies of nationalism in Latin America see, Nicola Miller 'The historiography of nationalism and national identity in Latin America', *Nations and Nationalism*, 12(2), April 2006, 201–223.

8   Alan and Knight (1986), *The Mexican Revolution*, 2 Vols (Cambridge: Cambridge University Press) and 1994, "Peasants into Patriots: Thoughts on the Making of the Mexican Nation", *Mexican Studies*, **10**(1), 135–163. Joseph Gilbert and D. Nugent (eds), *Everyday Forms of State Formation: Revolution and the Negotiation of Rule in Modern Mexico*, Durham, Duke University Press, 1994.

nation formation has given room to a fascinating area which has now been explored by creative and original research; this is the study of national identity expressed in art, architecture, literature, popular culture[9] The newly academic interest of nationalism connected to ethnicity has also been an approach undertaken in Latin American scholarship[10] well before the present chain of political mobilizations of indigenous peoples pressing for state recognition.

From different perspectives and through different approaches to viewing the national phenomenon of Latin America, my aim in this book is to put forward a typology of nationalisms underlying three concerns. Firstly, to establish conceptual differences between processes, that is to say, often labelled as nationalism are national liberation movements, national identity and nation formation. Secondly, to highlight the importance of historical research done on the making of the Latin American nation, which may not contain modern categories emerging in the context of the ethnic visibility brought by the collapse of the Soviet state. Nationalism in Latin America has been certainly well studied but from other perspectives. Thirdly, to provide a methodological framework to explain, another issue neglected by current theories and debates: the roles of women in nationalisms.[11]

We then distinguish three types of nationalisms distinctive to Latin America from the early nineteenth century up to the present.

1. The wars of independence
2. The nation – building process
3. The construction of the multicultural nation.

Each one of these types would be fully approached in Chapter 1, for the moment it would be enough to say, that they would interact with the typology of gender and nationalisms proposed by Anthias and Yuval-Davis (1989).

The book, then, follows four axes. The first identifies the way in which women have contributed to build the different stages of a nation, as it interrogates the processes by which the state and its institutions have, by means of racial and ethnic arguments, excluded women from the nation. The second explores the ways in which women have participated in the ethnic and nationalist movements of the present. The third shows that, if nationalism and the national culture are unimaginable without an array of subjective factors such as myths, traditions, symbols and icons, these at the same time glorify and idealize the female body. The female body has been

---

9   William Rowe and Viviane Schelling, *Memory and Modernity: Popular Culture in Latin America* (London: Verso, 1991). Sara Radcliffe and Sallie Westwood, 1996, *Remaking the Nation: Place, Identity and Politics en Latin America* (London: Routledge).

10 Mallon, F., *Peasant and Nation: The Making of Postcolonial Mexico and Peru* (Berkeley: University of California Press).

11 George L. Moss in his *Nationalism and sexuality* (University of Wisconsin Press, 1985) explored the gender category in the nationalist imaginary. Anthony D. Smith also made an account of the importance of women and female icons ('El papel de las mujeres en el nacionalismo', *Nacionalismo y Modernidad*, Istmo, 2000) as his theoretical approach concedes weight to subjective factors such as symbols, *Myths and Legends* and these cannot be fully understood if separated from gender and its far reaching symbolic associations.

portrayed to represent such essentialist features vital for the making of ethnic or national identities as mother-nature, as a symbol of homeland and belongingness, and as the mother-patria/fatherland. The last axis explored in this book emphasizes the incessant dynamic of the nation, its identity and culture by studying those groups of women who are closely linked with intellectual, academic and artistic endeavours, and who have initiated the conceptualization and socialization of their own ideas of thinking and envisaging culture, history or political sovereignty.

The book starts by addressing the main theoretical corpus of gender/nationalism and their intersections according to recent bibliographical sources. Chapter 1, written by Natividad Gutiérrez focuses on a methodological proposal for the complementary study of the roles played by women and the different types of nationalism. Although the chapter elaborates the Mexican case, it sheds light on the nationalist stages of other Latin American nations dealt with in this volume such, as Ecuador, Bolivia and Argentina. The first type of nationalism addresses the issues of planning and further struggle upon independence from the colonial regime; the second refers to the processes set in motion by the sovereign state with the aim of building up a nation; the third type, which is not necessarily defined as a political movement seeking the emergence of a new state, concerns the political and cultural expressions that interrogate the basis of the homogeneous or monocultural project of nationhood – the main idea structuring the nation of the new millennium. The methodological device of these three types of nationalism introduces and guides the discussion throughout the sections of the book; it imposes, moreover, a conceptual order on the many meanings of modern nationalisms all over Latin America.

The empirical cases included in the first section, Struggle and Independence, show the long span trajectory of conflict, demand and struggle, as well as the different collective efforts on the part of women to create ideas of common origin, to access natural resources and participate politically in the taking of decisions in their community organizations. Gabriela Bernal, in Chapter 2, undertakes a discourse analysis of the Quechua heroine Dolores Cacuango (1881–1971). Her written discourse underpins her vision and ideas of reconciliation between classes and factions, as well as an apology of pride of belongingness. An ethnic discourse of unity, contradicting the nationalist discourse delivered by the political and intellectual elites of the state in this Andean region has not facilitated the integration of popular classes and indigenous peoples within a pact of national unity. This shortage of the nationalist rhetoric on the part of the Ecuadorian state is undermined by the discourse concerning the common origin of the Ecuadorian peoples. Such discourse of unity 'which understands and includes everyone' deals significantly with the whole nation, and her proposal plants a common seed of origin which is at the beginning of any nationalist project. The following chapter, by Elena Lazos pertinently shows the construction of an empowering process among Nahua women of the Santa Marta Sierra, Veracruz. This example on the sustainability access, points as a specific way of understanding the process of constructing autonomy or independence which is at the core of this book. According to Lazos's analysis, the opening of political spaces of representation is an activity that is giving visibility to Nahua women of Tatahuicapan but certainly it could be well expanded to other organizing experiences of indigenous women. This theme gains consistency throughout the book as the discussion on the types of relation that indigenous women have established with the nation-state is progressing.

In the section, 'Nation-building and Identity', the book explores the second type of nationalism by means in which culture and national identity have used, celebrated or invented feminine stereotypes and archetypes. This section examines the many approaches to visual languages and discourses, that is to say, calendars, scripts and narratives which contain information and different possibilities of interpretation that may lead to new and fruitful lines of analysis. For example, the calendar popularizes 'Mexican-ness', through the idealization of the body of the mestiza woman or the legend of the 'sleeping woman' (Iztacihuatl volcano), which forms part of the central Mexican landscape. This is the perspective Gutiérrez utilizes to understand the popular imagination of nationalism. Using the same visual resource of the calendar, Arnd Schneider presents a creative approach to the construction of stereotypes of indigenous woman in the Argentinian society. Through the analysis of the photographs illustrating a calendar of the year 2000, Schneider shows how the photographer and the producer seek to recreate a nostalgic yearning for the durability of indigenous cultures in the Argentinian present, despite its European structures of cultural and racial types. His concern is the exclusion of indigenous women from the visual discourse of the nation and the attempts to reinstate an authentic origin by exploiting the female body to portray stereotypes of European beauty and glamour within rustic, primitive or even wildly exotic contexts, which recreate romanticized scenarios of indigenous life.

Further chapters offer new explorations of situations in which nationalism (as a doctrine, theory or movement) is no longer a masculine sphere alone and of the ways in which women have transformed nationalism creatively. The case of the first Mexican filmmaker, Mimí Derba, and her own ideas of 'Mexican-ness' are discussed by Irene García. Derba's vision and cinematographic discourse were pioneering acts in creating nationalistic aesthetics, which would later be consolidated during the so-called golden age of Mexican cinema. Derba, like the journalist Anita Brenner (Gutiérrez, Chapter 1), lived in the post-revolutionary ambience and contributed to its construction. At this time, Mexico began to gain cultural prestige by researching and recreating themes of Mexican national identity through culture, such as the landscape, pre-Columbian art traditions and values. The singer, Astrid Hadad (Gutiérrez, Chapter 1), can be added to this discussion; these women, Mimí, Anita and Astrid, at different times and by different means were able to forge their own visions, symbols and artefacts of Mexican 'originality', themes intrinsic to the understanding of the complex architecture of the national culture, a complementary aspect of the structural nation-building. Chapter 5 refers to a fictitious heroine, Eréndira. Ana Cristina Ramirez discusses the visual language of an Indian woman resisting the impact of the Spanish conquest on horseback. The murals painted by Eduardo Ruiz, and analysed by Ramírez, present a refreshing reading on the roles and stereotypes associated with women and heroism. The nation's unity in the vision of Dolores Cacuango, the political consciousness of Josefa Ortiz de Dominguez at the eve of Mexican independence and the symbolical empowerment attributed to an indigenous woman, Eréndira, are examples showing heroic roles of defiance, disobedience and bravery. The final chapter of this section brings to the core; the political involvement of women in building their own routes of membership with respect to political parties and the formation of leadership and voting promises among the Maya women of Yucatan, according to the study presented by Leticia Paredes.

The policy to construct and develop the nation-state without the participation of women in general and indigenous women in particular, renders visible a gender exclusion that crosses ethno-racial boundaries. It is evident, however, from the mobilizations and political rallies of the last 10 years, that women are in the process of finding not only a voice of their own but also new identities by means of retelling the current theme of autonomy and adding their particular significance to it. Autonomy from the gender and ethnic perspective has shared purposes of transforming traditional practices based on oppression, domination and patriarchy, and substituting them with collective and individual power to take decisions, as we shall see in the final section of this book, 'Multiculturalism and the Revival of Ethnicity'.

The debate of multiculturalism and gender in the construction of an inclusive nation is a theme of theoretical significance in this book. Margarita Zárate in Chapter 8 initiates the discussion by addressing that a multicultural or plural nation faces the structural and legal challenge of including the politics of recognition towards indigenous peoples, women and, consequently, indigenous women. Such double recognition adds complexity to the debate and thus, the importance of revising the meanings of nation, power and localisms from a gender perspective. This section provides also the ground to highlight the argument connecting education, information, and identity reconstruction. Education and literacy for women as discussed in Chapter 1 helped to push to the front ideologies and projects for defence and emancipation, the same ideas and concepts that are behind female collective action for constructing an inclusive and diverse nation. In this light, Chapter 9 foregrounds the resurgence of indigenous oral narratives. In this case, it is the intellectual creativity of Andean women that substantiates the third type of nationalism. The intellectual production of women, that is, the transmission of the oral or written words, is another theme explored in this book. Such a field is even more than necessary when a fourth element can be added to the so-called triple oppression of indigenous women (gender, ethnicity and poverty): 'lack of information'. Thus, Delgado and Choque make an outstanding contribution with their chapter on the 'ethnic feminisms', which inspire the new leadership of indigenous women through the revisited analysis of collective mythologies in the Quechua language aimed at questioning the ethno genesis and historical revisionism of Bolivian official nationalism. The final chapter of this section is that of Maylei Blackwell, who offers a detailed and up-dated discussion of the way in which indigenous women interact with political movements, which have, since 1994, gained momentum through the analytic axes of collective rights, habits, customs and the double practice of autonomy from the perspective of ethnic women.

Natividad Gutiérrez Chong
IIIS, UNAM, Mexico City

Acknowledgements

This volume has received financial support from CONACYT SEP-2004-C01-46149/A1. Yeni Briones Saldaña is acknowledged for the major task of putting together all chapters with remarkable efficiency and skill.

Thanks to Charlotte Broad for her editorial advice.

Translations of non-English terms and languages are by authors.

Chapter 1

Women and Nationalisms

Natividad Gutiérrez Chong

Introduction

'All nationalisms and national projects are gender-oriented' (McClintock, 1993, p. 61; Walby, 2000). However, there is not a single definition of nationalism that can be applied to the range of events, ideologies, movements or collective expressions of defence and/or pride that relate to the national subject. Also, we can draw up a double side scope of women and the nation. On the one hand, the use of the female body in a mythology, symbolism and iconography of national identity; on the other, the set of tensions, paradoxes and contradictions prevalent in the concepts of nation and nationalism. In other words, what we have is intense nationalist idealization contrasting sharply with a more trouble-prone field of analysis characterized by the interrelationship of women and the nation state.

Our purpose in this chapter contemplates an innovative proposal: to put forward a methodology for the complementary study of the roles played by women and the different facets of nationalism in Mexico. We refer to types of nationalism and we distinguish three stages: the wars of independence, the nation-building process and the multicultural nation. We have identified these types reflected in the research literature produced from an historical perspective in Mexico (Brading, 1998; Knight, 1986; Lomnitz-Adler, 1992; Gutiérrez, 1999; Van Cott, 2000). After identifying each type, the strategy then would apply for each stage the typology of gender roles and intersections of nationalism proposed by Floya Anthias and Nira Yuval-Davis in 1989. This methodology or approach to the different types of nationalism and women's roles illustrates the need to develop a system of classification, given the multidimensionality of the phenomenon of nationalism. This perspective allows us to mitigate the inevitable risks of interpretation should one attempt to demonstrate that one nation and its corresponding nationalism are the same as any other. Accordingly, the roles of women in the public and nationalist domain historically have not been always the same.

This chapter has two sections. The first identifies the main types of nationalism in Mexico, and their inter-relation with gender roles as defined by Floya Anthias and Nira Yuval-Davis. The second section leads on from this initial identification, and illustrates it with specific characters and situations taken from history.

Women and Nationalisms

The history of nationalism has revealed the notable absence of women, which was one of the reflections made by Catherine Hall in Bellagio (1992), in a gathering of women and the results were later published in the *Feminist Review* (4, 1993). 'If nationalism is not transformed by the analysis of gender power, the nation-state will remain a repository of male hopes, male aspirations and male privileges' (McClintock, 1993, p. 77). Or, 'Until gender is taken up as a matter of course by historians of nationalism and international relations, the preferences for masculinity and the form of sexual difference inscribed in the theories and practices of nationalism will continued to be exercised even in epochs where they appear to be absent' (Sluga, 2000, p. 517).

These opinions have contributed to highlighting the question of nationalism as hegemonic mode/discourse/practice whilst feminists and colonized natives began to find channels to claim their inheritance and their place in history as well as in national projects. What has been done so that nationalism ceases to be the exclusive terrain of masculine dominion? What findings does feminist research report? Previous to the Bellagio symposium on 'Gender, Nationalisms and National Identities' (July, 1992), two seminal texts had appeared: that of Kumari Jayawardena (1986) *Feminism and Nationalism in the Third World*; and, in 1989, *Women-Nation-State* by Floya Anthias and Nira Yuval-Davis. Jayawardena's book opened the discussion between two ideologies and movements which had not until then been linked, feminism and nationalism, and which, apparently, belonged to fields of analysis in which dialogue was not possible. It also managed to present the policies and aspirations of women in the Developing World in the context of their struggle for rights and the civil movements which differed from the concerns of the Western feminist academy and its interlocutors, white middle-class women. For their part, Anthias and Yuval-Davis (1989, p. 7) identified the five principal ways in which intersections between women and nationalism could be found, as we shall see later in this chapter.

Gender and nationalism were the focus of the special edition of *Nations and Nationalism* (Vol 6. 4, 2000). Criticism of the forms of exclusion of the national project, its genderisation and, as a result, the ambiguity in which women find themselves with respect to the nation and nationalism, are recurrent main ideas in authors such as Cusack (2000); Kandiyoti (2000), Sluga (2000) and Walby (2000) and those who implicitly or explicitly have elaborated on the ideas of Anthias and Yuval-Davis (1989). The contradictions of nationalism, modernity and backwardness, the urban and rural, tradition and culture, reappear and intensify upon tackling the situation of women, although almost immediately, it will be evident that women are housed in the most conservative niches.

There is a tendency to stress, the passive and traditional role of women as opposed to a more dynamic and enterprising project of the masculine world. For McClintock, men and women have different trajectories vis-à-vis the modern nation: 'while women present the traditional face of the nation (inert, backward-looking, and natural), men represents the progressive feature of national modernity (forward-thrusting, potent and historic)' (1993, 66). Women are the repositories of authenticity and originality which all nations pursue, while their rights in the political terrain of legality are delayed. We do not find elements in these affirmations that undermine the importance of nationalist symbolism, which, were it not to exist, would make any nationalism unthinkable. In other words, in spite of feminist criticism and its focus on denouncing the 'backward', 'traditional', 'excluded', and, of course, scarcely privileged situation of women, we believe their role as 'guardians', 'custodians' or 'carriers' cannot be ignored. In fact, there is no nationalism lacking symbolism and, if such symbolism incarnates the exaltation and celebration of domestic space, then the body or the heroic feat of women is neither a trivial not minor affair. In short, there are several roles which women assume in nationalisms, it is not only a question of seeing women as symbols or 'garments', but as social actors who are implicated in national processes in differing ways (Walby, 2000, p. 527 and Kandiyoti, 2000, p. 490).

Nationalism

It is wide spread the assumption that nationalism, has 'typically sprung from masculinized memory, masculinized humiliation and masculinized hope' (Enloe, 1989, p. 44 in McClintock, 1993, p. 62), or that it is a doctrine invented in Europe at the beginning of the nineteenth century (Kedourie in Leuossi, 2001, p. 230). The term, however, is multidimensional in the span of time and embraces a multiplicity of meanings. It is current thought that the modern world cannot be conceive without the impact of nationalism and its different forms and manifestations, namely, ideology, doctrine, state of mind, feelings of loyalty, ideals of independence, ethnic resurgence and folklore. Nevertheless, a certain consensus does exist regarding nationalism as a modern doctrine bestowing legitimacy on a nation. For Schoplin, the principals of nationalism are 'the proposition that the world is divided into nations and only nations, that each nation possesses a shared past and a future, and possibly that each nation is connected to a particular territory, which may also be symbolic' (in Leoussi, p. 25). Certainly, for 'the world to be divided into nations', the strategies of both colonies and metropolis, from the end of the eighteenth century, have been numerous, unpredictable and profoundly complex. Furthermore, they have not occurred at the same time nor pursued the same logic, which makes it difficult to coin a unique definition or a sole route of access to nationalism.

The doctrine of nationalism, however, seeks the fulfilment of independence and the capacity for self-government by a population (ethnic group or nation) in pursuit of recognition or differentiation vis-à-vis other populations. The sociology of nationalism has placed Europe in a privileged position as the cradle of the doctrine, mainly on account of the ideals of freedom and fraternity of the French Revolution, but the doctrine's first expression of colonial emancipation takes place with North America's War of Independence. The Declaration of Independence, on 4 July 1776, contributed to the creation of a political atmosphere that would put an end to colonial tutelage and disintegrate the viceroyalties and captaincies of the Americas. In our definition, nationalism is the quest for and consolidation of a state and, with it, self-sufficiency, sovereignty and self-determination.

If there is no one nationalism, but rather different types (see Hall, 1993), let us now look at possible characterizations for Latin America.

Table 1.1   Types of nationalisms in Latin America

1.   The first type of nationalism or the creation of the sovereign state
Wars of independence which marked the end of colonial rule
Territorial neigbouring disputes and territorial delimitation
Formation of the state and government popularly elected
Draft of Constitution
Defense against foreign intervention
2.   The second type of nationalism or the nation-building process
Nationalization of economies
Cultural homogeneization and linguistic unification
Socialization and standarization
Infraestructure and comunication
Assimilation of indigenous peoples
National identity formation
3.   The third type of nationalism or the multicultural nation
Economic neoliberalism
Indigenous uprisings, revivals and claims for recognition
Ethnic and gender awarness for self-defense
Democratization of the state
Human rights
Recognition and legitimation of difference of ethnic and gender boundaries
Constitutional rights for free determination and autonomy

Source: Proprietary based on 'Nacionalismos y conflictos etnicos', CONACYT. Gutiérrez, N. (2006).

1. **The creation of a sovereign state**   Achievement of self-determination of a people (emergence and consolidation of the state stemming from anticolonial struggles for freedom, popularly elected governments and constitutions, 18th–19th centuries).

2. **The process of construction of the nation by the state**   The forging of the nation-state by means of an official nationalism and institutions, 19th–20th centuries.

3. **The construction of the multicultural nation**   The capacity for negotiation and leadership of those ethnic movements or projects which question the homogeneity of the contemporary nation-state which in its turn recognizes plurality as a condition for greater participatory democracy, end of twentieth century up to the present.

In what follows I will identify some of the main process or situations that characterize the three types above mentioned in an effort to add conceptual clarification. (See Table 1.1.)

    In each of these types, it is likely to be applied the five principal ways in which intersections between women and nationalism could be found according to the typology of Anthias and Yuval-Davis:

Table 1.2 Three types of nationalism with the five intersections of women's roles in Mexico

Types of nationalism	Women's roles	Characters
1. Independence	A. Biological reproducer	Mothers
	B. Reproducers of national boundaries (honour/shame complex)	Creole *Mestiza* Indian
	C. Transmitter of national culture*	No role of women
	D. Symbolic signifier of national difference**	No role of women
	E. Active participant in national struggles	Josefa Ortíz de Domínguez

* *The intellectual production of women on the concepts or ideas of nation was not visible in the pre-nationalist era.*
** *It is still ambiguous to identify a nationalist symbol of gender before independence.*

2. Nation-Building	A. Biological reproducer	Mothers
	B. Reproducer of national boundaries	*Mestiza* / Miscegenation
	C. Transmitter of national culture	Anita Brenner (Journalist) Frida Kahlo (Painter) Female School Teachers Malinche (Symbol of *Mestiza*) Patria/Motherland in free textbooks (Mexican Educational System)
	D. Symbolic signifier of national difference	Iztacchiuatl. The Volcano symbolising a sleeping woman (Almanacs and calendars)* Virgin of Guadalupe (Highly popular symbol as the Mother of the Mexican people)
	E. Active participant in national struggles	No role of women
3. Multicultural Nation	A. Biological reproducer	Mothers
	B. Reproducer of national boundaries	*Mestiza* / Miscegenation
	C. Transmitter of national culture	Astrid Hadad (Singer) Margo Glantz (Writer) Female School Teachers
	D. Symbolic signifier of national difference	Malinche Virgin of Guadalupe
	E. Active participant in national struggles	Commander Ramona (EZLN) Marta Sanchez (ANIPA Leader)

Source: 'Patriotic thoughts or intuition: roles of women in Mexican nationalisms', *Nations and Nationalism*, Issue 12.2. Permission granted by the editors of *Nations and Nationalism, Journal of the Association for the Study of Ethnicity and Nationalism* (London School of Economics).

as biological reproducers of the members of national collectivities
as reproducers of the boundaries of national groups (through restrictions on sexual and
marital relations)
as active transmitters and producers of the national culture
as significant symbols of national difference
as symbolic signifiers of national difference
as active participants in national struggles (1989, p. 7)

Our methodological proposal is to build up a model of explanation able to identify the interaction of women and nation by combining the inter-relation of the three types of nationalism with the five intersections of women's roles. (See Table 1.2.)

Such model aims at a double purpose. First, to demonstrate the different historical routes implied in nation formation, from struggles against colonialism to the present political claims for the recognition of ethnic and gender differences. This exercise helps to establish theoretical separateness between periodization of historical stages and their corresponding definitions thus, avoiding confusion when confronting an 'ideal of independence' which is not equivalent or interchangeable with the category of 'nation-building' also widely understood as nationalism. Second, the typology of the five intersections regarding women's roles is likely to be applied to each one of these types. And this typology informs us in greater detail about the various ways in which women have been involved in the multiple dynamics and process of inclusion and exclusion of nationhood. As a result, we aim to build a theoretical approach capable of responding to numerous enquiries on how women have interacted with the nation. Anthias and Yuval-Davis's typology is applicable to every national formation; however, we are to focus on its relevance when applied to the case of Mexico and for extension to Latin America.

To be able to locate Mexican women's roles in the three types of nationalism, Table 1.2 shows in columns 1 and 2, their participation in various fields and their invisibility, or exclusion. By adding the third column 'character' we are providing clear cut identity to either 'real historical woman' or to 'symbols'. Furthermore, our exercise helps to identify them in more than one role in the three types of nationalism, and, as previously stated, these roles can be simultaneous, combined or separated.

In each type of nationalism, women have participated in various roles; the unmistakable female role of *biological reproduction*, appears obvious, while others display a degree of variance. The *symbolic signifier of national difference* and the *participation of women in national struggles* are not always present in all nationalisms. The emergence of women as *transmitters of national culture* within the second type of nationalism is also worth noting, and to this we must add their creative ability to imagine, think and articulate their own ideas of nationalism and identity, as we shall see in the section of the nation-building process.

The First Type of Nationalism or the Creation of a Sovereign State

Towards 1809, the first uprising for independence takes place in Quito. A year later, urban districts in Buenos Aires, Caracas and Santiago witness large-scale mobilization. In the central provinces of Mexico, too, the peasants revolt. The wars of independence continued for a period of 20 years, with millions of civilian deaths and cruel repression for rebel leaders and their followers (Lynch, 1986; Brading, 1991, Mallon, 1995). Were there women whose libertarian deeds sought to abolish colonialism and attain the independence ideal? Or is it only possible to identify pre-nationalist women in the domestic milieu and delimited by a patriarchal and sexist structure? (see Gutiérrez, 1995; Stern, 1999)

In a section of a previous study 'Women in revolt or creating the homeland' (Gutiérrez, 1999) we referred to the 'heroines of independence'. This particular study led us to formulate the following question, which we now develop here: was nationalism in Mexico and in Latin America introduced as 'an European doctrine' or did it acquire form as 'protonationalism', that is, collective feelings of belonging, even at the macro-political level, without confining itself to the modern nation-state (Hobsbawm, 1990, p. 46), or as racialized and sexualized feelings of exclusion? That a generation of women born during the final decade of the 18th century and the beginning of the 19th acted knowingly in support of independence ideals is beyond question. Fernandez de Lizardi (1776–1827) dedicates his 1825 Calendar to the patriotism and sacrifice of the heroines, whose 'act of love for the homeland has filled the weaker sex with courage and fragile women have achieved extraordinary deeds' (Agraz García de Alba, 1992, p. 14).

If the only way of knowing about nationalism was by spreading its doctrine, then where did these women acquire or learn about the ideals of independence? If the conclusion is that such a doctrine can only be accessed via the transmission and diffusion of ideals, then we are inclined to think that it had less impact among women. The nation, or the homeland, the latter term now in disuse but greatly popular in the period we are dealing with, are linked to the access of ideas, if we base ourselves on B. Anderson's frequently cited phrase of the 'imaginary community' (1990). A deductive argument indicates that only male Mexicans in the 18th century onwards were in a position to share in the current of ideas and, therefore, form part of the nation under construction. Why only males? Three centuries of colonial life had restricted women to the home, the convent or the church. Men from elite families received ecclesiastical instruction or attended colleges or universities. Reading and writing, in Spanish and Latin, provided access to ideas and discussion, and this was determined by gender and ethno-racial stratification. An estimate of the high levels of illiteracy among women in Mexican society in the nineteenth century has been sketched by Arrom (1985). The number of women who could not sign their own wills, in a period from 1802 to 1803, was 80 in a sample of 100 (p. 21). This criterion is even more significant if we consider that wills and dowries were the exclusive concern of white, middle- and high-class women. An analysis of two newspapers from Mexico City concludes that those articles on 'feminine culture' included subjects solely related to the interests of a privileged class. Although these articles appeared with certain regularity – 1,875 were recorded in *El Diario de México*, – 'not one was written by a woman' (Lavrín, 1978, p. 201). What is more, women from the Mexican elite did not write personal diaries, much less novels (Arrom, 1985, p. 13).

In an effort to describe in greater detail this astonishing panorama of intellectual sparsity among Mexican women, a widespread search I carried out on those publications signed by women from the second half of the nineteenth century. Two publications were unearthed: *Albún de la Mujer* (1883–1990), whose editor was a Spanish woman,

Concepción Gimeno de Flaquer, and *Violetas del Anáhuac*, under the direction of Laureana Wright de Kleinhans. I selected articles from both publications which, implicitly or explicitly, referred to the 'homeland', 'heroes', 'prominent women' and 'legends'. My selection also included literary production, poetry to be precise, the genre common in this kind of publication (National General Archive (AGN)).

Female illiteracy (see Muriel, 1974; Sefchovich, 1999) was overwhelming, while the few women capable of reading were restricted to texts of a religious nature. Thus, in spite of the 'imaginary community's' great popularity, this included men only, and if colonial women became informed of nationalism, it was not by reading newspapers and novels. Let us now review the political action of women performing independence-related deeds by taking a look at the most famous heroine of Mexico's civic pantheon, Ortiz de Domínguez (1768–1829).

Speculation and legend play a part in her story. Married to a 'corregidor' (a magistrate appointed by the King), she helped organize the outbreak of the popular revolution of independence (15 September 1810). Some twentieth century historians have attempted to minimize the role played by Josefa Ortiz. For example, a work written in 1909 by Luis Gonzalez Obregon alleges that she acquired her political awareness and patriotism by earwigging conversations between the writer, Joaquin Fernandez de Lizardi and a Creole supporter of independence at the latter's house where it is said Josefa worked as a maid (difficult to believe, if Josefa was the wife of the Corregidor Domínguez) (Agraz García de Alba, 1992). It is interesting to note the emphasis that biographers and historians have put on the fact that the ideas of liberty which Josefa pursued were heard clandestinely. The 'cry of Independence' ('Grito de Dolores')[1] is avoided due to Josefa's well-timed intervention, who had heard, as wife of the 'corregidor', that the conspiracy has been uncovered.

This lack of recognition of patriotic sentiment (or intuition), attributed to women, has been refuted by a biographer of Josefa Ortiz, Gabriel García Agraz. Josefa, like any other person not born in the Spanish peninsula, of mestizo and mulatto origins, was naturally sensitive to daily experiences of humiliation, contempt and segregation. Why should it be difficult to imagine that such a markedly adverse situation were capable of creating the need for liberation and self-government among women, Josefa among them? The biographer in question, García Agraz, notes that, curiously, Lizardi does not include Josefa in his commemorative calendar, and ventures the hypothesis that there was never any contact between them. Josefa is, for conventional historiography, the woman who contributed to independence, by the simple act of listening to the conversations of the insurgents from behind closed doors or screens.

> While the Corregidor (Josefa's spouse) was running the prison of Epigmenio, his wife (Josefa), conscious of the risk that the conspiration ran of coming to nothing and that those involved in it might be apprehended, if prompt and effective measures were not taken, tried to give Allende immediate warning of the point which things had reached. Her bedroom was above the dwelling of the prison warder, which was, as in nearly all the capitals of the province, in the basement of the Government building. The warder was called Ignacio

---

1   It refers to the beginning of the armed struggle of Independence (16 September 1810).

Perez and he was one of the active agents of the conspiracy. The Corregidor's spouse, careful and vigilant, had agreed with him that, on any urgent occasion, she would call him by giving three blows on the ceiling of the room which he occupied. Upon hearing that signal, Ignacio Perez hastily went out into the street, drawing near to the hallway of the Corregidor's spouse, where she, having rapidly come downstairs, was waiting for him. There, through the lock and with her lips to the keyhole, she told him what was happening, entrusting him to immediately warn Allende, who was to be found at the villa of San Miguel el Grande. (Wrigth de Kleinhans, 1910, p. 293)

For official historiography, her heroic act was not the transmission of ideas or ideals, of winning violent battles or making one's mark, it was rather the ability to emit a whisper at precisely the right time. How do we explain this heroic deed, typified in gender role in studies of nationalism? In the initial phase of the building of a separate identity, it is not surprising to find confusion between racial or cultural hatred, on the one hand, and the conscious need to defend a territory, a village or a history, on the other. Characteristic of the former are feelings of humiliation, deprivation, outrage, discrimination, while for the latter, we count on projects, ideologies or strategies.

In the twentieth century, further historians added their names to the list of those who tended to underestimate the patriotic feelings of women, seeing these as manifestations of simple racial hatred. This is understandable insofar as patriotism is a rational intellectual construction, rooted in the knowledge of rights, and a reaction to the usurpation of these as well as the awareness of the differences. On the other hand, 'simple racial hatred' is an emotional manifestation caused by rejection and discrimination. Thus, the prominent liberal, Jose Maria Luis Mora, made this comment about Josefa's patriotism: 'The wife of Domínguez, whose only idea of independence was to feel hatred towards the Spanish, having conspiring against them, then joined the rebels' (cited by Agraz García de Alba 1992, p. 56).

Josefa died in 1829. It was not until 1885–1890 that a journalist circulated a portrait of Josefa in a special publication designed to celebrate the events of September 1910 so that her patriotism could be more widely known. In her book *Mujeres Notables Mexicanas* (1910), Laureana Wright de Kleinhans, on the subject of the most eloquent period of the 'invented traditions' of Mexico in the 20th century, states:

> From that moment on, as a result of one of those inconceivable ingratitudes on the part of peoples, the veil of oblivion fell heavily and coldly upon the memory of the Heroic patrician. When celebrating the anniversary of Mexican National Independence, her name would no longer figure alongside those of Hidalgo, Allende, Abasolo and Aldama, whom she had saved in her perilous enterprise, not to mention the cowardly consciences of those who were scandalised that a woman should have the audacity to become involved in political affairs and should have endured the stigma of general excommunication heaped upon the insurgents. (p. 303)

In the long war of independence, other examples of patriotism are attributed to maternal abnegation and the sacrifice of the home and the family. An interesting passage in Wright's book exemplifies a moment of intense patriotic idealization:

> On the memorable morning of 16 September, 1810, the honourable family (Maria del Rosario Diaz, married to Ignacio Acevedo, weaver of wraps) was awoken from its

tranquil sleep by the roll of drums and bells, which announced the proclamation of the independence cause and, hardly had Ignacio understood what was happening, he told his wife that he was going to talk to the priest, Hidalgo, taking his eldest son with him.

The heroic Rosario, feeling the sacred fire of patriotism well up in her soul, far from bursting into faint-hearted complaints and tears, or opposing the departure of her husband and son, like vulgar women, not only approved of their fulfilling their duty as citizens, but, full of enthusiasm, exclaimed with spartan courage: "Ignacio, take my son Lorenzo, too; he is big already and can defend his country".

The husband hesitated a moment, but then, combining in his mind what he owed to the homeland with what he owed to the home, he replied: "No; we are going to war and may not come back; let Lorenzo stay so that, if that happens, he can look after the weaving and support you".

The two patriots left, and the heroic woman, satisfied with her behaviour sat before the loom, replacing the absentees in the work and keeping house for the whole period of Hidalgo's revolution, until, with the death of the leader, her husband and her eldest son came home, having had the luck to be respected by the Spanish bullets. (Wrigth de Kleinhans, 1910, p. 243)

Women displayed not so much ideals but acts, which subsequently favoured the plan for independence. To judge by the high levels of illiteracy prevailing among them, the ideas of independence were believed to be a matter for men only. Patriotism and independence were not only ideals and doctrines imported from the French Revolution and the Enlightenment. Had this point of view been enough, then we would not have had women fighting so as not to be left out. But they too felt solid affiliation, which was seen in sentiments produced by the injustice of discrimination and because Mexico was governed by the Spanish crown. It was not necessary to know what a political ideal was to sense the injustice and embrace the need for sacrifice and defence. Using ingenuity, common sense, physical strength, fate or discretion, these women were instrumental in establishing a network of communication between one group of insurgents and another, sounding the alarm when conspiracy was at risk, helping soldiers injured, providing food and, above all, managing to master the terror of torture, capital punishment and imprisonment. For these women, it was never a question of glory but of martyrdom. Were they found out, their faith in the patriotic cause remained steadfast. In an anonymous document entitled 'A call to women to fight for independence, 1812', women were urged to join the struggle by taking up 'cruel swords' and joining Morelos and Hidalgo against usurpation, domination and the loss of male relatives. The handwritten document, with the spelling and syntax of the period, carried moreover an illustration of two women adorned with hats and drawn swords. (AGNM, Ramo Operaciones de Guerra, vol. 406, fc 195).

After prolonged struggles to gain independence, struggles which were spurred on by unrelentless desire and a project for self-government, the new republics now faced an endless number of difficulties and obstacles in the construction and delimitation of independent and sovereign collectivities with their own identity based on common origins and shared future goals. At different times, and with varied intensity and complexity, the incipient republics overcame factional and leadership disputes, as well as painful and costly territorial conflicts (The Pacific War, 1879–83: confrontation between Chile, Peru and Bolivia; the Chaco War 1865–1870, in which

Paraguay loses half its population to Brazil, Argentina and Uruguay, the secession of Texas, the Treaty of Guadalupe, and the war between Mexico and the United States, 1846–48, in which Mexico loses what is California, Nevada, Utah, Colorado, Arizona and New Mexico today) (Gutiérrez, 2001a, p. 724). To this is added the difficulty of defining a constitution of one's own and the dependence on foreign capital. Situations which point to a nationalism not of liberation, but of construction.

The Second Type of Nationalism or the Construction of the Nation by the State

The construction of the nation by the state presents us with a process of great importance in this discussion. And one of the outcomes of such process is national identity which has engendered vast and multiple themes on the study of the cultural histories of Mexico and Latin America. The nation-building process, is the type of nationalism that brings together or transforms intense processes of the most diverse kind: it has sought to unite a collectivity at the cost of the linguistic and ethnic disappearance of the indigenous peoples, it has attempted to eradicate the backwardness of huge masses through education and assimilation, it has introduced technology and modernity leading to unity and communication.

We find three key themes that highlight and give permanence to women in the nationalism of the second type: women teachers (Gutiérrez Chong, 2004), the exaltation of the female figure in art inasmuch as she is depicted as a significant representative of national identity and, lastly, the women as intellectual creators of ideas of homeland and nation.

National Identity

Women are depositaries of the authenticity and originality that every nation desires and embody an array of symbols and mythological accounts (Smith, 2000).[2] Also from the typology proposed by Anthias and Yuval-Davis (1989); we discover that the most evident intersection is that which identifies 'women as symbols of national differences and active transmitters and creators of national culture'. This discovery comes as no surprise, in that the culture and identity of the nation are areas which generously permit, favour and adapt imaginary feminine icons. Let us begin with national identity. I define this phenomenon of collective identity as a 'cultural system of information which injects historical meaning and social cohesion into modern nations' (Gutiérrez, 2001, p.xix). National identity does not arise spontaneously, nor is it exclusive of a specific group or generation. It is assimilated and transmitted

---

2   An excellent historiography, from the transformation of Creole patriotism (themes and symbols that justify Mexican independence) to Mexican nationalism (national union which seeks the incipient liberal state) (see Brading, 2001), places great importance to powerful religious symbols inspiring social cohesion, the Virgin of Guadalupe. Other studies had focus on the impact of the Malinche and the myth of *mestizaje* (Glantz, 1994; Gutiérrez, 1999). Two female symbols emanating from a patriotic and nationalist universe have provided the inaugural character of the Mexican nation, the spiritual protection of Mexicans and the myth of ethnic origin of mixed descent, European and Indigenous.

Figure 1.1   José Bribiesca, No title, oil on canvas
Courtesy of Soumaya Museum (Mexico City). Photograph by Javier Hinojosa.

on a large scale. It has precise and defined limits, that is, it has cultural, historical and territorial markers. In addition, it constructs its own archetypes and stereotypes. The goals of national identity include the attainment of levels of assimilation and socialization, which allow citizens to discover similar characteristics and a common culture and thus express a shared identity. National identity can thus make people aware of themselves as a unique collectivity and a defender of its possessions or historic patrimony, such as territory and culture (Gutiérrez, 2001, p. 9). If national identity is the information which the integrants of the nation-state reproduce, then this has three objectives: the standardization of practices, communication and norms; the construction of homogeneity; and the delimitation of cultural originality.

Why does nationalism favour imaginary feminine icons? Nationalism has recourse to what is female, but only in so far as this is 'woman's body', serving as a multiple, creative and adaptable marker with which to construct archetypal images of national identity. To illustrate the nationalist use of the body, let us look at the simple and popular example of the calendar and the picture card.[3]

---

3   The Soumaya Museum (México) and the Mexican Fine Arts Centre Museum (Chicago), organized an exhibition of calendars, entitled 'La leyenda de los Cromos. El arte de los calendarios mexicanos del siglo veinte', I develop this section on the basis of the 2000 catalogue.

Since the early decades of the twentieth century, we have learnt to identify the images of the almanacs, very Mexican expressions of daily life, colourful picture cards, accessible, popular, attractive, decorating the walls of who knows how many houses and shops throughout the country. Images drawn with 'maximum extremes of idealization', voluptuous bodies in the style of Hollywood, adapted to dark skinned mestizo women, or rehashed productions of Aztec monumentality depicting architectures adorned with mystery-charged goddesses and priestesses. (See Figure 1.1.)

Next to the fleshy *Malinche* (the legend of the Indian woman who helped the conqueror, Hernan Cortes), are there other idealized drawings, figures such as the banner-waving woman or the woman-homeland. From the 1960s onwards, the public became familiar with such images, for they appeared on the covers of the first collection of textbooks to circulate in primary schools, from third grade (Mi libro de tercer año) to sixth grade. This was a transcendental task of socialization, using predetermined and precise images, an objective of national identity, materialized in the large scale diffusion homeland icons employed in the textbooks issued in mass by the Ministry of Education. In official textbooks, the woman-homeland figure reveals a female grasping the national flag with great solemnity and intent, while the picture card version illustrates a smiling naked female wrapped in a green, white and red shawl (Jose Bibriesca 'Mexico lindo' (detalles), 1954, *La leyenda de los cromos*). The flag-waving woman is also displayed for advertising purposes. Here, her nakedness (bare arms) is wrapped in the flag, while in the background, we have the symbol of the foundation of Tenochtitlan. She covers her breasts with crossed arms in a gesture of protection and integrity (Rodolfo de la Torre Sin titulo, s/f, *La leyenda de los cromos*). Another picture card representing yet another popular image is that of the woman-homeland. Here, she is seen walking through the countryside, hand in hand with a young child, in the background, the legend of the volcanoes. The *patria* is here depicting a devout, patient, feminine figure, who orientates and protects (Jesus de la Helguera 'Oh! Patria Mia', 1963 *La leyenda de los cromos*).

Numerous symbolic associations between the female body and nationalism are drawn in the craft of illustration or in the plastic arts (see Fox, 1987). The object and context of illustrations involving idealizations and exaggerations such as 'impossible beauties' or 'fantasy landscapes' offer representations of idealized Mexican-ness so archetypical that, in contemplating these images the beholder immediately assimilates nationalist information. Another example derived from the same genre of calendar and picture card is the famous legend of the volcanoes drawn by Jesus de la Helguera ('La Leyenda de los Volcanes', 1941, *La leyenda de los cromos*). The voluptuous sleeping woman wrapped in snow, lifeless, representing the impressive nature of the volcano Iztacihuatl, mourned by the ever-vigilant active volcano, embodying the imposing warrior figure of Popocatepetl. With his numerous illustrations of volcanoes and related themes de la Helguera succeeded in transforming 'his utopias into signs and signals of identity' (La leyenda de los cromos). His images from provincial life, conjured up female mestizos with happy faces, dressed in stylized indumentary of the indigenous type, with long plaits and softened features. These invented dark skinned women were placed in rural settings or in domestic environments (Alfredo Gonzalez Sin titulo, n/d, and Jorge Gonzalez Camarena 'Amecameca' detail n/d).

Creation

If the female body, idealized and stripped of its own ideas, is a favoured resource of nationalism, let us now take a look at an altogether different phenomenon: what did women actually think of the nation? Mexico is in a continual process of transformation and, with time, its patriotism, as well as its nationalism, take on other meanings. Mere praise for patriotic awareness is replaced by an urgency to provide the nation with its own identity. The beginning of the 20th century sees the unification of the masses, endowed now with invented traditions and rituals of civic loyalty. Monuments are erected and cities revamped. Streets, squares and public places are named after heroes (Knight, 1986; Garner, 2001). Women, a select group, appear on the scene and reveal a passionate interest in inventing, reconstructing or celebrating ideas of Mexican-ness. An heterogeneous group of women played a part in the history of the country as *freethinkers* (to use a term fashionable at that time), although they were little known, tolerated or understood. We are keen to identify those women who possessed their own ideas on the homeland and the symbolic construction of the nation (Gutiérrez Chong, 2004).

In these first signs of intellectual interest in the nation, a question is wanting: to what extent did a woman's view of Mexican-ness have an impact in society at large? Is national identity, with its archetypes and stereotypes, a rationality or creation pertaining exclusively to the male domain? In the same way, are women experiencing a different kind of Mexican-ness?

In replying to this question, we have chosen two female artists[4] who have approached the theme of Mexico from very different perspectives: the anthropologist and journalist, Anita Brenner (1905–1974), and the creator of spectacles figuring archetypes and stereotypes of national culture, Astrid Hadad.[5]

The Diva of Post-Modern Cabaret

Astrid Hadad's spectacles conceptualize and stage a range of icons or archetypes of Mexican-ness. Far from humorously venerating these icons, her artistic originality, evident in her musical style and theatricality, instils them with new meanings by transgressing and exploring all the possibilities that a symbol, archetype myth or

---

4   Other women who contributed to build up the concept of Mexicaness by artistic means or because they were related to male personalities in the making of national identity were: the Uruguayan Blanca Luz Brum (1905–1985) wife of the Uruguayan poet Juan Parra del Riego and lover of the Mexican muralist, David Alfaro Siqueiros (Achugar Hugo 'Falsas Memorias' *La Jornada* 5 August 2001). The photographer Tina Modotti (1896–1942) (Poniatowska, 1996), Nahui Olín (1893–1978) (Malvido, 1993), the painter Frida Kahlo (1907–1954) (Herrera, 1985) and Antonieta Rivas Mercado mistress of Jose Vasconcelos (Bradu, 1991), the architect of official nationalism.

5   This section is based on my article 'Patriotic thoughts or intuition: roles of women in Mexican nationalisms' *Nations and Nationalism. Journal of the Association of Ethnicity and Nationalism*, **12**(2), 2006, 339–358. Permission granted by the editors of *Nations and Nationalism, Journal of the Association for the Study of Ethnicity and Nationalism* (London School of Economics).

icon enshrines. It is not surprising that some have said of her that 'it is as if the Virgin of Guadalupe suddenly opened fire on maguey plants or as if Frida Kahlo decided to abandon her wheelchair and start playing the electric guitar' (www.astridhadad. com). Any nationalism can appear banal at the best of times, but Hadad provides us with an innovative experience in which we can recognize and value the emotive power of symbols. Her work is detailed, intellectual. As she herself says, 'I like something, I look into it. I let my mind wander'.

For Hadad, the most important element of her theatrical art is the phenomenon of Mexican-ness, which never fails to be a hybrid formula: 'nationalism, tragic Mexican religious delirium and fatalism, in a cabaret-type explosion with intellectual overtones'. Her work is also 'an excellent synthesis of kitsch art'. So, while there is coherence and chaos, the national subject itself is never lost from view, never evaporates. Hadad gets her very artistic best out of the theme, exploring every possible angle. There is not just one discourse, then, but a combination or recombination, invention or fabrication of manifold modes of expression. Openness to every possibility is the optimum moment to define postmodernism and this is how Hadad is seen the scenic arts.

If, in this chapter, we have seen that women have been used by and for nationalism, today there is a fact that points to the contrary: originality in conceptualizing and expressing Mexican-ness. The language that Hadad has identified and refined for this purpose is, without doubt, unique, the language of wearing, in a daring manner and 'in some other precise moment', as in the case of Josefa's whisper, a particular attire.[6] What can be more stereotypically feminine than a woman fascinating and being fascinated by a dress? In Hadad's case, the fascination is not an individual experience, but the ability to transmit to the public the language of her dress, her long hair and her somewhat exaggerated make-up.

Nationalism is so charged with symbolic triviality and complexity that Hadad has discovered the ways and means of expressing these in the feminine language of dress. From a report in the *Reforma* newspaper (Mexico City, 14 September 2001) which circulates in an electronic format, we are informed that the main elements that inspire her magnificent attire[7] are: the heart (carmine coloured), Mexican cacti (*maguey* and *nopal*) and *the Coatlicue*(the Aztec goddess with her skirt of serpents.). In addition, she has subverted and combined anew in 'live' paintings the popular compositions of Diego Rivera and his arums, adding at the same time, epaulettes and petticoats in recalling the revolutionary epic of Emiliano Zapata. She has recreated the attire of Jose Maria Morelos carrying the Guadalupan emblem which gives us our independence. Hadad's work is said to be inventive, creative, but it also reveals

---

6   Frida Kahlo profusely used indigenous dress to highlight her sense of Mexicaness. Kahlo's sophistication of such way of dressing is today's a symbol of identity which interacts with media technology, see for example the section 'Welcome to Frida Kahlo's Interactive Wardrobe' (web page *The World of Frida Kahlo*) where *Frida* can be dressed according to our desires.

7   It is worth mentioning the making of Hadad's vestments which made using great creativity using fabric, sponge, paper. Her collection made up of twenty different dresses is first conceptualized by Hadad and later materialized by Rocina Conde, Laureano Ruiz y Víctor Susarrey. (Velasco Beatriz, 'Astrid Hadad, mexicana de corazón' *Reforma* 14 September 2001).

a deep understanding of Mexican-ness from a woman born in Chetumal and clearly influenced by Mayan and Lebanese cultures. Which begs the questions: how can a woman, who is both Mayan and Lebanese, from the distant peninsula of Yucatan, subverts and exalts the central nationalism of baroque Mexican-ness?

Idols behind the Altars

Anita Brenner is like a lighthouse whose light shines on many parts, all of which lead us to a particular understanding of nationalism. Anita was not a victim, nor was she a stereotype fashioned by *machismos*, patriarchies or official nationalisms. Nor did she seek her own vision of the national theme, although she did strive to defend it passionately. Anita revealed with great intensity her own creativity and understanding by embracing the importance of 'belonging', that is, she understood the value of different cultures. In following that light which shone on many places, let us take a look at whom Anita Brenner was by according to the story told by her daughter, Susan Glusker, in her book, *Anita Brenner. A Mind of Her Own* (1998).

The second of five children of Jewish parents, immigrants from Lithuania, who had settled in Aguascalientes, Anita played a key role, from the early age of 20 until her death, in ensuring that Mexican art emanating from the post-revolutionary wave of muralists and intellectuals became known and appreciated in the United States, and later, in all the world. Here we have just one prism of that light. Another is her vehement defence of Mexico seen in her writings, in her profession as journalist, in face of the attacks and calumnies from the United States against Mexico, the latter accusing the former of being an unsophisticated settlement for noble and affluent Jewish immigrants fleeing European persecution and the fight against anti-Semitism.

So, the young woman born in Aguascalientes of Jewish parents with family and professional ties in San Antonio, Texas, and in New York, begins, from an early age, to articulate a coherent defense against the attacks and disqualifications of 'barbarous' Mexico, a country that had only just recovered from a prolonged revolution.

With respect to the prisms of light, let us add another, her writings. Three books with revealing titles: *Idols behind the Altars* (1929), *The Wind that Swept Mexico* (1943), and *Your Mexican Holiday* (1935). Five books for children, from 1955 to 1972, were edited and published by *Mexico This Month*; another notable contribution was her column in *Mademoiselle*, magnificently named to reflect critical feminist thought, and personal autonomy, a mind of her own. Another aspect of this extraordinary woman was that 'family of artists and intellectuals' (Glusker, 1998, p. 43) with whom Anita interrelated, on many different levels, documenting such friendships and professional relations in her diaries, the photographers East Weston and Tina Modotti, her friendship with Nahui Ollin, Diego Rivera, Tamayo, Doctor Atl, Xavier Guerrero, that whole period of Mexican cultural life which, with nostalgia and admiration, was considered the 'golden age' of Mexican-ness. There is, however, another prism. Her contribution to the development of anthropology and archaeology, viewed as disciplines with which to better understand, the Indians of Mexico whose presence contributed significantly to the authenticity and originality of Mexican culture.

There are other prisms of course, encompassing impeccable journalistic work, art criticism and academia. The titles of her journalistic work tell us at once of her interest in spreading the word about Mexico and Mexican-ness in the United States, frequently referring to the latter as the other Promised Land.

Perhaps the prism that continues to intrigue us is the title and, consequently, the content of *Idols behind the Altars*. Glusker concludes that it is a book about various aspects and facets of Mexico written for a foreign public, but the book also condenses a way of seeing Mexico, as well as an understanding of its many contradictions and conflicts. In Mexico, one can find every day and on every corner idols behind the altars. There is no way of knowing exactly what happens when an individual reveals his/her true self, in a non-public arena. The power of discretion is a fascinating phenomenon, while the Indian imagination would seem to know no bounds (Gruzinski, 1993), and it is for this reason that the title and content of Anita Brenner's book encapsulates the paradox of a cultural and religious continuity, while there is an acceptance of a modernity that has been perhaps implanted at the same time as loyalty to the past or what went before continues to prevail. The title, reflected in the intense cultural life of Brenner, is a formula that synthesizes a classical paradox: imposition of the new, persistence of the past.

The Third Type of Nationalism or the Nation in the New Millennium

The nation-states of Latin America have gradually begun to recognize the presence of indigenous as well as immigrant ethnicity. In this premise, two possible trends of analysis can be identified. On the one hand, that the formula of homogeneity on the part of official nationalism, or the construction of the nation by the state, has reached saturation point. On the other, that there is growing evidence of greater democratization of political life. The number of significant mobilizations, claims by indigenous groups for official recognition, greater visibility of ethnic politicization, as well as the direct participation and leadership of women in these new, popular demonstrations, constitute powerful reasons which point to debate and to the construction of legal bases capable of administering the recognition of differences.

The metanarratives and official histories upon which nation-states are founded are beginning to be the target of serious criticism from sectors once excluded from official nationalism, for example, women and ethnic groups and, above all, ethnic women (see Grewal and Kaplan, 1994). This phenomenon, therefore, can be interpreted as a matter of conscience and a revaluation of the different identities. In effect, far from assimilating and homogenizing the different groups or ethnicities under the formula of a powerful, official nationalism, together with its well-organized institutional backing, ethnic groups and indigenous women have benefited from modern innovation via a nationalist strategy, for example, increased educational opportunities and the spread of technological know how (Gutiérrez, 1999, 2001).

Indigenous cultures face a stage of reappraisal provided by bilingual skills and contemporary Indian consciousness as a result of modernity and the spread of globalization. Indigenous writers are taking advantage of technology to convey and disseminate new themes and ideas such type of work can be appreciated in the essays and poetry by Briceida and Flor Marlene. An innovative manner of getting close to modern Maya identity is recognizing and admiring the intellectual production of women writers in the Maya language of the Yucatan Peninsula. To be able to have writings and publications of women creators, who possess a specific consciousness of being Maya gives other clues of how to approach diversities. It also means to have reading materials and imagination to understand cultures detached form symbolism of oppression or dominance. The incursion of indigenous women, as 'transmitters of national culture', into the realm of intellectual production aimed at creating, inventing, fabricating has a short history. Not always have there women writers in indigenous languages. Thoughts, ideas and sentiments that now are emerging from the mind and heart of these women are of recent provenance.

The nation now emerging is increasingly less authoritarian, less restrictive in its vision and more prepared to include the many different ways of participating in the collective imagination. In this line of thought, the nation is perceived anew as 'territory of struggle between competing subject's positions, narratives, and voices where nationalism or nationalisms may win, as they have indeed won in many parts of the world, but cannot wipe out the traces of such struggles' (Liu (1994, p. 27).

We could add more ink to the impact of the Zapatista movement but it is a subject that has been dealt with in studies elsewhere (Tello Díaz, 1996; Levario, 1999; Wimmer, 2002). Here, we recover what we consider most significant to highlight the new arena upon which a plural and inclusive nation must be constructed. Among other facts, we point to the negotiation of the San Larrainzar Agreement (February 1996), as well as the passing of the Law in Matters of Rights and Indigenous Culture (April, 2001) (Gutiérrez Chong, 2003) and the participation of the female Zapatista commander *Ramona* on the legislative rostrum of San Lazaro (29 March). The symbolic importance that commander *Ramona* of the Zapatista army, acquires by taking the legislative stand in her famous speech as an Indian woman, lies in the construction of discourse and the creation of a moment of great symbolic value, effective in convincing and moving the general public, legislators and media alike, regarding the double subordination of gender and ethnic origin, which, from Fraser's viewpoint, it is a matter of cultural assessment and economic redistribution (1998).

The indigenous woman is profoundly degraded. Proof of this are the multiple acts of daily and political life providing evidence of mistreatment, discrimination, rejection and ridicule. As in the case of the pre-nationalist heroine, Josefa, Ramona, and millions of women of different generations, have lived through the intensities of injustice and hostility; they have confronted the disapproval of voice and acts anchored in machismo and the patriarchal structure. Voices and interests which are not prepared to lose ground nor do privileges, nor share options or possibilities, much less seek shared solutions. Thus, in this new millennium, the trend towards a more open minded vision on the part of the nation stems from the relentless claims which ethnic groups and growing numbers of women have been capable of implementing (see Barrera Bassols and Massolo, 1998) and not exclusively from institutional action and public policy aimed at correcting and solving such historical degradation.

For the indigenous women of the nation in the new millennium valuation and redistribution (Fraser, 1998, p. 29) will still involve processes of questioning, struggle, reflection and experience, all of which can be put forward at the political level (see

Lovera and Palomo, 1999, 2nd edn). The multicultural nation includes visibly indigenous women as 'active participants in struggles'. The promising leadership of an Amuzgo woman from Guerrero, Martha Sanchez, has emerged on the political scene. She has led the most broad-indigenous organization to date to the discussion of regional autonomies within pluricultural democracies. The politicization of women is intertwined in a network of identities of gender and ethnicities, or as the 'result of the conflicts between self-affiliation and affiliation by others, between self-recognition and hetero-recognition' (Oehmichen, 2000, p. 93).

Conclusion

Mexican women in their different roles, as discussed in this chapter, have been instrumental in creating a homeland, in forging an inclusive nation, or in taking up contemporary indigenous claims for the whole recognition of the ethnic group. The nation, as a result of self-determination, was conceived to unify, to give feelings of and reasons for cohesion to an incipient citizenship, based on the ideals of equality. This has contributed to the nation being identified as a project led by the state and whose purpose is cultural homogenization and linguistic unification. More recently, as a result of social mobilization and the legal recognition of ethnic and minority groups, the nation has started to abandon its previous monocultural formula and is beginning to take on board projects of diversity, plurality and multiculturalism.

We have proposed a methodological exercise for the complementary study of women and nationalisms in Mexico. The broad scope of nationalisms implies to differentiate them accordingly, bearing in mind their political and historical context. We have discussed three types of nationalisms: the independent movement, the nation-building process, the democratization of the nation and the recognition of its cultural plurality. In analysing each one of these types we have found the typology of Anthias and Yuval-Davis concerning the five roles of women in nationalism, useful and applicable.

1. *Independence*
   Biological reproducers
   Reproducers of national boundaries
   Active participants in struggles.
2. *Nation-building*
   Biological reproducers
   Reproducers of national boundaries
   Transmitter of national culture
   Symbolic signifier of national difference
   Active participants in struggles.
3. *Multicultural Nation*
   Biological reproducers
   Reproducers of national boundaries
   Transmitter of national culture
   Symbolic signifier of national difference
   Active participants in struggles.

Our methodological proposal allows flexibility when it comes to identify the more frequent roles of women in the arena of nationalisms. Inverting the list above provides the following results.

Roles of women   Biological reproducers and reproducers of national boundaries
Types of nationalism   Independence, nation-building and multiculturalism

Roles of women as biological reproducers and reproducers of national boundaries are ever present in the three types discussed here. Women's centrality in the reproduction of the nation, and its continuity, is of paramount importance. Thus, the feminization and sexualization of symbols representing the nation are richly and profusely expressed in every possible form of art, including religious art and decoration. We have included in this chapter the example of the calendar to illustrate the popular consumption of archetypical images and symbols of Mexican womanhood depicting popular legends such as those of the male and female volcanoes, idealized rural settings of mestizo people, and interpretations of Mexican flags and female bodies.

Roles of women   Active participants in national struggles
Types of nationalism   Independence and multiculturalism

Women as participants in struggles were found particularly relevant in the stages of independence and multiculturalism. From the very birth of nationalism, many women became involved in a process that implied a break with the existing colonial order. The decision to take part in such a process stemmed from personal conviction, as well as from experiences of prevailing injustices and discrimination. Mexican women did not openly voice or defend their ideals as supporters of independence based on discussion and systematic access to ideas (Enlightenment or the independence of North America). However, it can be affirmed that their ability to react in the face of disadvantage or exclusion, to defend what was theirs, clearly transcends what a conventional school education was capable of offering at that time. Women of the pre-nationalist world were not taught to be patriotic. Instead, their patriotic awareness was shaped by the denial of self-determination and, subsequently, by an end to centuries of colonial rule, that is Josefa. A similar context of open participation is currently in the making, given the political assertiveness and ethnic awareness of women of indigenous origin. With the exhaustion of a homogeneous cultural nation, and the recognition of rights and diversity, women have played, and continue to play, leading and significant roles in these struggles, contributing to and advancing the democratization process of Mexico and Latin America.

Roles of women   Transmitter of national culture and symbolic signifier of national difference
Types of nationalism   Nation-building and multiculturalism

As nationalism was progressing in the form of nation-building, we can now see the celebration of national identity – planned, executed and created by women – including ethnic women, attaining its plenitude. National identity, the hegemonic nation and official speeches may belong to the masculine arena but the incursion of women engaged in intellectual and artistic creativity has broadened the spectrum of nation's styles of representation. While Astrid Hadad's theatrical shows, today are subverting and ridiculing the banality of nationalism, or highlighting the beauty of a symbol, a heroine, or the national flower; the journalist Anita Brenner centred her passion in contributing to the 'golden age' of cultural nationalism, transmitting abroad the innovation of Mexican painting movement (murals) and archaeology as unique and original expressions awaken by the revolution of 1910. The written stories of Briceida and Flor Marlene are contributing to exerting cohesion, cultural reproduction and then, identity. The system of information that women writers are accumulating would indeed endorse their many roles as women reproducing and disseminating the Maya culture of the future and the construction of a multicultural nation.

In this chapter I have taken the stand that the success of nationalism depends on its transmission and diffusion. However, one clarification is required. If we were to limit the argument that nationalism exclusively pertains to the field of ideas, then it would be entirely a masculine domain and a masculine competence given the overwhelming illiteracy of pre-nationalist women; but, as we have seen, the first nationalist ideas took root in colonial societies where women were illiterate. Of course, the nation is also a facilitator of modern culture. Evidence of this can be seen in the emergence and expansion of not only political, but also literary women's organizations, and the proliferation of writings signed by women from the nineteenth century up to date.

Our combined model has proved its malleability when attempting to define and explain the three types of nationalism common to Mexico examined in this chapter. To be able to identify women's roles in nation formation we constructed a methodological exercise, and the result has not been only a more comprehensive understanding of nationalisms outside Western academic debates, but also proved to be a path breaking tool for future research on gender, sexual identity and the nation.

Women from Mexico and Latin America as we shall see throughout the chapters of this book have been instrumental in creating a homeland, in forging a national identity, in defending natural resources, multiple facets of nationalisms that provide us with independence, sovereignty and recognition.

References

Agraz García de Alba, G. (1992), *Los Corregidores Don Miguel Domínguez y Doña María Josefa Ortiz y el Inicio de la Independencia* (Mexico: Tomo I).

Anderson, B. (1990), *Imagined Communities. Reflections on the Origin and Spread of Nationalism* (London: Verso).

Anthias, F. and Yuval-Davis, N. (eds) (1989), *Woman-Nation-State* (London: Macmillan).

Arrom, S. (1985), *The Women of Mexico City 1790–1885* (Stanford: Stanford University Press).

Barrera Bassols, D. and Massolo, A. (eds) (1998), *Mujeres Que Gobiernan Municipios: Experiencias, Aportes y Retos* (México: El Colegio de México).

Billig, M. (1997), *Banal Nationalism* (London: Sage).

Brading, D. (1991), 'The First America', *The Spanish Monarchy. Creole Patriots and the Liberal State (1492–1866)* (Cambridge: Cambridge University Press).

Brading, D. (2001), *Mexican Phoenix Our Lady of Guadalupe. Image and Tradition across Five Centuries* (Cambridge: Cambridge University Press).

Bradu, F. (1991), *Antonieta, 1900–1931* (México: Fondo de Cultura Economica).

Cusack, T. (2000), 'Janus and Gender: Women and the Nation's Backward Look', *Nations and Nationalism*, **6**(4), 541–561.

Enloe, C. (1989), *Bananas, Beaches and Bases: Making Feminist Sense of International Politics* (London: Pandora).

Florescano, E. (1987), *Memoria Mexicana* (México: Joaquín Mortíz).

Fox, J. (1987), 'The Creator Gods, Romantic Nationalism and the Engenderment of Women in Folklore', *Journal of American Folklore*, **100** (398), October–December, 563–572.

Fraser, N. (1998), 'From Redistribution to Recognition?, Dilemmas of Justice in a 'Post-socialist' Age' in *Theorizing Multiculturalism. A Guide to the Current Debate*. Willett, C. (ed.) (Massachusetts: Blackwell Publishers).

García, M. (ed.) (1995), *José Joaquín Fernández Lizardi, Heroínas Mexicanas (María Leona Vicario, M. Rodríguez Lazarín, María Fermina Rivera, Manuela Herrera y Otras)* (México: Vargas Rea).

Garner, P. (2001), *Porfirio Diaz* (London: Longman).

Gellner, E. (1983), *Nations and Nationalism* (Ithaca: Cornell University Press).

Glantz, M. (ed.) (1994), *La Malinche, Sus Padres y Sus Hijos* (Mexico: Facultad de Filosofia y letras, Universidad Nacional Autonoma de Mexico).

Glusker, S.J. (1998), *Anita Brenner. A Mind of her Own* (Texas: University of Texas Press).

González, E. and Barrios, E. (1995), 'Notas para comprender los orígenes de la rebelión zapatista', *Chiapas, Vol. I* (México: Era).

Grewal, I. and Kaplan, C. (1994), 'Introduction: Transnational Feminist Practices and Questions of Postmodernity' in *Scattered Hegemonies*. Grewal, I. and Kaplan, C. (eds) (Minneapolis; University of Minnesota).

Gruzinski, S. (1993), *The Conquest of Mexico, Westernization of Indian Societies, 17th to 18th Centuries* (Cambridge: Polity Press).

Gutiérrez, N. (1995), 'Miscegenation for Nation-Building: Native and Immigrant Women in Mexico' in *Unsettling Settler Societies*. Yuval-Davis, N. and Stasiulis, D. (eds) (London: Sage).

Gutiérrez, N. (1999), *Nationalist Myths and Ethnic Identities. Indigenous Intellectuals and the Mexican State* (Lincoln and London: University of Nebraska Press).

Gutiérrez Chong, N. (2000). 'Mujeres patria-nación. México: 1810–1920', *La Ventana, Revista de Estudios de Género*, **II**(12), 209–243.

Gutiérrez, N. (2001), 'The Study of National Identity' in *Modern Roots. Studies of National Identity*. Dieckhoff, A. and Gutiérrez, N. (eds) (Aldershot: Ashgate Publishing).

Gutiérrez, N. (2001a), 'South and Central America', *Encyclopaedia of Nationalism*, **1** (San Diego: Academic Press).

Gutiérrez Chong, N. (2003), 'La autonomía y la resolución de conflictos étnicos. Una perspectiva de los Acuerdos de San Andrés Larráinzar', *Nueva Antropología*, **XIX**(63), October, 11–39.

Gutiérrez Chong, N. (ed.) (2004), *Mujeres y Nacionalismos en América Latina. De la Independencia a la Nación Del Nuevo Milenio* (Mexico: Instituto de Investigaciones Sociales).

Gutiérrez Chong, N. (2006), 'Patriotic Thoughts or Intuition: Roles of Women in Mexican Nationalisms', *Nations and Nationalisms*, **12**(2), 339–358.

Hall, C. (1993), 'Gender, Nationalism and National Identities', *Feminist Review*, **44**(summer), 97–103.

Herrera, H. (1985), *Frida: Una biografía de* (México: Frida Kahlo).

Hobsbawm, E. (1990), *Nations and Nationalism Since 1780* (Cambridge: Cambridge University Press).

Jayawardena, K. (1986), *Feminism and Nationalism in the Third World* (London: Zed).

Kandiyoti, D. (2000), 'Introduction: The Awkward Relationship: Gender and Nationalism', *Nations and Nationalism*, **6**(4), 491–494.

Kedourie, E. (1960), *Nationalism* (London: Hutchinson).

Knight, A. (1986), *The Mexican Revolution*, 2 Vols (Cambridge: Cambridge University Press).

Lafaye, J. (1985), *Quetzalcóatl y guadalupe: la formación de la conciencia Nacional En México* (México: Fondo de Cultura Economica).

Lavrín, A. (1978), 'Women in Convents: their Economic and Social Role in Colonial Mexico' in *Liberating Women's History: Theoretical and Critical Essays*. Carroll, B.A. (ed.) (Chicago: Chicago University Press).

Leoussi, A.S. (ed.) (2001), *Encyclopaedia of Nationalism* (London: Transaction Publishing).

Levario, M. (1999), *Chiapas, la guerra en el papel* (México: Cal y Arena).

Liu, L. (1994), 'The Female Body and Nationalist Discourse: The Field of Life and Death Revisited', in *Scattered Hegemonies*. Grewal, I. and Kaplan, C. (eds) (Minnesota: Minneapolis University of Minnesota).

Lomnitz-Adler, C. (1992), *Exits from the Labyrinth: Culture and Ideology in the Mexican Nation Space* (Berkeley: University of California Press).

Lovera, S. and Palomo, N. (coords) (1999), *Las Alzadas* (México, Comunicacion.e Informacion de la Mujer, Convergencia Socialista).

Lynch, J. (1986), *The Spanish American Revolutions, 1810–1826*, 2nd Ed. (New York: W.W. Norton).

Mallon, F.E. (1995), *Peasant and Nation: The Making of Postcolonial Mexico and Peru* (Berkeley: University of California Press).

Malvido Arriaga, A. (1993), *Nahui Olin: La mujer del sol* (México: Diana).

McClintock, A. (1993), 'Family Feuds: Gender, Nationalism and the Family', *Feminist Review*, **22**(summer), 61–80.

Muriel, J. (1974), *Los recogimientos de mujeres: Respuesta a una problemàtica social novohispana* (Mexico: Instituto de Investigaciones Històricas: UNAM).

Oehmichen, C. (2000), 'Relaciones de etnia y género una aproximación a la multidimensionalidad de los procesos identatarios', *Alteridades*, UAM, **10**(19), 89–98.

Poniatowska, E. (1992), *Tinísima* (México: Era).

Schöpflin, G. (2001), 'Ethnic and Civic Nationalism (Hans Kohn's Typology)', in *Encyclopaedia of Nationalism*. Leoussi, A.S. (ed.) (London: Transaction Publishing).

Sefchovich, S. (1999), *La suerte de la consorte, las esposas de los gobernantes de México: Historias de un olvido y relatos de un fracaso* (México: Océano).

Sluga, G. (2000), 'Female and National Self-Determination: A Gender Re-Reading of the "Apogee of Nationalism"', *Nations and Nationalism*, **6**(4), 495–521.

Smith, A.D. (1986), *The Ethnic Origins of Nations* (Oxford: Basil Blackwell).

Smith, A.D. (2000), *Nacionalismo y modernidad* (Madrid: Istmo).

Smith, A.D. (2001), 'Ethno-Symbolism', in *Encyclopaedia of Nationalism*. Leoussi, A.S. (ed.) (London: Transaction Publishing).

Stern, S.J. (1999), *La historia secreta del género, mujeres, hombres y poder en México en las postrimerías del poder colonial* (México: Fondo de Cultura Economica).

Tello Díaz, C. (1996), *La rebelión de las Cañadas* (México: Cal y Arena).

Van Cott, D.L. (2000), *The Friendly Liquidation of the Past. The Politics of Diversity in Latin America* (Pittsburgh: Pittsburgh University Press).

Walby, S. (2000), 'Gender, Nations and States in a Global Era', *Nations and Nationalism Journal of the Association for the Study of Ethnicity and Nationalism* (Cambridge: Polity Press).

Wimmer, A. (2002), *Shadows of Modernity* (Cambridge: Cambridge University Press).

Wrigth de Kleinhans, L. (1910), *Mujeres notables mexicanas* (México: Topografía Económica).

Documents

de la Helguera, J., 'La Leyenda de los Volcanes', 1941, *La leyenda de los cromos El arte de los calendarios mexicanos del siglo veinte* México, Soumaya Museum and Telmex Foundation, Mexico, 2000.

de la Torre, R., No title, no date, *La leyenda de los cromos El arte de los calendarios mexicanos del siglo veinte*; México, S., Museum and Telmex Foundation, Mexico (2000).

Archives

Archivo General Agrario, 23/25 10214, File 2 to 12. (Mexico City).

Archivo General de la Nación, Ramo operaciones de guerra, Vol, 406, Fc, 195.

Web page

http://www.astridhadad.com/

Articles from newspapers

Astrid Hadad: 'Mexicana de corazón', in *Reforma*, 14 September 2001, México, electronic format.

PART 1
Struggle and Independence

Chapter 2

Dolores Cacuango and the Origin of the Mother Country:Seed for the *Kichwización* of the World[1]

Gabriela Bernal Carrera

Oh, these wawas of today, what they say!
But a time is coming of much suffering; although you all don't believe, a time to cry will come.
But it will always be the Indian who will rise up (...)
That's how my grandmother told it; that's how the ancient ones spoke. Later, my grandmother told me:
- Neither you nor I are going to see what is to come; your children will be the ones who will see, they will be the ones who will endure that. With those words she told me. And whatever she has said, so it has come to pass. Everything my grandmother spoke of is coming true, without fail.

Matilde Colque de Jach'a Qullu in Rivera Silvia (ed) 1987, p. 286.

In present-day Ecuador, a cursory bibliographic revision serves to show that the subject of indigenous women leaders is enjoying a period of great productivity. Many reasons may be attributed to this; the two most important being, on the one hand, the emergence of the Ecuadorian Indigenous Movement as a powerful interlocutor of the Ecuadorian State, and, on the other, the singular feminine participation in the processes of ethnic leadership.

Ethnicity and gender synthesise, in many ways, the political and academic concerns of recent years. Some Non-governmental organisations (NGOs) view this relationship with apprehension, in which they don't perceive equilibrium (Cervone et al. 1998). The specific demands of the peoples these women belong to, and the 'gender-specific' proposals favoured by financial and political organisations

---

1   This work is the fruit of many long conversations with Fernando Garces, Armando Muyolema and Fabian Potosi. To them, who made this work possible with their data and reflections, a special vote of thanks for their friendship and for those long talks. Also, a special thank you to the students of the Jatari Unancha school, Centro Tigua, who taught me more about myself and my 'incomplete mestizaje', than I ever could have while we were together. Much of the ethnographic data, especially those present in the analysis of the text, were taken from my own experience as an educator in the Indigenous Education System of Cotopaxi (SEIC) (1994–96), and from the research for my master's thesis, undertaken during December and January of 1999–2000 and the same months of 2000–2001.

external to the indigenous communities, represent a game of multiple interests with increasingly more complex players.

During the first months of 2001, it was much more evident that the indigenous women were protagonists in the political life and proposals of their peoples. In the mobilizations, at the negotiation tables of the Indigenous Movement and the government, in the National Congress, in the halls of local power, in the Second Grade Organisations (SGOs), the feminine indigenous participation and authority was all too obvious. However, these women at the dusk of the twentieth century and the dawn of the twenty-first century are not exclusively fruits of the work of political and gender-specific awakening of state-level organisms or NGOs.

Ecuadorian history records the data of some indigenous women who, because of their courage and tenacity, marked not only the course of their peoples, but also saw their words being echoed by the national society. One of them is Dolores Cacuango (San Pablo Urcu-Cayambe, 1881–1971).

The present work is an approach to Dolores Cacuango, not as the legend that many speak of, but to her own discourse on *the Fatherland*, a subject directly linked to the motivation for this book. For the singularity of the present elements, for its narrative structure, this story about *the origin of the Fatherland* is a prodigious example of how the cultural elements specific to its ethnicity play together to sustain the struggles and demands for the land, and the cultural specificity of the Indigenous Movement of the first half of the twentieth century. On the other hand, Dolores' words are being recycled to propose the possibility of *expanding* the indigenous culture, not as in the past, but as an alternative civilizing possibility from and for the indigenous peoples of Ecuador. However, the proposal is not limited to indigenous peoples, but the entire population of that country.

The Context

Between the close of 1871 and the beginning of the following year, Fernando Daquilema was proclaimed king of Cacha, in the province of Chimborazo. In the middle of a complete reordering of the indigenous tributes and contributions, the nation-state was favouring those elements that would permit the articulation of both the economic and social organization of the indigenous peoples. After the Great Andean Rebellion, led by Tupac Amaru II (1780–1781), Daquilema's rising was 'a sort of rehearsal for ethnic independence and, in consequence, for non-recognition of the State in the era' (Fuentealba, 1990, p. 71).

Moreover, it constitutes the framework of the continuity of a tradition of indigenous rebellion during the colonial period and shows the new republic that the indigenous cultural presence would not be an easy element to deal with. This is because in the Daquilema rising may be seen not only an indigenous reaction in face of economic impositions of the State, but also the use and defence of 'ancient symbols and millennia-old rites' (Almeida Vinueza, 1990, p. 174).

The history that surrounds Dolores Cacuango is a continuance of indigenous insurrections and rebellions. For the nation-state, it is also an important moment: the Liberal Revolution that becomes firmly established in 1895. These changes, which sought the transformations necessary for the country's ingress into the global capitalist market, were not fully crystallized. Even after its triumph and implementation, the traditional hacienda land rights system continued controlling large areas of power, both at the local and national levels. The monopoly of the mountain lands and the control of the large indigenous masses was its greatest advantage in face of a bourgeois coastal sector agro-exporter that attempted to attract labour for its plantations (Almeida Vinueza, 1990; Ibarra, 1992).

Thus, the close of the nineteenth century and opening of the twentieth century are witnesses to many economic, social and political reorganization processes. On the coast the first worker unions begin to arise, and while the mountainous population is attracted toward the coast with wages and salaries that, in the traditional hacienda land rights structure, are indispensable, the indigenous insurrections and protest continue unabated.

During the first century of the Republic's existence, the process of formation of the national identity finds no element around which it can agglutinate its population. It is only in 1942, with the dramatic territorial loss to Peru, that an identification reference is generated, which, however, is limited to averring *we are not Peruvians*, but at the same time deepens the disharmony that *what is it to be Ecuadorian* generates.

Thus, in a territory having a profound cultural ethnic diversity, variegated by hard class conflicts, the nation-state does not manage to propose, not even as a function of the necessities linked to its articulation to global capitalism, a real process of construction of the national identity.

At the same time as the state is not seeking its immersion in the international markets, the bourgeoisie from the sierra or the coast, are disposed to cede their political or economic privileges, depending on the case, as a function of the construction of a long term national project.[2] The mestizo, as a member of the new nation, does not enter into the discourses of 'Ecuadorianism', as in the case of Mexico. The two biggest existing population groups, the indigenous and the other that, for now, we will call the 'non-indigenous', remain, from the point of view of the state, unrelated to each other, therefore, unable to provide a common ground for national identity formation.

From 1897 to 1968, 18 individuals assume the constitutional presidency of the Republic. For 71 years military dictatorships usurped power; with some of the presidents lasting not more than a few months or days,[3] and others acceding to power on more

---

2   This perception that the leading classes of Ecuador are incapable of articulating themselves as a nation project is still apparent today and is summarized in the ideas presented by Andres Crespo Reinberg, a guayaquileno personality with a prominent political participation: '.../... But the business leaders from all over Ecuador, like all the political parties, very imperfectly represent their constituents and do not defend the interests of the majority.... /... I think it is easier to identify with the indigenous than with the ruling class and Ecuadorian economics. The majority of the business class neither understand nor are interested in the profound Ecuador'. *El Comercio*, 25/02/01.

3   Cases are recorded, for example that of Lizardo García: September 1905–January 1906; Mariano Veintimilla Suarez 3 September to 16 September, 1947. The other extreme is Velasco Ibarra, five-time president of the Republic: from 1934 to 1935, 1944–1947, 1952–1956, 1960–1961, 1970–1972.

Table 2.1 Dolores Cacuango's text about the origin of the mother country

	Introduction	Baby	PERIOD 1
1. Who was the owner of the Fatherland? Baby Manuelito. He formed the Fatherland.		Manuelito	PERIOD 1
2. Holy Mary of Bethlehem gave birth to the Baby Manuelito in the prairie.	Where and of whom was he born.	Elders	PERIOD 1
3. He is the owner.	Possessor (master)	Baby Manuelito	PERIOD 1
4. The planet thus was born. Only pure water, pure water. Thus rumour has said Baby Manuelito.	Origin, who gave the origin	Baby Manuelito	PERIOD 1
5. And Holy Mary of Bethlehem has married. Our Lord Jesus Christ has married.	Parents, origins of Baby Manuelito	Elders	PERIOD 1
6. Then he has said. But I don't know how to work, I do nothing, only a carpenter. Him working as carpenter and Holy Mary follows with lunch.	Parents' occupation, young men's and women's functions within the world of the hacienda.	Elders	PERIOD 1
7. Thus, passing through humiliations she feels her belly.	Labour pains	Elders	MOMENTO 1
8. There then has gone Jesus Christ. To my house, I am ashamed, saying	Taken from the father of a feminine period.	Elders	MOMENTO 1
9. Fleeing Holy Mary has given birth on the mount.	Spatial situation (mountain) of the birth of Baby Manuelito	Elders	PERIOD 1
10. And then there jumping, Baby Manuelito is born	Birth of Baby Manuelito	Baby Manuelito	PERIOD 1
11. And the rumour has said: Look after my mummy's diet my daddygrandfather. I am going to form this Fatherland.	Beginning of the task. Placing his mother in the care of his grandfather	Baby Manuelito	PERIOD 1
12. No, we do not have power, little one, what power do you have? Mary has said.	Distrust of the elders in the capacities of the Baby Manuelito	Elders	PERIOD 1
13. No, I'm going to see, I'm going to see my daddy there, at eight in the morning, there on slope of Josafan he is about to.	Reunion of father and son (elders and youth) for the formation of the Fatherland	Baby Manuelito and Elders	CULMINATION

Table 2.1 Continued

	Introduction	Baby	PERIOD 1
14. If I can form it, it has to be at 12 noon.	Time fixed and date	Action	PERIOD 2
15. There, flag has to stop, music has to stop, band, for when it nears 12 o'clock sharp, rumour has said, Baby Manuelito.	Promise of a party after the triumph	Party	PERIOD 2
16. And the Baby Manuelito goes on to form the Fatherland	Actions for forming the Fatherland, manage to do it.	Action	PERIOD 2
17. and then, forming the Fatherland, he has made function, has made wedding, has made drink, has made everything.	Solidification of promises	Party	PERIOD 2
18. And you have done everything, the little plant, little barley, little wheat, little oca, little potato, all that he makes no more.	Party with eminently Andean elements	Party	PERIOD 2
19. Thus forming that he sees, ca, ahura, ca, the Fatherland.	Conclusive phrase	Action	PERIOD 2
20. Little Daddy God, Baby Manuelito, Holy Mary so all have a Fatherland.	The Fatherland for all, divinisation of the possibility that the Fatherland is for all. Baby Manuelito and elders	Divine backing for the story (Implicit promise of party)	CULMINATION
21. But now ca, they do not give ps, they do not give for everyone.	Injustice, actual reality	Reality	PERIOD 3
22. And we have to protest, although he punishes so, master.	Action to be taken	Action	PERIOD 3
23. Making protests already punish.	Risks	Reality	PERIOD 3

than one occasion. In the midst of the instability of personalities the projects don't gel, they are not completed. What the coastal bourgeoisie propose as new trajectories directly affect the interests of the mountain landowners,[4] who insist in maintaining pre-capitalist power relationships.[5] The death of Eloy Alfaro (1912), leader of the Liberal Revolution, dragged and burned in Quito, is a clear example of the incapacity of the dominant sectors to subjugate their regional interests to a project that transcends them.

The mestizoism has been thought of as an abstract category, according to which the mestizo would come to be the child of a Spaniard and an Indian, the homogeneous synthesis of both heritages. However, the mestizo, the Cosmic Race (1925) that Vasconcelos talks about, does not represent a real project for the Ecuadorian nation-state. This does not find points of accord among that amorphous and still to be defined (that which we have called indigenous) mass, the 'belligerent' indigenous people and the classes that engendered it. The nation-state does not feel capable of regaining possession of the inheritance of any glorious people of the past: because the Indians are not past in their present (see Table 2.1). There were revolts, rebellions and constant uprisings. That is, they don't even have, as in the case of Mexico, the elements necessary to invent origins that legitimize them as heirs of the original owners of their land.[6] On the other hand, the visible and constant demands of the indigenous peoples, not only for their land, but also for the survival of their myths, traditions and cultural rationalities, distance even more the possibility of assimilating them into the *mestizo*. If in Mexico, the glorious and magnificent indigenous past was expropriated from the indigenous peoples by the Creoles, in order to support the Mexican national identity (Gutierrez, 2001), in Ecuador, the political and cultural processes of nationhood, did not allow for that process to happen.

The myths and symbols still form part of the everyday indigenous experience. On the other hand, the indigenous heroes did not fall within the parameters of the new nation-state. The so called heroes were the leaders of large and small rebellions that had caused both the national order and the everyday life of small settlements to tremble.[7]

---

4   In search of attracting labour for the agro-exporter plantations, for example, agricultural wages were revamped, which seduced a considerable percentage of the migrant indigenous population (Ibarra, 1992).

5   Several forms of non-capitalist economic relationships are seen; among the most well-known, 'el concertaje, occasional recruitment of indigenous labour that, later, is converted into permanent labour as the worker and his family become indebted to the hacienda' Ibarra (1992, p. 52). Thus, it is within the traditional hacienda system that non-capitalist forms of worker exploitation take shape: huasipungos, yanaperos, partidarios among others. For more information, see Guerrero (1983); Ibarra (1992).

6   Bolivar clearly summarizes, the feeling of the creoles and their heirs: 'Americans by birth, and Europeans by rights, we find ourselves in the conflict of disputing with the natives their titles of possession, and of maintaining ourselves in the country that we saw born in face of the opposition of the invaders; thus, ours is the most extraordinary and complicated case'. *Bolivar's Discourse in the Angostura Congress* (15 February 1819) Cited in: Harrison (1996,p54). In this context, the cultural adscription is not the only origin of the problem. The legitimacy of access to the land is one of the fundamental points that underline Bolivar's doubt.

7   Weismantel (1994), affirms that, until the decade of the '70s, the hacienda owners did not sleep on their properties for fear of being murdered.

Table 2.2   Some indigenous uprisings of Dolores Cacuango's era

Year	
1872	*Indigenous Uprising In Chimborazo. Fernando Daquilema, King of Cacha
1907	*Patateurcu (Tungurahua)
1913	*Chillanes (Bolívar)
1914	*Quina-corral and Espino (Bolívar)
1916	*Tisaleo (Tungurahua) *San Felipe (Tungurahua)
1920	*Quingeo, Sitcay y Sinincay (Azuay)
1921	*Guano, Cujibíes, Guamote y Columbe (Chimborazo)
1923	*Julian Revolution, calling for "the dignification of the indigenous race" (Brought about by young military men) * Repression in Juan Montalvo (Cayambe-Pichincha) of a movement in demand of lands. *Sinincay and Jadan (Azuay) *Urcuquí (Imbabura) *Leito (Tungurahua)
1925–1930	* First indigenous unions in Otavalo - Imbabura (Impelled by Ricardo Paredes and Luis F. Chavez).
1926	*Jesus Gualavisi, indigenous peasant representative: Peasant Workers Union of Cayambe. (Pichincha) *Formation of the agricultural unions of Cayambe: The Inca, Free Land, Bread and Land, in Pesillo, Moyourco and la Chimba respectivamente. (Pichincha)
1930	*Calling of the First Indigenous Congress in Cayambe. (Pichincha)
1930–1945	*Indigenous uprisings and unionisation of field workers.
1931	*Violent prohibition of the realisation of the "Congress of Agricultural Workers and Peasants" *The Yaguachi Battalion violently represses the protests in the Cayambe area. *Simiatug (Bolívar)
1932	*Palmira (Chimborazo) *Pastocalle (Cotopaxi)
1933	*Mochapata (Tungurahua)
1934	*Rumipamba (Imbabura) *Llacta-urcu (Cotopaxi) *Salinas (Bolívar)
1935	*First National Worker Peasant Conference *Licto, Galte and Pull (Chimborazo) *Regional Rebellion in Chimborazo under the leadership of Ambrosio Lazo, indigenous leader with links to the Communist Party.
1953	*Massacre of Indigenous of Gualte and La Merced.
1954	* Massacre of Indigenous in Guachala and Pungalá (Pichincha) *Foundation of the Federation of Agricultural Workers of the Litoral.
1961	*In Columbo Grande (Chimborazo), national forces enter to support the landholders who had accumulated a debt for non-payment of wages to the huasipungo workers.
1963	*Military Junta in Power
1964	*First Agrarian Reform Law
1968	*Grant of 9,700,000 acres. In the Amazon region to foreign oil companies.
1972	*Military Government of Guillermo Rodríguez Lara
1974	* Second Agrarian Reform Law

Sources: Albornoz Peralta, 1983; Icaza, 1984.

The personalities that the Creole imagination, synthesized by the Jesuit Juan de Valasco (1727–1792), had created in order to legitimize the independence, were soon overtaken by events. In the *Historia del Reino de Quito* (History of the Kingdom of Quito), published after the death of the Jesuit, a royal indigenous dynasty of Quito was established, finally united, by marriage, to the Inca dynasty of Peru. The legends at the foot of today's school posters still tell a story of matrimonial alliances and valiant warriors who resisted the 'Peruvian invader' (see Table 2.2).

One historical detail should be recognized, Juan de Velasco, upon recording the matrimonial alliance between a princess from Quito and Huayna–Capac, in the *Historia del Reino de Quito*, was legitimately uniting the destinies of what would, in the future be known as Ecuador, and Peru. But beyond the constant allusions to the 'valiant defence' and sacrificial death in defence of their territory, Juan de Velasco unwittingly recorded another of the myths regarding those that later would be articulating the notion of the national identity: *la raza vencida* (the vanquished race). Silva (1995) maintains that this was constructed upon two basic ideas: the impossibility of the indigenous person's dominating the geography, and the fact that, 'historically', the Indians of the Northern Andes would have been defeated constantly by the 'expansionism of the Cuzco people' or 'the Inca imperialism'. As such, the Ecuadorian nation-state was articulating nothing more but *an identity in negative.*

It was until the decade of the 70s that the military clarified, from its position of power, the idea of the mestizo as emblematic figure of national unity (Silva 1995, 29). Until that time, the nation-state neglected its primordial task, of unifying the 'non-indigenous' and indigenous populations as a function of its own project. Moreano (2000) pointed out that the importance of the indigenous peoples in Ecuador, compared with other countries having a high proportion of indigenous population, such as Mexico, Peru and even Bolivia, is owed to 'a sort of incomplete mestizo'. This feeling that the mestizo has not been completed is evidenced in a traditional expression, used when one acts unconsciously: *me salio el indio* (the Indian in me came out). The *Indian comes out* when conscious censure suddenly disappears. However, there is evidently an implicit recognition that the person making this affirmation is repressing the Indian that inhabits him/her.

In the midst of this deviation, the indigenous peoples continue using their symbols, rites and myths in the constant insurrections against the nation-state. As Almeida Vinueza (1990) accurately points out, the basic reason for the indigenous uprisings is not found exclusively bound to the processes of the defence of the land; there is a component that demands respect for, and self-determination of, their own 'cultural rationality'.

Thus, despite the fact that the first indigenous and peasant unions are organised by the Socialist party (see Table 2.1), the existence of the ethnic element within their struggles cannot be discounted. Dolores Cacuango sums this idea up very well.

The Woman

Dolores Cacuango was born in San Pablourco, one of the haciendas in the Cayambe zone, on October 26th, 1881. Her parents, Juan Cacuango and Andrea Quilo were *huasipungueros.*[8] Upon the death of her father, the members of her family became *arrimados.*[9] At around 20 years of age, Dolores runs away from the house of the hacienda where she worked after the land-granted priests tried to marry her off to someone that she didn't want. She flees to Quito where she works as a domestic servant. There, she learns Spanish. After a while, she returns to Cayambe where she marries Rafael Catucuamba, son of Jose Catucuamba and Juana Chirana, also *huasipungueros*. The civil ceremony takes place on August 15th, 1905. She had several children, of which the only survivor is Luis Catucuamba, later to become the first teacher at the Cayambe Indigenous Schools.

Throughout the twentieth century, the indigenous people are involved in constant uprisings. Many of them in the Cayambe area (see Table 2.1). Dolores Cacuango is introduced into the indigenous struggles by Ignacio Alba, another indigenous leader of the era. Until 1926, Dolores participated in the formation of the area's indigenous unions and, by 1931; her leadership was being publicly identified. Thus, when in the same year, the Yaguachi battalion violently repressed the zone's indigenous protests, Dolores' house is one of those burned down and her family is expelled from the *huasipungo*.

In 1944, she participates in the founding of the Ecuadorian Indian Federation (EIF), together with Jesus Gualavisí, who is also its first secretary. In that same year, Dolores forms part of the Central Committee of the Communist Party. The following period (until approximately 1950), Dolores is the General Secretary of the EIF. In 1946, she creates the Cayambe Indigenous Schools, in collaboration with members of the Communist Party and her son; the experience last approximately 20 years.

Later, although still linked to the Communist Party and the EIF, she is accused of fomenting divisionism and arrogance, and her influence gradually diminished. She died in Olmedo (Cayambe area) on April 24th, 1971. This brief glimpse into the life of Dolores hides the tremendous force behind her motivations for struggling. Muriel Crespi, who during the 1960s had a chance to interview her, affirmed: 'This remarkable woman has become one of the rural workers' most celebrated cultural heroes, and, I gather, is their only heroine' (Rodas, 1998, p. 131).

We will attempt now, a brief review of some important details regarding the personality of Dolores Cacuango. On one hand, this woman must be situated in front of her own people, and on the other, in front of another cultural tradition, represented not only by the nation-state, but by the left wing parties of which she was an active member and which she took part in long debates over the indigenous question.

Leading her people, Dolores follows a rear guard of woman *cabecillas*, that is, ring leaders. In some cases, this apprenticeship is passed down from mother to daughter, as happens with Transito Amaguana, another leader and contemporary of Dolores (Bulnes, 1943; Yanez, 1984; Rodas, 1998). That is, the presence of a woman as leader was not a serendipitous occurrence. Neptali Ulcuango (see Yanez, 1984, p. 166) indicates how the leadership selection proceeded: 'Leaders were chosen according to their activities, their spirit of struggle, their thinking. Thus, the youths, *the male or female individuals* who among the group were conspicuous for greater activity, greater knowledge and clarity, were chosen as leaders, as directors' (emphasis mine).

---

8   See Figure 2.1.
9   The hacienda structure was quite complex and divided by sex and age. See Figure 2.1.

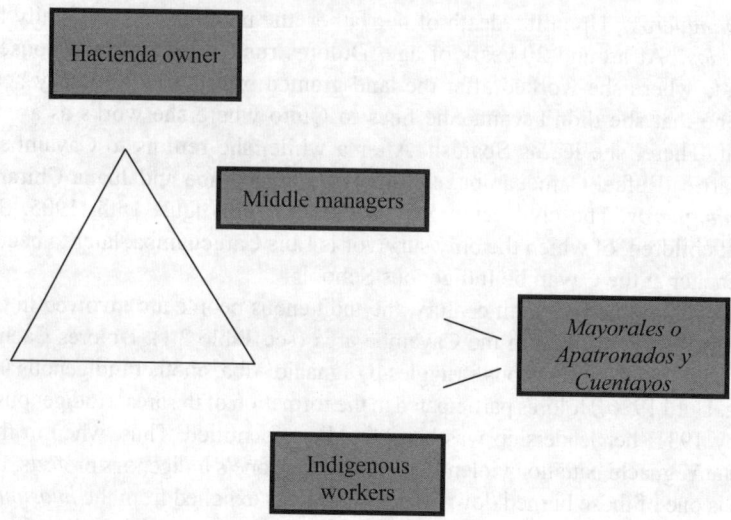

Figure 2.1   The hacienda structure

An important point is the consideration that the communities make of the capacities of their leaders. Knowledge and management of the greatest quantity of possible elements, and the character of the individuals, among other things, would permit the leaders to better tackle the negotiations with the hacienda's intermediaries and, later, with the authorities of the nation-state.

Following this reasoning, an important detail must be borne in mind. When Dolores escapes from the hacienda, unmarried, *she learns Spanish*. This signifies access to the code for relating to the nation-state.[10] In the Ecuadorian haciendas, up until the first Agrarian Reform, Quicha constituted the language of communication, no matter the 'ethnic classification' in the rural highlands.[11] It would not be strange, therefore, that the women, in their native tongue, were able to lead the entreaties and demands, given that their listeners understood what they were saying and the community did not disqualify their action. The use of language is, perhaps, in Dolores Cacuango, the most expressive and lasting of her actions.[12] In Quicha or

10 Considering the present-day women leaders, it should be borne in mind that the migrations, generally realized by the men, facilitated access to the Spanish language. The present-day indigenous women leaders have had the chance to learn Spanish, a fact which augments their visible political participation for the national society. However, this does not signify that those women that do not speak Spanish remain on the margin of political activity. Harvey (1987, 1989, 1991) tabled some suggestive reflections on this subject.

11 Fernando Garces, personal communication.

12 The fact that is a woman who speaks about the origin of the Fatherland is not out of outside of the Andean cultural context. In the area of Zumbahua, it is the women who write the song lyrics that are sung. Depending on the occasion, it is they who take charge of developing the stanzas that they will speak about the party or celebration. The men add the music, but those who narrate it are the women. On the other hand, Fernando Garces, analysing one of the most significant poems of the Ecuadorian Quichua, the *Atahualpa Huañui*, asks: '¿What may be said of the author when, in v. 33, we have a call to the brothers in the <turicunalla>

in Spanish, the force, the images that she created with her words, have seduced 'whites', 'mestizos' and indigenous people ever since she pronounced them.[13] What interests our work is that all of her discourses, all that has been gathered or preserves the memories of other personalities, records the use of metaphors and elements belonging to her cultural system. She never used foreign symbolic forms to express what she wanted. Not even as a Communist Party activist did Dolores sideline her own system of representation. On the contrary, the production of her discourse was measured by a tacit knowledge (her culture) that allowed her to create significant expressions for her indigenous and, curiously, 'mestizo' colleagues.

Synthesized in brief, Dolores Cacuango, upon personifying, in her political discourse of confrontation towards the state, the cultural elements of her own people, is creating a *positive* indigenous identity. The act of recovering the cultural elements that make her words significant for her people (and for that population considered 'non-indigenous'), implies a pride in being who she is. Of the spaces (the high, cold and bare *paramo* region),[14] of the experiences (the get together). Faced with a nation-state that cannot count on anything other than negative elements for proposing a national identity, Dolores *uses* those significant cultural elements in order to regain the unity, the pride of her culture and her experience in the struggle. With significant metaphors, she permits those hearing her *to feel like they belong*.

We are like grains of quinoa if we are alone, the wind takes us far, but if we are united in a sack, the wind cannot reach us, it will blow, but it won't cause us to fall.

The naturally alone, the master kicks and insults. He is like the fibre of a poncho that is easily broken. The naturally united, like a knitted poncho, boss will not be able to bend.

---

format? Given the Quichuan semantic structure, whoever pronounces that will be a woman. One may object that, for reasons of metre, that term would have to have been used. However, this objection is not pertinent because the wawkikuna format would fit perfectly in the metre cited. It is, then, the intention of the author (s), to place the gathering call to the brothers in the mouth of a woman (vv. 33–34)' (Garces,1998, p. 99).

13 Thus, the mural of the National Congress, made by Oswaldo Guayasamin, he paints it and locates one of his most well-known phrases: *We are the paramo grass that is torn up and grows again, and in paramo grass we cover the world.* Upon this same phrase, Muyolema (2001), explores in the indigenous 'expansionist' project of Dolores Cacuango's discourse. '.../.... The metaphor of the Indian as an historic root also operates as a denial of the co-ethnicity of the indigenous peoples: every political proposition of the so-called Indians is disqualified by the non-Indians because, according to them, such propositions embody "archaic utopias" and pretensions of "return to the past". The national historical narratives that silenced the peoples' political and cultural processes that identify with the voice of Dolores Cacuango, suffer from a chronic evolutionism that would be surprised by the possibility of reverting the process and proposing an indigenization of the world..../... against these narratives and in spite of them, we can interpret Mama Dulu's proposition as wagering on a counter-cultural process opposed to the "whitening": "sow or cover the world in grass" would imply a process of indigenization or kichwizacion of the world' (Muyolema, 2001, p. 355).

14 Which leads us to think of 'the crazy geography' that the nation-state falsifies in order to propose the myth of the vanquished race (Silva, 1995).

Sacks and ponchos form part of the everyday experiences of both the indigenous and non-indigenous, but, moreover, are signs of identity.[15] The listener can understand the sense of unity and belonging. It is the indigenous way. It is their culture. Dolores does not propose a halfway point for meeting the non-indigenous population, she waits for it in the pride of knowing who she is, and she then proposes that positive identity that the nation-state is not capable of offering. This expansionist sense of her proposal, as Muyolema (2001) has already affirmed, is present throughout her discourse and wisdom. Intelligently, around the exploitation of the indigenous, non-indigenous, blacks and half-castes, Dolores manages to establish points of consensus that the nation-state had not been able to find. She explains it thus:

> I have struggled in all areas of the nation. I have gone to the Congress. I have gone to Bogota. I have gone to Cali. I have gone to Guayaquil. I have gathered all the colleagues. I have gathered blacks and half-castes. I have struggled for everyone.
> I am not alone, I am not an orphan, I am not lying down. Now, the struggle-unity for all equally. For all we have struggled, for the poor, blacks, half-castes, carpenter, baker, barber. Seeking a future for all.

This idea of the struggle for *all* is present in the indigenous movement of today. It is the population excluded by the nation-state, but included in Dolores's view.[16] Two parallel political processes are perceived, but while the one does not forget Daquilema, the other does not manage to present itself as a national project.

We have tried to present the production context of this history and a brief portrait of Dolores Cacuango, to position what will be our analysis of her story concerning the origin of the Fatherland. In this narration, that notion of the Fatherland, understood as land of birth, and the elements that particularize it as part of an Andean cultural system, are joined together. The question of the origins, the struggles and the idea of a new order, in synthesis, represent the purpose of this history.

The Text

For the text analysis of the narration made by Dolores Cacuango on the origin of the Fatherland, we first present the narration recovered by Muriel Crespi at the beginning

---

15 One of the elements most indicative of identification, up until now, is clothing.

16 After the initial disquiet that the 1990 Indigenous Uprising produced among the country's non-indigenous population, little by little they have been questioning this, increasingly with more force. In the last uprising January–February, 2001, the scenes captured for national television were impressive, when, among others, one woman wept upon bidding farewell, on the highways that leave Quito, the indigenous people returning to their communities, while she said that they are the only ones who worry about the poor. However, the situation is still surprising to the country's ruling classes. Vice-president of the Republic, Pedro Pinto, a few days after the end of the indigenous uprising, affirmed: '.../... another thing that impressed me very much is that in the discussions, when the government offered advantages for the indigenous sector, the made it clear to us that they were not struggling exclusively for the indigenous sector, but for all the poor of the country' (Programme La Television, Sunday, 11 February 2001).

of the 1970s. This version is revisited both by Rodas (1998) and Yanez (1988). We will now attempt a series of edited cuttings according to periods and personalities, with a view to establishing minimum units of significance within the discourse. Linked to these minimum units of significance (which will be located in the first box on the left, Table 2.1), we will present the periods, elements and personalities of the narration, in order to facilitate locating the part referred to during the analysis. Finally, we will attempt an interpretation of this story.

Who was the owner of the Fatherland? Baby Manuelito. He fashioned the Fatherland. Holy Mary of Bethlehem gave birth in the prairie to Baby Manuelito. He is the owner. The planet thus was born. Only pure water, pure water. Thus rumour has said Baby Manuelito. And Holy Mary of Bethlehem has married. Our Lord Jesus Christ has married. Then he has said. But I don't know how to work; I do nothing, only a carpenter. Him working as carpenter and Holy Mary makes lunch. Thus, passing through humiliations she feels her belly. There then has gone Jesus Christ. To my house, I am ashamed, saying fleeing Holy Mary has given birth on the mount. And then there jumping, Baby Manuelito is born and the rumour has said: Look after my mummy's diet my daddy grandfather. I am going to form this Fatherland. No, we don't have power, little one, what power do you have? Mary has said. No, I'm going to see, I'm going to see my daddy there, at eight in the morning, there on slope of Josafan he is about to. If I can form it has to be at 12 noon. There, flag has to stop, music has to stop, band, for when it nears 12 o'clock sharp, rumour has said, Baby Manuelito. And the Baby Manuelito goes on to form the Fatherland and then, forming the Fatherland, he has made function, has made wedding,[17] has made drink, has made everything. And everything he has made, the little plant, also little barley, little wheat, little oca, little potato, all that he makes no more. Thus forming that he sees, ca, ahura, ca, the Fatherland.

The Analysis

The foregoing narration has been collected in Spanish, which has been interspersed with Quichua. Probably, the most evident is the presence of particles, such as 'ca', topic marker, used to re-table the subject being discussed or to emphasize the section of the discourse to which attention is drawn. Also noted is the absence of a numbered concordance which is unnecessary because of the Quichua linguistic structure being taken as read when there is an element that indicates it. Finally, perhaps the sense of some words in Spanish does not bear a relation to the sense given to the same by the Quichua communities. In the story, such is the case of 'advance', which is used in the sense of power. However, it is possible to discover and follow the logic of the discourse.

---

17 According to the testimony of Neptali Ulcuango, indigenous leader, contemporary of Dolores Cacuango from the same area, "For the meetings primarily – as they were accustomed to even before the initiation – the peasants in the employ of the hacienda were talking and convening a meeting, not directly saying that we were going to have a meeting, nor a session, nor in such and such a house. They said: –'This evening we're going to the wedding. This evening there will be a wedding at such and such a house, so let's all go to the wedding. Thus, everyone understood. They met at night because they were busy at work during the day and also to avoid persecution' (Yanez, 1988, pp. 164–165).

The narration is divided into three periods, linked to each other by what has been called culmination (Figure 9.1). Each one describing a specific situation. In the first, an introduction is made (phrases 1–4), positioning the topic of the origins and, as such, the owners of the Fatherland. The father and mother of the Baby Manuelito are presented. It tells of their marriage and the activities of these two characters (phrases 5–6). Next, it narrates the birth of the Baby Manuelito himself. Mary alone on the mount gives birth to the Baby Manuelito, who is born 'leaping' (phrases 7–10). Then the dialogue between the Baby Manuelito, his paternal grandfather and his mother is produced (his father has gone away before Mary gives birth). In this dialogue, Baby Manuelito delegates charge of his mother's diet and goes to form the Fatherland. The mother doubts the capacity of the child, as she also doubts her own capacity: (we have no power, little one, what power do you have?) (phrases 11–12). However, Baby Manuelito says that he will not go alone, that he is going to find his father. This is the moment that has been called culmination, when finally the Baby and the adults (his father) are together.

In this first moment, there are several important elements. We will begin an approximation to the characters that are basically two: the adults and baby Manuelito. Within the adults are, the paternal grandfather, the father, represented in the story by Jesus Christ and the mother, Holy Mary.

In the communities, the relationships between young and old are extremely important and a source of constant interrogations from one side to the other. Respect for the word and the instructions of the elders carry great weight with the young. There used to be problems with the migrants because, upon returning, they try to flaunt the authority of their parents and grandparents, generating disharmony and/or rejection among those who do not migrate, who, on the other hand, are generally women. But in the story, the doubt of the elders regarding the capacity of the young is overcome in the culmination, when Baby Manuelito affirms that he will not be alone, but that he will have his father with him, that is, the elders. This produces the union between those who seemed to be opposed.

Almeida Vinueza (1992, p. 263) collects the following scene: a Quichuan child, member of a musical group in a festival in Otavalo said: 'We are the root of our ancestors', a fact that had occasioned general laughter. But the situation would have been saved when the host – a professional journalist, also Quichuan – affirmed: 'Yes. It is in us, in the new generations, to make our ancestors *come to life*, to make them issue from our hearts in order to illuminate our path to freedom' (emphasis in the original).

The conflicts between the elders, the past, the tradition, and the young, the future, the modernity is a subject of political and academic debate. However, the dilemmas presented by the topic of 'tradition and modernity' are shaped not only in the political or academic exercises, but also in the development projects. With a rather evolutionist vision, what is in the past is held as something that must be overcome. To go forward, *to develop oneself*.

Emilia Ferraro (*s/f*) stated that the notion of development, conceived and applied between 1950 and 1960, had as a central focus, rapid economic growth and capital creation. Action that was not produced from the standpoint of the survival economy of the indigenous communities (Mayer, 1994). But moreover, modernization was conceived as being the step toward technologies and methods of social organization coming from the West; with this, the traditional world and the modern world, characterized by different economic structures, values, familial organization, and so on, would be at opposite poles. Of course, the process would be directed by 'privileged national groups, via political initiatives'.[18]

The tradition, the past, the elders, located on the end of that which heads toward the future, the young, the modernity, would have to be overcome en route. Nevertheless, the story achieves the symbolic union of the two poles. The Baby Manuelito and his daddy, who will go on to form the Fatherland.

On the other hand, the activities discharged by Mary and Our Lord Jesus Christ, are events that are easily positioned in the indigenous and non-indigenous cultural universe. Jesus Christ the carpenter and Holy Mary who follows him with the lunch, are characters who fulfil roles that correspond to indigenous people, but also to poor 'mestizos'. Additionally, the care of the diet is an activity that is undertaken not only in the indigenous communities, but also in the so-called 'mestizo' communities.

In this first part of the story, there is also a fundamental element: the place of birth of Baby Manuelito. The point of origin. This is the *paramo*, the *mountain*. An exclusively indigenous place where the non-indigenous can easily get lost or consider it abandoned. The story positions it as the key point for the birth of the Fatherland. From there emerges its founder, its creator. In the national narratives, the paramo is positioned as a barren desert, where only grass grows, and sterile. Nevertheless, Dolores positions it as the place where the Fatherland will originate, thus, a far cry from the image of the arid, useless and empty paramo that circulates in the non-indigenous imagination.[19]

Throughout all of the narration, it is interesting to note that not only the places, but also other elements, such as the food: potatoes, oca, barley, and wheat are directly linked to the indigenous world. They are foods that are consumed daily in the communities. But moreover, they belong to the world of the indigenous foods that sustain and strengthen the indigenous identity.[20] The party, the band, the flag, are another type of elements connected to important events within the indigenous communities.[21] The magnitude of the celebration of the party marks the importance of the occasion.

---

18 As a critic of this model, is that Muyolema (note 11), proposed his *indigenization* process.

19 This feeling of loneliness and aridity, probably inspired by the landscape, has resulted in, on some occasions, sacks of potatoes, 'abandoned' at the side of the Zumbahua highway, being 'taken' by travellers. Nevertheless, they are immediately recovered by the owners who, although not being visible, are looking after them. While I worked there, some occasionally violent confrontations took place in the area due to situations like this.

20 Weismantel (1994), points out, as in Zumbahua, that they are revealed by way of the classification and consumption of foods, visions and conflicts of indigenous and non-indigenous identity between the communities of the area.

21 The ethnography offers a piece of information worthy of reflection: in the 'mestizo' parties, the band, the food, the party in general has a strong parallel with indigenous experience. And, in general, when they have drunk quite a bit, they end up dancing to 'Indian music'. Once more, when the conscious censure disappears, the repressed Indian emerges.

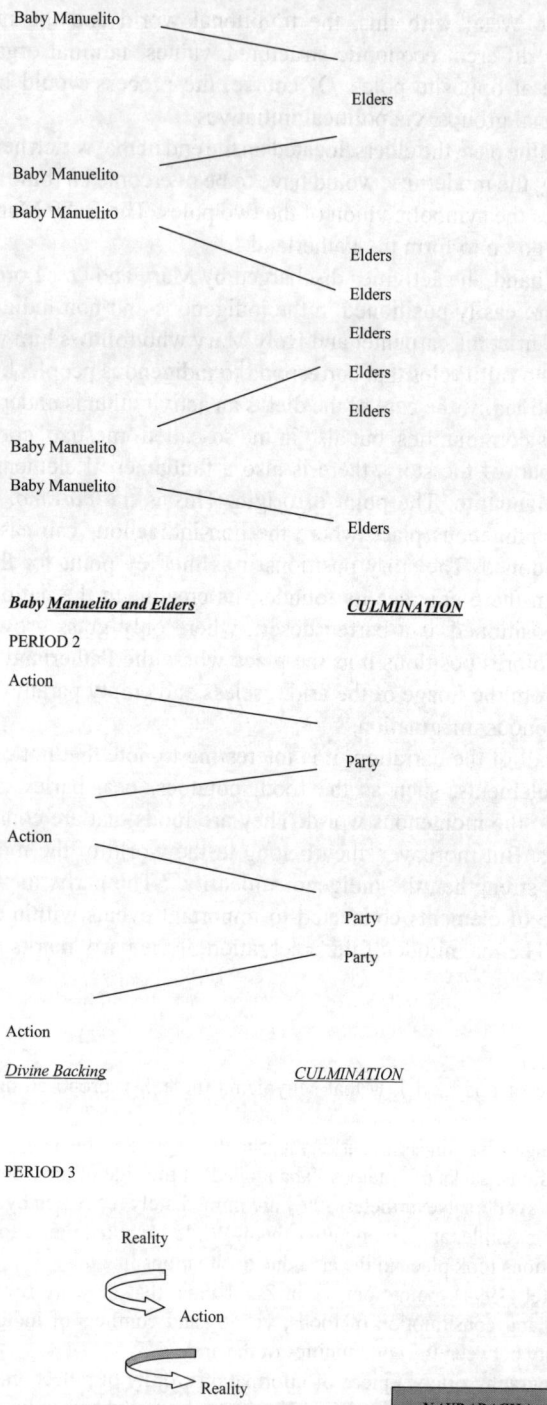

Figure 2.2   Moments, elements and prominent figures of Dolores Cacuango's text about the origin of the mother country

If in that first period of the narration it is possible to position the elders and the young people as two opposing poles, in the second period, the actions destined towards the formation of the Fatherland and the party thrown in its honour, represent the two extremes between which the story oscillates. I have positioned the culmination of this period in phrase 20. In that phrase, the supernatural characters (Little Daddy God, Baby Manuelito, Holy Mary), grant divine support to the possibility of a Fatherland for everyone. With this period, the story itself is brought to a close, giving way, in the third period, to the conclusion where two counterpoints are restored: the situation that is being lived (phrase 21), what must be done (phrase 22), in order to return finally to what is being lived.

Trying for a simpler graphing, we confirm that the movements between the characters and events generate a zigzag. (See Figure 2.2.)

The zigzag formed by the narration is repeated both in the fabrics and the songs. It is a design that is very diffuse in Andean culture. Gutmann (1993, p. 247) calls this *Andean cultural design*. The zigzag or *q'enqo*, symbolizes the continuity of life and the water current (idem.). In Dolores' story, water is present as the beginning (phrase 4), but, at the same time, in itself, this is a narration about origins. It is the story that legitimizes a group of actions that flow and are destined toward the formation of a 'Fatherland' for everyone. Water, the life-giving element, sustains both the narration of the origin and the search for life: *we need a little house, we need something to wear, to eat, to feed ourselves. We are humans, we want them to treat us well*, said Dolores on another occasion.

The symbolic articulation of the elements that concern a people is that which makes them unique. In the case of the Andean cultures, the systems of representation differ substantially, for example, from the Mexicans.[22]

For that reason, the elements present within the narration must not be analysed in isolation. Everything that is present within the story links together in order for it to make sense. Thus, water, time, space is presented together, because together they give emphasis to the message.

> The water current, the symbol of the continuity of life, includes also the notion of time; in the water current, as in the course of life, the past is chained to the present and the present to the future. One time is not separated from another; they intertwine, the interweave, they form a unity. It is the unity, it is the life that pulses (Gutmann, 1993, p. 250)

In itself, the entire story is a narration about the origins of an element foreign to the indigenous cosmovision: the Fatherland. The Fatherland that is an idea generated from the nation-state and assumed by the left as a battle flag. But Dolores makes it her own; *she reads it* as part of her codes. If in many Andean communities, the Fatherland is assumed a synonym for state (Cutipa Lima, 1993, pp. 20–21), this story shows how the indigenous communities process these foreign elements, integrating them into their

---

22 Such is the proposal of Thomas Cummins who suggests that the Andean representation systems with which the Spanish were met upon their arrival, were so abstract that events and memories saved on the quipos had to be 'translated' to pictures or stories. On the contrary, in Mexico, the mesoamerican written and pictorial tradition would have been clearer for the European conceptual universe. See Cummins, 1993.

cultural schema from their own logic. However, a debate still rages: does the nation-state, the ideologues of the left and right, realise that their codes have been made over?[23]

This is most evident if we note the conclusion of the story and that we have graphed at the bottom of figure two, and that we synthesize as Nayrapacha. This concept has been introduced in the analysis on the Andean culture by Carlos Mamani and then revisited both by Silvia Rivera and Muyolema, in some of their works.

Carlos Mamani explains: '...Nayrapacha: ancient times. But they are not ancient in terms of being long dead, lacking functions of renovation. They imply that this world can be reversible, that the past can also be future' (Rivera Cusicanqui, 1991, p. 1). This 'past-as-future' is 'a renovation of pacha (time space-plenitude). It deals with a past that in its to-come future is capable of reverting to the already lived situation transforming it' (Muyolema, 2001, p. 352).

The past, the origins of the Fatherland, sustained by Baby Manuelito on indigenous land, with elements destined to reinforce the idea that every thing indigenous are the centre of that 'new' Fatherland, it is that past that is going to be made future. In the midst of the protests, nayrapacha permits the overcoming of the present of punishments that the indigenous organizations experience. As Muyolema affirms, the situation of 'punishments' that is being lived, is reverted to transforming it, to make present the past narrated in the myth of the origin of the Fatherland, in the voice of Dolores Cacuango. The struggles of the indigenous organizations of Dolores Cacuango's day, violently repressed most times (see Table 2.2), permit an understanding of the reasons for the narration. We consider the myth becomes the vehicle for a social representation, with the intention of generating certain behaviour. The past, made present in the figure of the narrated myth, permits the expression of that social representation and the generation of a social conduct, linked to the work of the organizations.

But only through 'Nayrapacha' is it possible to conceptually articulate the memory and the utopia of the indigenous movements, that utopia that must be understood as something to-come. The idea of a historically linear time, diffused among the western societies, scarcely allows the understanding of the implicit agenda in Dolores' story. The concept of Nayrapacha permits the understanding that it does not desire to go backwards, but to be future out of the past. For this reason, the testimony of the indigenous boy, recorded by Jose Almeida,[24] is not a momentary error, on the contrary, reflects a full conception of the time space, but above all, a combination of these notions to life and the specific political struggles.

The epigraph of this work, which is another prophesy in the voice of a Quechuan woman of Bolivia, is alluded to here because, within the Andean indigenous peoples, there exists an extensive tradition of myths and symbols linked to a change in

---

23 The complex relationship that was established in the reading of the indigenous and non-indigenous cultural codes, has not been a subject studies from an anthropological viewpoint in Ecuador. Many events take place in them, which in foreign codes similar phenomena are read. It is not a case of thinking which type of elements are incorporated into the social life of the communities, but how are they used within them. Warnier (2001, p. 98), to provide a more ample context, points out: *Without doubt, the market globalises the flow of objects and behaviours, but in the same movement, it supplies the societies with infinitely diversified goods that serve to construct the difference and the identity.*

24 See p. 305.

the social and cultural structure. Both the voices of Matilde Qolque and Dolores Cacuango shout the indigenous processes that they have been already living. With this work, we have desired to reinforce the idea that the Ecuadorian Indigenous Movement has more history than just the last 11 years, and that the feminine participation should not be understood as a modern undertaking of the governmental and non-governmental organizations having a 'gender focus'. On the contrary, the Andean feminine participation is framed in its own cultural tradition and should be understood from and within that viewpoint.

Conclusions

The events of the last 10 years have had an effect on those of us who have grown up watching the huge indigenous mobilizations, whether on television or in the streets. The public visibility of the indigenous movement, at a national level, has allowed us to listen to the 'historical' directors, as well as to the new ones. Many of us 'mestizos' have participated in indigenous assemblies. Many of us have voted for indigenous candidates, and with the help of those of us not recognized by either the government nor the indigenous organizations as being indigenous, the candidates for Pachakutik, the party of the Indian organizations, have been re-elected in the diverse municipalities where they carry out their public administrations.

In 2000, the dollarization of the Ecuadorian economy was decreed; the country was thus transformed into an economic laboratory of the future plans for the Americas. From the heights of power, the myths, the symbols, the mythified heroes continue to be considered second-class elements. And while the country's economic crisis fails to unite those who wield power in the nation-state, the indigenous organizations undertake a task that began several years ago, not only with the indigenous population, but also with the 'mestizo'. Little by little, the barrier of racism and discrimination is being weakened. The process is far from completion; it has just begun and promises to be difficult.

Nevertheless, the weaknesses of the nation-state in proposing a national identity that includes at least a considerable portion of the Ecuadorian population represent ruptures that the indigenous movement has been taking advantage of. In the face of a state that has not bothered to educate, generate channels of communication or media such as a nationwide television network, the endogenous resistance of the indigenous communities is beginning to show signs of its centrifugal potential.

Anthropologically speaking, the cultural distances between the indigenous and the mestizo are short.[25] The limits that should be positioned are, better stated, political in nature. The cultural concurrences, such as shared expressions of symbolic systems, allow Dolores Cacuango's texts to be understood, assimilated both by the indigenous and the non-indigenous. The question mark is not really at the cultural level, however, like since the times of the colonization, the question revolves around who considers himself to be mestizo and as a function of what. Politically, this is the

---

25 See the text of Espinoza Apolo, 1995 that makes a very specific synthesis regarding the Ecuadorian mestizos.

interesting part. Who stops considering himself indigenous or mestizo, to assume as a political act, in face of the nation-state, an identity that grants him advantages or disadvantages in such and such situations, is making a choice that is more political than cultural. As a function of what is the choice undertaken to assume an identity that involves estrangements, in the case of 'ceasing to be indigenous'? When does one cease to be indigenous? The political option may be expressed in the use of dress or language, however, the mental symbolic structures that allow for the articulation of the difference cannot be limited to dress or the public use of Spanish.[26] But, what is to be done about the increasingly frequent questions of the population considered non-indigenous regarding who they are?

During the events of January 2001 in Quito, many pieces of graffiti appeared saying: 'They're Indians and we are.... ?' 'Who is the minority?' This without taking into account that, to the surprise of those who classify them, many people openly, with or without doubts, declare themselves to be indigenous. What made these people opt for declaring themselves to be indigenous?

Dolores Cacuango is a woman who is not alone. Several indigenous women of this century have actively and publicly participated in the indigenous movement. They represent an open question to those positions that suggest that indigenous women should not participate in the public affairs of their communities. Within the indigenous movement itself, Dolores Cacuango represents a challenge and a reference point. Her words sustain uprisings and generate debate and reflection. Because throughout all of her texts she efficaciously refutes that generalized idea, both in academia and in political circles that the so-called Indians (altered like foreign and distant) want to, in some way, as Muyolema would say, 'Go back to the past'. She allows in this present, but clearly facing the future, a possibility of *being* for the indigenous people and its culture.

With large headlines, it is constantly repeated in newspapers and magazines: *the Indians want power*. The events of January 2000 corroborate it. The warnings and the fright come out of the impossibility of thinking of the indigenous people as a real future, and not simply as still open crevices of a past that must be overcome. Dolores Cacuango was sure about wanting a future as an indigenous person and, in that, the political power, the control of the state, is not excluded. In some way, in the measure in which the indigenous peoples are proving capable of carrying out successful local administrations,[27] the grass of the *paramo* is covering, openly, the world of the Ecuadorian nation-state.

The voice of the women extends over the entire Andean region. The idea that the time has to change for their people subsists among the narrators. Mama Dulu,

---

26 Evidently, language is one of the elements around which the demand for respect of the difference is articulated. Discounting the linguistic and political importance of the use and growth of the indigenous tongues, our interest is in demonstrating that the cultural peculiarities do not dry up when the languages are no longer used.

27 Like Guamote or Cotacachi, to cite the most representative examples. The mayor of Cotacachi won, in November of 2000, a world prize for best local administration, to the astonishment and surprise of those who didn't believe that an Indian was capable of making a good administration.

Table 2.3   The indigenous heroes of history of Father Juan Velasco according to modern school poster details

PACCHA CHIRI XVI	Upon the death of his father Chiri XV at the battle of Hatum-Taqui (Prov. of Imbabura), the army proclaimed him Chiri XVI and he married Huayna-Cápac, with this he assured the total conquest of the Kingdom of Quito and the expansion of the "TAHUANTINSUYO".
NAZACOTA PUENTO	With the Quiteno warriors that did not surrender at the battle of Hatum Taqui (Prov. of Imbabura), he resisted the army of Huayna-Cápac for 17 years, dying in the Yaguarcocha (Imbabura) lagoon, together with his 30,000 brave warriors.
TOMALA	Headman of the punáes, who, seeing the impossibility of resistance to the Túpac-Yupanqui conquest, set a trap and, upon failing, died with his people.
PINTAG	Warrior who put up fierce resistance to the army of Huayna-Cápac at the battle of Hatum-Taqui (Prov. of Imbabura)- Imprisoned, he preferred death to loss of his independence and selling his soul.

or Matilde Colque's grandmother, remember the stories that maintain the certainty that things are going to change, they did not see them, but their children are seeing them and are participants in the new political and cultural processes of the Andean indigenous peoples.

The participation of women in these new processes has other angles and new trajectories. But it must not be forgotten that their action should be understood within the Andean cultural logic, and not as an exclusively western political events. The rules, codes or conventions that intervene in the production, construction or employment of the symbolic forms produced by indigenous women, are not the same at the moment of codification as those used for the decoding. How is the feminine indigenous participation read in the national society, or in the left wing parties, or in the NGOs?

It would be an error to try to understand the participation of women, from a standpoint external to the Andean cultural logic. Or worse even, to politically formulate them outside of it, as several NGOs do. Dolores Cacuango represents the clearest example that feminine participation is possible within the indigenous organizational processes. Otherwise, the processes of conquering and domination would have to be repeated, where that *kichwización* of the world that Mama Dulu herself sought and brought to us, as an alternative civilizing process, renewable today more than yesterday, is not possible.

Glossary

Middle Managers

Administrator, mestizo brought from the city to look after the interests of the hacienda owner.
Scribe, kept the accounts and production records of the hacienda.
Overseer, generally, mestizo who oversaw the work.

Mayorales o apatronados, indigenous assistants of the overseer.

Cuentayos, indigenous responsible for the reproduction and raising of livestock, crops and cheeses.

Indigenous workers

Ordeñadoras

Huasicamas women, in charge of laundry and food preparation in the hacienda main house.

Huasicamas men, care and feeding of horses, provision of firewood, minor errands.

Servants, girls of 11 or 12 years who did housework and served the masters and hacienda employees.

Yanaperos, occasional casual hacienda workers in exchange for favours (use of water, grass or thoroughfares).

Arrieros, transporters of products to the markets or to the destination of the masters' choice. Arrimados, landless peasants who lived with relatives in the hope of one day obtaining a parcel of land. Volunteer labour for hacienda work. For them remained the chucchir, grain collection after the harvest.

Peasants unbound o free, not having a great link to the hacienda or fixed residence there, with wages paid in cash or produce and subject to free hiring.

Own peasants, those who lived permanently on the hacienda land.

Huasipungueros, in exchange for unpaid work on the hacienda lands, they were given a small plot of land, the huasipungo, for their personal use, along with use of resources such as water, firewood and pasture.

Source: Rodas, 1998.

References

Albornoz Peralta, O., *Osvaldo Historia del Movimiento Obrero Ecuatoriano* (Quito: Letranueva).

Almeida Vinueza, J. (1990), 'Luchas campesinas del siglo *XX* (primera parte)' in *Nueva Historia del Ecuador. V. 10. Epoca Republicana IV*. Ayala Mora, E. (ed) (Quito: Corporación Editora Nacional), 163–185.

Almeida Vinueza, J. (1992) 'Quinto Centenario y resistencia Indígena' in *Indios*. Cornejo, D. (ed) (Quito: Abya Yala), 263–292.

Bulnes, M. (1994), *Hatarishpa Ninimi, Me Levanto y Digo. Testimonio de Tries Mujeres quichuas* (Quito: El Conejo).

Cervone, E. et al. (1998), *Mujeres contracorriente. Voces de líderes indígenas* (Quito: CEPLAES).

Cueva, A. (1990), 'El Ecuador de 1925 a 1960' in *Nueva Historia del Ecuador. V. 10. Epoca Republicana IV*. Ayala Mora, E. (ed) (Quito: Corporación Editora Nacional), 87–112.

Cummins, T. (1993), 'La representación en el siglo: La imagen colonial del Inca' Urbano Henrique (Comp.) *Mito y Simbolismo En Los Andes La Palabra y la Imagen, Cusco* (Centro Bartolomé de las Casas).

Cutipa Lima, J. (1993), *Reflexiones críticas sobre el pensamiento andino. Puno* (Universidad Nacional del Altiplano).

Espinosa Apolo, M. (1995), *Los Mestizos Ecuatorianos y Las Señas De Identidad Cultural* (Quito: Tramasocial).

Ferraro, E. s/f, Notas sobre Desarrollo: un Enfoque Histórico-Teórico, Fotocopias, Quito.

Fuentealba, G. (1990), 'La Sociedad Indígena En Las Primeras Décadas de la República: Continuidades y Cambios Republicanos' in *Nueva Historia del Ecuador. V. 8. Epoca Republicana II.* Ayala Mora, E. (ed) (Quito: Corporación Editora Nacional), 45–68.

Garces, F. (2000), 'Aportes para un análisis lingüístico de la poesía quichua: Atahualpa Huañui', *Revista Educación Intercultural Bilingüe A*, **2**(4), 89–104 (Quito: UPS-Programa Académico Cotopaxi).

Guerrero, A. (1983), *Hacienda, Capital y Lucha De Clases Andina* (Quito: El Conejo).

Gutierrez, N. (2001), *Mitos Nacionalistas e Identidades Étnicas los Intelectuales Indígenas y el Estado Mexicano* (México: CONACULTA. IIS. Plaza y Valdez Editores).

Gutmann, M (1993), 'Relato sobre el agua', *Urbano Henrique (Comp.) Mito y Simbolismo En Los Andes. La Palabra y la Imagen* (Cusco; Centro Bartolomé de las Casas).

Harrison, R. (1996), *Entre el Tronar Épico y el Llanto Elegíaco: Simbología Indígena en la Poesía Ecuatoriana de los Siglos XIX y XX* (Quito: Abya Yala).

Harvey, P. (1987), 'Lenguaje y relaciones de poder: Consecuencias Para una Política Lingüística (1)', *Allpanchis*, **XIX**(29/30), 105–101 (Cusco: Instituto de Pastoral Andina).

Harvey, P. (1989), *Género, Autoridad y Competencia Lingüística Participación Política de la Mujer en Pueblos Andinos* (Lima, Instituto de Estudios Peruanos).

Harvey, P. (1991), 'Mujeres que no hablan castellano Género, Poder y Bilingüismo En Un Pueblo Andino', *Allpanchis,* **XXIII**(35), 227–260 (Cusco: Instituto de Pastoral Andina).

Ibarra, A. (1992), *Los Indígenas y el Estado en el Ecuador* (Quito: Abya Yala).

Icaza, P. (1984), *Historia del movimiento obrero ecuatoriano. De su Génesis Al Frente Popular* (Quito: CEDMIME).

Mayer, E. (1994), *Notas del Seminario: Economía Campesina en los Andes* (Quito: CELE/Pontificia Universidad Católica del Ecuador).

Moreano, A. (2000), 'El Ecuador: simulacro o renacimiento', Saltos, N. (Comp.) *La Rebelión Del Arcoiris Testimonios y análisis* (Quito: Fundación José Peralta), 159–186.

Muyolema, A. (2001), 'De la "cuestión indígena" a lo "indígena" como Cuestionamiento, Hacia una crítica del latinoamericanismo, el indigenismo y el mestizaje' in *Convergencia de Tiempos. Estudios Subalternos / contextos latinoamericanos estado, Cultura subalternidad.* Rodriguez, I. (ed.) (Amsterdam/ Atlanta: Editions Rodopi Books), 327–363.

Rivera Cusicanqui, S. (1987), 'La mujer en la lucha comunaria en Bolivia: historia y memoria por el Taller de Historia Oral Andina', in *Ciudadanía e Identidad: las*

Mujeres en los Movimientos Sociales Latinoamericanos. Jelin, E. (Comp.) (Ginebra: Instituto de Investigaciones de las Naciones Unidas Para El Desarrollo Social).

Rivera Cusicanqui, S. (1991), *Pachakuti: Los Aymara de Bolivia Frente a Medio Milenio de Colonialismo Chukiyawu* (Taller de Historia Oral Andina).

Rodas, R. (1998), *Dolores Cacuango* (Quito: GTZ/EBI).

Silva, E. (1995), *Los Mitos de la Ecuatorianidad* (Quito: Abya Yala).

Stolen, K.A. (1987), *A media voz. Relaciones de género en la sierra ecuatoriana* (Quito: CEPLAES).

Warnier, J.P. (2001), *La mundialización de la cultura* (Quito: Abya Yala).

Weismantel, M.(1994), *Alimentación, Género y pobreza en los Andes ecuatorianos* (Quito: Abya Yala).

Yanez del Pozo, J. (1988), 'Yo Declaro Con Franqueza' in *Memoria Oral de Pesillo–Cayambe*. Causashcanchi, C. (ed.) (Quito: Abya Yala).

Chapter 3

Nahua Women's Struggle: Small Spaces, Enormous Restrictions[1]

Elena Lazos Chavero[2]

...I don't tell anyone what I think, because I don't know anything. I can't read, I didn't go to school, we were poor, I can't talk to people from the city, so who wants to know what's going on in my head?   (Doña Mauricia, old Nahua woman from Tatahuicapan)

What are we supposed to do? They leave us with no support. I wanted to file a complaint, but I went dozens of times and they never paid me a blind bit of notice. Now I've lost the land, I don't have anywhere to plant my corn.   (Adelfa, Nahua woman from Tatahuicapan)

Introduction: Struggles and Inequalities

Nowadays, despite the incorporation of the concept of gender as a discursive element in the links between indigenous population, environment, poverty and development and in the discussions on sustainable development, integral policies have yet to be devised to ensure the wellbeing of rural domestic units that engage in participatory processes. Even less has been done to promote policies which, despite involving social actors as a whole, focus on indigenous women in impoverished rural settings. Despite the rural effervescence of the 1970s, it was not until 1986 that peasant women from the *Coordinadora Nacional Plan de Ayala* were able to organize their first national encounter and discuss their own role in rural struggles. Despite their continuous marginalization, various women from a number of organizations have managed to open up a political space for devising projects and experiences that reflect their specific problems (Hernández, 2004). However, engaging in collective action in public and political spheres has not been easy. At this point, it is worth recalling some experiences of the 1990s, such as the First Meeting of Coffee Producing Women, organized by the *Coordinadora Estatal de Productores de Café de Oaxaca* (CEPCO), the San Cristóbal Women's Group, the Chiltak Organisation.

1   This research was carried out thanks to financing from the Head Office for Academic Personnel Support (DGAPA) at UNAM as part of the project on 'Depletion of Natural Resources and Productive Alternatives for Sustainable Development in the Sierra Santa Martha, Veracruz' coordinated by Elena Lazos and Luisa Paré.
2   I would like to thank the Nahua women from Tatahuicapan in the Sierra de Santa Martha with whom I shared their lives and with whom I experienced a deep sense of solidarity.

The women in these organizations participated in all kinds of assemblies, promoting recognition of their role and living conditions. However, despite that women's guidelines have become a key part of these organizations, women are still faced with countless difficulties; family restrictions, excessive workload, incredulity and lack of respect from various authorities, financial difficulties, lack of education and health services (Aranda, 1996).

In this chapter, I would like to discuss the limitations and possibilities that exist regarding the construction of sustainable processes to enable one of the poorest, most marginalized sectors of the rural setting-women to participate in the decision-making concerning the development of their communities and access to and use of their natural resources.

Through this study, I would like to reflect on the enormous social inequalities that exist for women, particularly indigenous women, in order to foster genuine participation and political openness in their own communities. The mosaic comprising indigenous women is based on profound inequities due to language, customs, education, forms of access to land, financial resources, and organization, but above all, the relationship with the state's political structures. Thus, although there are organizations of independent women, and others that may form part of larger organizations, with shortages and difficulties, but with the experience of a collectively, there are also women who have never participated in community decision-making or had the experience of an organization, nor do they have right of access to land, meaning that they feel devalued and marginalized within their own communities. The case described in this paper concerns the latter, in other words, Nahua women from the Sierra de Santa Marta in the south of Veracruz whose prescribed role is to operate within their domestic groups and who have been overlooked by institutional, legal and organizational mechanisms.

Divergent Positions: Contradictory Policies

Since 1975, when the United Nations declared the decade of women, whose aim was to achieve the 'integration of women into economic development', various positions have emerged, which have translated into intervention models and different public policies. In the 1970s, populationists pointed to demographic growth as the main cause of maldevelopment in countries. They posited that economic growth alone would generate demand for the use of birth control methods, which in turn would eliminate poverty. After the World Conference on Population in Bucharest in 1974, economic growth was replaced by economic development as the universal panacea. This trend also emphasized a population control policy, but through the improvement of health and education conditions. However, the economic crises of the 1980s led to a drastic decline in social spending.

Within this scenario of an economic development policy, in which women were merely regarded as the depositories for the implementation of birth control, new approaches emerged. These proposals showed the importance of incorporating women into development programs. This view, known as WID (Women in Development), has been criticized because of its instrumental nature, its overtly financial approach, and the fact that it regards women as the only object of development, without contextualizing the social, political and cultural relations in which they are immersed.

In the debate on the links between population-environment-poverty, environmentalists reformulate the demographic thesis by attributing ecological deterioration to population growth. Criticism of these postures hinged on two issues: ignorance of the complex social relations that govern population processes and the mathematical reductionism that attempts to use a single model to explain the variety of links that exist between population and environment. This approach ignores the environmental impact produced by differences in the patterns of consumption between rich and poor.

Other environmentalists, academics and feminist activists have created new approaches focusing the relationship between population and environment. They generally regarded population growth as a secondary factor in the explanation of environmental deterioration and poverty, attributing these problems to the unequal distribution of wealth and a predominantly male social structure.

During the 1970s, the WID view incorporated proposals that included the relationship between women and the environment. This approach, known as Women, Environment and Development (WED) has been criticized in similar ways to the theoretical bases of WID. Firstly, its reflections focus on the role played by women, rather than on gender relations. Secondly it regards 'women' as a homogeneous whole and finally, it fails to consider the different perceptions of women regarding the environment due to generational, ethnic and class differences.

Several authors criticized these trends, arguing that women's problems are the result of the subordinate position they occupied, primarily in power relations. They therefore suggested that in order for the policies to be really effective, in addition to improving women's living conditions, they should focus on changing their position in society through their empowerment.[3] This trend is known as GID (Gender in Development).[4]

In analysing relations with the environment, the Gender, Environment and Development approach (Ged) introduces two key aspects. Both the environment and gender relations are social constructions that occur within a dynamic fabric in which various sectors with often contrasting interests and values intervene. The power structure, at both the micro and regional level, will serve as the framework for understanding the relations between gender, environment and development.

---

3   Empowerment is understood as a process of political education that challenges existing power relations through the dialogic praxis between action and reflection. A process of empowerment encourages and requires people, organizations and groups without power to a) be aware of the dynamics of power in the context where they live and work, b) develop skills and capacities to gain reasonable control over their lives, c) exercise this control without infringing the rights of others and d) support the empowerment of others actors in the community. The strategies for women's empowerment must increase their skill in controlling resources, determining agendas or programs and decision-making (Kabeer, 1998 p. 241).

4   The GID trend has been broadly represented by the WAD (Women for Alternative Development) group.

All these debates and achievements, but more, the pressure of women's movements have translated into the occupation of political spaces by women. Within their own communities, women have gained access to tasks involving social responsibility through cooperatives, as health promoters, by creating savings banks and in their negotiations with the authorities (Hernández, 2004). All this has modified women's position in the community sphere and created appropriate forums for their demands. However, although they have gained significant social spaces, enormous gaps still remain.

The implementation of these ideas into social, political and economic practices raises a number of questions. Whereas for external agents the strategic objective is the empowerment of women and other subordinate sectors, the latter's attention focuses on solving their needs. If these points of view are not oriented towards the same direction, it undermines the respect for the methodological principle of social participation. At the same time, there is the methodological difficulty of coordinating all the dimensions in the conditions of poverty in which developing countries live.

In this respect, poverty should become the starting point for constructing processes of sustainability linking gender and environment. Much of the bibliography on the issue has talked about a 'vicious circle' between poverty and environmental degradation, in which peasants, driven by the population increase and the need to satisfy their requirements, occupy more marginalized land that can easily become degraded. However, one should recall that poverty is not a homogenous phenomenon. Reardon and Vosti (1995, 1495) suggest that there are different types of poverty in rural settings, according to the types of resources that a person lacks, be they: a) natural resources, b) human resources c) financial and material resources related to agriculture or d) financial resources unrelated to agriculture. These authors state that when a 'vicious circle' between poverty and deterioration is posited, the structural complexity of the environment is overlooked, meaning that when problems involving environmental changes are discussed, the problem tends to be over-simplified. They suggest that the criteria for poverty should include the capacity to invest in order to improve or maintain the natural resources to which people have access. A domestic group may be above the poverty line and yet be below it as regards its capacity to invest in the maintenance of natural resources.

In studies on the interrelationship between gender, population, poverty and the environment, these considerations are crucial. We start with the idea that female poverty, from a gender approach, requires the study of absolute poverty, which both men and women have the right to satisfy. However, there is also a need for approaches involving relative poverty, which refer to the specific states of deprivation of women, which are gender-based (Salles and Tuiran, 1999). Gender inequalities, which place women at a disadvantage in aspects such as access to power, decision-making, and resources, inhibit the development of their capacities and rights, making them more vulnerable to conditions of extreme poverty, by trapping poor women in circles of precariousness from which it is difficult to escape. It is essential to consider the 'deprivation trap' proposed by Chambers (1983) in order to understand the significance of female confinement within their domestic sphere which makes women dependent, and often leads to their having high levels of malnutrition, low levels of schooling, vulnerability and a lack of power in relation to male family members and male authorities (Bonfil, 1996; González Montes, 1997). The feminization of poverty should therefore be analysed within both the family and the region. There are households above the poverty line within women can experience enormous economic and social inequities which in turn forces them to depend entirely on male members of the family. Thus, there is not only a need for approaches that will study poverty from a socio-demographic and economic point of view, but also cultural studies that will help one understand the gender dynamic engaged in by men and women, indigenous or mestizo people in impoverished rural settings.

Populations from the Sierra: Who Loses Out?

As part of these reflections, I would like to provide elements for explaining the possibilities and social, political and cultural limitations that prevent rural women from taking part in the decision-making process regarding two aspects: the development of their own communities and the access to and conservation of natural resources. How have women lost the productive space and territory in the sense of the communal use of natural resources? What implications does this loss have for women's position in their communities? How could communities govern the access to, use and conservation of natural resources in order to guarantee equity in environmental management? What opportunities are there for women to participate in the political and cultural context of indigenous communities in the Sierra de Santa Martha in the south of Veracruz? To answer these questions, we constructed a collective experience with the Nahua community of Tatahuicapan in the municipality of Tatahuicapan de Juárez.[5]

A section of the sierra territory constitutes part of the recently declared Los Tuxtlas Biosphere Reserve, since it still contains remnants of an enormous biodiversity. The relief of the sierra, which rises from sea level to 1,720 m.a.s.l., the heavy rainfall and a mosaic of different types of soil creates a variety of atmospheres that favours the development of 14 types of vegetation (from mangrove swamps, palm groves, savannahs, tropical pine groves and oak woods, to evergreen high and low forests). The paradox of the sierra is that, within this region of rich biodiversity, the population lives in conditions of extreme poverty and marginalization. The municipalities (Mecayapan, Pajapan, Soteapan and Tatahuicapan) which are home to 69,218 inhabitants according to the 2000 Census (INEGI, 2000) have been categorized as highly marginalized.[6]

5　Tatahuicapan is a community of Nahua origin with over 9,000 inhabitants. However, since the last decade of the twentieth century, it has been populated by *mestizo* families from the center and south of Veracruz (1995) Municipal Census). The *ejido* has 11,234 hectares, whom which only 466 ejido members benefit, as a result of which there is a broad contingent of families that have settled there without having legal access to land. Nowadays, as a result of the purchase of lands, there are just over 700 owners with plots of land varying in size from 2 to 20 hectares (Community Archive, 1997). Their land is primarily used for extensive cattle-raising or maize growing, in small areas.

6　By 1995, Pajapan had an index of 1.245, Mecayapan had an index of 1.396 and Soteapan had an index of 1.579 in 1995, Tatahuicapan was still included in the data

The sierra dates back to ancient times, when the Populucas utilized this enormous range of atmospheres. The subsequent arrival of the Nahua from the centre of Mexico led to the creation of shared spaces (Velázquez, 1997). The productive system of the Nahua and Popoluca developed in various spatial units, such as the forest, the savannahs, the milpa and the lagoon. A peasant family could support itself on 2 hectares of milpa, in addition to what the lake and streams provided. The high diversity of crops in the milpas (numbering up to 30) afforded peasant families the basic diet (Foster, 1942, pp. 16–26). Growing coffee, rice and sugar cane and raising pigs produced a small-scale monetary income. Each ecosystem was used (hunting in the mountains, fishing in the rivers, picking mushrooms in the oak forests and obtaining fruit and wood from the forest) (Stuart, 1978; Perales, 1992; Chevalier and Buckles, 1995).

For many years, the Popoluca and the Nahua defended their territory from those attempting to occupy their land. In 1906, peasants from the sierra joined the movement led by Ricardo Flores Magón's Liberal Party. Until the 1930s, the region saw the beginning of agrarian distribution. Peasant farmers' applications for plots of 'ejido' land within the Populucas' communal land led to the start of agrarian measures to regularize the legal situation of land.[7] Likewise, the monopolization of land triggered the struggle for better distribution (Velázquez, 1992; Chevalier and Buckles, 1995; Lazos, 1996). During this period, the population began to increase at an annual rate of 1.3 per cent, as opposed to what had happened when the revolutionary struggle had prevented any increase.

Between 1930 and 1950, the population slowly increased. Throughout the 1950s, the demand for labour in the Minatitlán-Coatzacoalcos corridor triggered a mass emigration of the sierra's inhabitants towards these points (Palma, Quesnel and Delaunay, 2000, p. 100). From the late 1950s onwards, the sierra was subjected to several waves of mestizo colonization-led by government programs such as 'the march towards the sea' that sought to meet the political demands of landless peasants in other parts of Veracruz. Between 1960 and 1970, 12 new 'ejidos' were created with landless mestizo and indigenous populations. In the mestizo communities, access to plots of land was granted on an individual basis, originally through the provision of ejido land and subsequently through informal contracts involving the sale and purchase of land. Thus, the sierra that had once been inhabited by Popoluca and Nahua was gradually turned into an ethnic mosaic intermingled with *mestizos* from various parts of the state of Veracruz (Figure 3.1). The establishment of the aforementioned agrarian policies and the colonization had demographic repercussions, since the period between the censuses (1960–1970) saw the recovery of an annual population growth rate of 3 per cent. During this period, most of the sierra was distributed among the ejidos.

In the Nahua communities, social conflicts, resulting from colonization by mestizos who brought with them a model of extensive cattle-raising, led to a sharp

---

for Mecayapan, since it formed part of that municipality. All three are among the 40 most marginalized municipalities in the country (Conapo, 1998).

7   For details of the agrarian struggle in the region, consult Foster, 1942; Paré et al., 1992; Chevalier and Buckles, 1995; Velázquez, 1992.

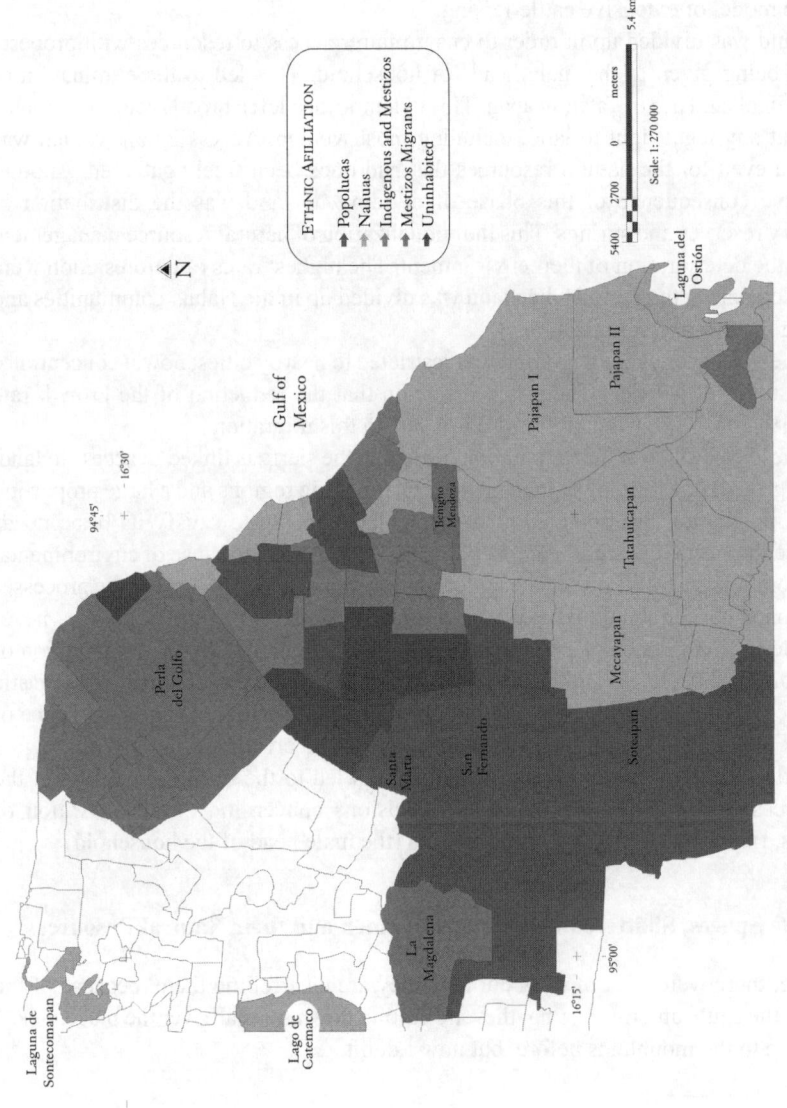

ETHNIC AFILIATION

↑ Popolucas
↑ Nahuas
↑ Indigenous and Mestizos
↑ Mestizos Migrants
↑ Uninhabited

Scale: 1: 270 000

5400   2700   0   meters   5.4 km

Map design by: Cynthia Trigos Suzán

SOURCE: SIG-PSSM

Figure 3.1   Ethnic affiliation according to land tenure during 1995 in de Sierra de Santa Marta, Veracruz, Mexico

conflict over the use of resources. Whereas before the milpa-forest system had formed part of a productive cycle, the spread of cattle-raising throughout communal land forced the milpa owners to occupy smaller areas (Velázquez, 1992; Chevalier and Buckles, 1995; Lazos, 1996; Vázquez, 1996). At the same time, through the squandering of credit, national agricultural policies promoted the conversion of 'infertile and unproductive lands' (that is rainforest) into a sea of pastureland based on the model of extensive cattle-raising.

Land was divided up in order to ensure fairer access to resources with property deeds being given to the male heads of household. This led to the elimination of communal land use in Tatahuicapan. This dynamic also left a broad sector of peasants without any legal right to land, including most women. Access by all women was limited even for the natural resources that had once been freely gathered. Another negative consequence of this phase of dividing up land was the distribution of forestry reserves and springs. This individualization of natural resource management led to the deterioration of their environment. The highest rates of deforestation were recorded during the period when land was divided up in the Nahua communities and during the mestizo colonization.

A few decades ago, emigration was restricted to nearby cities; now it concentrates to the north of Mexico. There is a suspicion that the reduction of the growth rate from 1995 to 2000, which fell to 1.35, is due to this migration.

These data suggest that population growth in the sierra is linked to access to land. Since growth rates are lower than in other surrounding regions and a large proportion of the population has obtained a supplementary income to satisfy its basic needs outside the sierra, the argument that population growth is the cause of environmental deterioration is invalid and that the interrelationship between the rest of the processes mentioned earlier should be explored in greater depth. Government policies never regarded the environment as a resource that should be maintain, the introduction of technological packages had negative consequences on the environment. The drastic changes in land use in mestizo communities took place within a very short space of time. Finally, the distribution of land gave rise to the creation of a large contingent of settlers without access to land, which in turn led to the over-exploitation of the resources, and on the other hand, left decisions concerning the conservation of forests, rivers and springs up to individuals (the male head of the household).

Private Spaces, Shattered Perceptions, Women and their Natural Resources[8]

Before, there were a lot of trees but now they are clearfelling them, because of the milpa, the cattle and for grazing, they are cutting down trees all over the place. I used to go up to the mountains before, but now I don't.

---

8   This section is discussed in more detail in the article by Godínez and Lazos (2003). It was constructed on the basis of interviews with 45 Nahua women from the community of Tatahuicapan. The sample was designed to include 50 per cent adults, 25 per cent old women and 25 per cent young people. Three age groups were established: old women (over 60), adults (between 26 and 59) and young women (between 15 and 25). We realize that these categories are somewhat arbitrary, since the local population does not define the stage of life

This quotation by an old woman from Tatahuicapan takes us back to the time when women used to go up to the 'mountain' (forest)[9] looking for the various resources to which they had access. Those times obviously refer to the period before the land was divided up. The most serious consequence of this change in land ownership is individual access to the forest. Before the land was divided up, all the inhabitants (both men and women) were allowed access to this communal resource. Afterwards, only *ejidatarios* whose plots of land had wooded areas or were located near the edges of the forest could continue to use the range of forestry resources.

This transformation of the access to land serves as watershed between the past and present. Previously, 75 per cent of the old women interviewed went up to 'the mountain' at some stage in their family cycle, as opposed to only 22 per cent who do so nowadays. Likewise, whereas before 44 per cent of the adult women used to go to the forest, at present only 10 per cent has access to these resources. This means that there has been a drastic reduction in women's interaction with their environment. It is worth noting that young women never go to these areas at any time.

What did women do in these forest areas? Whereas adult men were responsible for cutting wood to build houses and hunting, women concentrated on gathering edible plants (such as fruits, mushrooms or inflorescences, the most important being a palm known as *Astrocarium mexicanum*), and occasionally ornamental plants. The fruits gathered in the rainforest such as the *totolochi* (*Cayaponia racemosa*), wild lime or tencualala (*Achatocarpus mexicanus*) and star tree or vaina (*Inga jinicuil*) were only consumed occasionally and did not form part of their basic diet. Other fruits and leaves used in the preparation of food were gathered in the secondary forests and along the riverbanks (list in Lazos and Paré, 2000). An important activity during the rainy season was mushroom gathering (yellow and white mushrooms) in the olm-oak groves, which was generally carried out by women once or twice a week during four months.

Female activity focused on the rivers and streams, which might be either near or in the heart of 'the mountain'. Previously, most of the old women (around 90 per cent of the interviewees) and adult women (75 per cent of the interviewees) used to fish regularly. The most highly sought-after species were river shrimp (*mayacaste*), conch (*tegogolo*) and various fish species and a sort of river crab.

> I used to go and collect conch everyday, I'd bring in about half a basket a day. When I started living with my husband, we'd go down to the stream for fish and we'd catch about two small bags. (Francisca)

> It was usually the women that went fishing, after they'd done the washing. You'd see them there, fishing. (Epifanio)

The frequency with which women went fishing depended on their household activities, the family cycle and the abundance of the agricultural cycle. In the households,

---

exclusively on the basis of age. However, we opted for this categorization in order to have a homogeneous criterion.

9   This is the term used by the local population to designate primary vegetation, regardless of whether it is rainforests or temperate forests (pine-oak associations). In Spanish, the local inhabitants name it 'el monte' o 'la montaña'.

during the first cycles when children were still young, women used to go two or three times a week. River fauna was regarded as a basic source of nutrition in the family diet. Conversely, during the more advanced cycles, they only went once a week.

The two processes that explain the decrease in activity among women in the forest are the drastic reduction of resources and the individual appropriation of forestland. Since these two processes occurred, women have stopped going up to 'the mountain'. The distance from the forest and the enormous amount of time required to find plants meant that women no longer felt it was important to look for them. Nowadays it is the men who, on their way to their plot of land or when they are looking for trees with suitable wood for construction stop off to pick fruit or inflorescences.

Elderly women have reasons for not going up to the mountains: precarious states of health and fear of venturing out on their own. Adult women have other activities (street stalls, child raising), which they regard as being more important than what they can obtain by going to the forest. Young women see no advantage in going to 'the mountain'. 'I'm not interested in finding out,' was what several of the young women from Tatahuicapan said. Unlike young men, who enjoy going fishing, young women are unfamiliar with the techniques involved and do not enjoy the activity.

Unlike other indigenous groups, Nahua women do not go into the forest to gather medicinal or ritual plants. Of the 45 women interviewed, only four said they knew of five to eight medicinal plants that were available in the forest, which were mainly used for curing digestive ailments, respiratory disorders and as antipyretics. The medicinal plants utilized are basically obtained from secondary vegetation and home gardens. In Tatahuicapan, very few women collected ornamental plants (orchids). Several elderly women told us about using vanilla and flowers (such as *flor de la loca*) to prepare fragrant ointments that they mixed with paste from the greasy fruit seed of zapote mamey to put on their hair.

Thus, fishing and gathering medicinal plants were restricted to male 'specialists'. The knowledge and preparation required to become hunters or medicine men were governed by rituals, diets, rules and codes that were obtained through divine revelation and learnt through the special powers of other specialists regarded as 'masters'. Women were excluded from both this knowledge and these activities.

Other female tasks were gathering firewood and cultivating in the maize field. Previously, most of the old women (9 out of 13 interviewees) and half the adults gathered firewood in the secondary vegetation and milpas. Nowadays, only a third of them engage in this activity. This reduction may be due to the women's advanced age and their health conditions or to the fact that when the men go up to the plot of land to tend the cattle, they assume responsibility for this activity. Young women do not engage in this task since they regard it as difficult and tiring.

Women's participation in the milpa has changed drastically. Before the land was divided up, most of the old women and the adult women (around 70 per cent) worked regularly in the milpa. A third of them used to take part in certain tasks or at certain stages of their life cycle while only 10 per cent of the women said that they had never been to the milpa to work. Several young women (40 per cent) stated that they had participated in a milpa cycle. Nowadays, this intervention has declined. Only one old woman and six adult women go to the milpa to sow or harvest the maize and none of the young women go. This means that on average, only 15 per cent of the 45 women

Table 3.1   Environmental concerns perceived by Nahua women

	Old women	Adults	Young
Climatic Changes	8	1	
	19		
Loss of river fauna	8	14	1
Loss of edible forest food	7	11	1
Loss of fauna	7	10	1
Deforestation	5	12	1
Reduction of the rivers	7	5	1
Loss of wood	6	5	0
Decrease in the milpa productivity	4	5	1
Loss of milpa diversity	5	7	0
Loss of useful plants	5	6	0
Decrease in firewood	7	0	
River pollution	7	0	
Increase of plagues	3	7	0
Soil erosion	1	2	0

N=45 women (13 old women, 26 adults and 6 young women).

interviewed contribute to work in the milpa. This transformation is primarily due to the displacement of the cultivation of a rich, diversified milpa. This has meant the exclusion of women from the decision-making process, since they rarely become involved in the work of cattle-raising. This change has also been detrimental to the family diet.

The consequences of environmental transformation are perceived very differently by the inhabitants, depending on their age group, social sector, sex, the activities they carry out, their ethnic group and their relationship with cities. For the Tatahuicapan women interviewed, the environmental concerns perceived were clearly differentiated by age group (Table 3.1). The old women (between 50 per cent and 60 per cent of the interviewees) were struck by the rapid loss of river fauna and fauna as a source of food and of the edible plants from the 'mountain'. If we combine all the comments on the reduction of the natural resources obtained from the forest areas used as a food source for peasant families, 10 out of the 13 old women interviewed are concerned about their reduction. This reflects the importance these resources once had for the basic Nahua diet, particularly during times of poor harvests. The old women referred constantly to the importance of fish in their diet. Likewise, they pointed to the loss of edible fauna as an environmental concern. They often regretted the decline of five species (deer, paca, agouti, brocket deer and wild pig), as well as the loss of birds and iguanas, once eaten on festive occasions.

In the cultivated areas, several old women bemoaned the replacement of multicropping in milpas with maize as monoculture. They regarded this change as a major environmental concern in their family dynamics. The abandonment of varieties of maize, with so many associated crops and plants grown in sown fields (such as *quelites*, *verdolagas*) is the subject of continuous reflections. The following quote from an old woman forces one to think about the consequences of the loss of food self-sufficiency for peasant families.

Now, there's no food but before there used to be. Now we eat bought food. Life has changed. Before, if there was nothing to eat, you'd grab a bag, go to the milpa and bring back a bunch of isquiote. Before the rainforest disappeared, we used to eat animals, and yucca is delicious. Now there's no food, in the water, or the forest, or in the secondary vegetation. They're using it all up, chopping it down, and that will be the downfall of this village, because there's nothing left to fill your stomach with, nothing. (Mauricia)

This loss is also significant for adult women, yet neither the fauna nor the edible plants are as important to them as they are for the old women. Cattle-raising and the continuous exchange with the cities through migration have obviously transformed women's concerns about these dietary changes.

...now *we* have transformed into cattle, now we buy all our food. (Jacinta B.)

Other environmental concerns continuously raised by the Nahua women include changes in the climate (particularly rain), which were regarded as the main environmental problem by many adults (three-quarters). These changes were also noticed by half of the old women, although not as insistently. Among these changes, the reduced rainfall and the more intense heat of recent years were the ones most commonly referred to. Conversely, changes in the wind pattern and the amount of early morning dew went virtually unnoticed. However, other changes have occurred within a very short space of time and the women's answers vary according to the amount of rainfall and the temperature of that particular year.

The water is drying up because there are no plants in the hills. The water gives the mountains life. If it doesn't have shadow, water shrivels up like us (Jacinta H.)

Half the old women regarded the reduction of the rivers as a major problem. Conversely, only 25 per cent of the adult women saw it as a cause for concern (Table 3.1). The changes the women noticed in the rivers included their smaller volume, and the increase in pollution and water temperature. Other concerns involved the loss of plant resources in the forest. There has been a sharp decline in wood suitable for building houses or firewood and ornamental plants. This reduction is perceived by both old and adult women as a problem for the future of their children. One point worth noting is the lack of perception of soil erosion by both old and adult women. Although they talked a little more about the increase in the number of pests, this was not a recurrent theme in the interviews. However, during the home garden workshops, pests were regarded as the main obstacle to growing crops.

The young women showed a surprising lack of concern about environmental changes (Table 3.1), because their world revolves around nearby cities rather than the village and the forests.

Various factors influence the diversity of perceptions and the importance given to each of the matters of concern. Age constitutes a breakwater in the Contact established with 'the mountain'. One of the main differences between old and adult women is the importance of edible products (from the mountain and the milpa) for the former and the change in the amount of rainfall for the latter. The old women's diet relied more on the food they gathered and products from the milpa, whereas adult women were already calculating the effects of a possible shortage of water in a region which once had an abundance of water. The activities carried out by domestic units also influence their environmental concerns. Although families that engaged in cattle-raising tended to minimize the importance of the loss of food, timber and firewood resources, they were worried about pollution and the reduction of the rivers. Conversely, the units without plots of land were increasingly concerned about the loss of natural resources, yet unable to find alternatives. Households with the highest number of migrants lost interest in preserving their resources while their concerns focused more on the reduction of rainfall and the lack of water for the community.

Women in the Sierra: Limitations on Their Participation and Development

The concerns expressed by women on the transformations of the rainforests and rivers revolve around two main aspects: the decrease of food resources and the poverty of their living conditions. The old women were aware of the loss of their self-sufficiency as regards food and the consequences of the latter on their families' living standards. Whereas before they used to depend on fishing as a primary source of food, nowadays, the decline of this activity has caused problems of malnutrition and external dependence on monetary resources to buy food products. In this respect, the women conceive environmental deterioration in ecological as well as social terms. The shortfall of food resources has been matched by women's loss of control over the former. 'What can we say to them? The boys chuck bombs and Butox into the river and all the shrimp die but nobody says anything.' Thus, women have lost a community space for collective decision-making on the management and conservation of resources. Women face impoverished environments that are difficult to restore, they say, without external intervention or honest authorities to enforce community agreements.

We shall analyse the limitations or expression of the different types of poverty in each of the women's spheres of action. Even in the space perceived as women's sphere of action par excellence, the home, women face a series of limitations. Cultural standards, in terms of kinship bonds, marriage rules and alliances, restrict them to a certain socioeconomic level and ethnic group, which obliges them to belong to indigenous or mestizo households with more or less financial resources. Female illiteracy continues to be the norm, since girls of school age have to replace their mothers in domestic tasks at a very early age (from 10 onwards). Of all the adult women, over 90 per cent are unable to read or write.

Within the community sphere, both indigenous and mestizo women have very little mobility or communication with each other. For many indigenous women, trips outside the community are restricted to family visits. Most mestizos lead extremely cloistered lives. Inter-community and extra-regional mobility are further reduced by the lack of experience and fear felt by women and the fact that it is contingent on being accompanied by a male member of the family. This restricts their reflections regarding other women, other social and cultural norms, and the possibilities of establishing links and exchanging knowledge.

This is not the case for the new generations. Although their movements are also restricted, access to school and the media offers them the possibility of other life references. Recently, migrations have created female circuits between the city and regional and extra-regional cities.

Two major regional activities constitute an exception to adult and old women's lack of mobility: trade and religious pilgrimages. There is a sector of Nahua women, some of whom have been abandoned and become household's heads while others belong to poor households, which sell farm products in nearby cities.[10] Among these, the street vendors from Pajapan and San Juan Volador operate within a trade union-like organization. Despite belonging to a union affiliated to another political organization led by men, for the women, this activity has meant having positive experiences and has satisfied certain demands, such as collective transport or spaces in urban markets and acquiring a certain degree of control over their organization. Moreover, in Mecayapan and Tatahuicapan, women have opted to trade basic products-produced in the small localities of the Popoluca zone – for industrial merchandise. During their trips, they exchange information and experiences with men and women from other localities.

On the annual pilgrimages to Catemaco to visit the Virgen del Carmen, many Catholic women of different communities of the sierra have can meet other women, exchange feelings, express desires and establish alliances and bonds of solidarity.

These images reflect the importance of the activities carried out by women to ensure the reproduction of the household in material, cultural and social terms in order to improve the living conditions of the household as a whole, while revealing the social forces that keep them in this marginalized situation. This marginalization is not only conceived of as the economic shortages of households, but primarily as the restrictions on the opportunities for personal development such as access to information, formal instruction or at least reading and writing. Not having the means to expand the network of agents with which they can communicate forces them to keep information only with the messages and reports transmitted by the media.

The lives of both indigenous and mestizo women in the communities are controlled by the men in their households. Male heads of household would appear to be the de facto representatives of the family in its dealings with community institutions. Women are thus virtually excluded from the spheres where communication and decision-making takes place, such as assemblies, committees and even school meetings. On the one hand, they do not feel able to express their opinions, while on the other, they have been relegated to a world in which no one is interested in knowing what they think. Consequently, when the possibility of participating arises, it causes fear.

At the traditional meetings of indigenous communities-assemblies or school meetings[11] women are not allowed to be physically close to the men. Female and

---

10 Around 130 women dedicate to the small commerce (Data of 2004). Their number oscillates depending on the market opportunities and on their own living conditions of the moment. In general, only mothers go selling. Nevertheless, in bad years, all the daughters, even the youngest ones (10 years old) go out to sell farm products in nearby cities.

11 We witnessed an extreme case of physical separation between men and women in the school meetings at the Cuauhtémoc bilingual primary school in Pajapan. When the women were in the classroom the men stood outside and when they were asked to come in, they said that as long as the women were inside, they would not go in. During the next session, the men sat inside the classroom while the women stood back. When the director asked the

male spheres are clearly delimited. In addition to the fact that they are a numerical minority, women are usually placed behind men. This spatial distribution reflects and reinforces the fact that this space does not belong to them and that they are outside the community decision-making process. In other spaces, where important decisions are not made, there is not such a clear division. The presence of mestizo women-except for widows-in these spaces, is nil.

In agricultural production, mestizo women have restricted access to this type of resources. In cattle-raising, regarded as a primarily male activity, although women are allowed to assume responsibility for certain tasks during the husband's absence, they are unable to make decisions concerning the handling and sale of cattle. For their part, until 20 years ago, Nahua women actively participated in farm work, but the loss of many of the crops in the milpa, which were regarded as women's responsibility, and the spread of cattle-raising, has displaced women from these spaces. The fact that certain women play an active role in productive processes does not mean that they are entitled to make decisions concerning the techniques used in production or the final destination of the latter; in the milpa, they could take the corn they needed for their own family's consumption, yet they were not allowed to sell the maize harvest. In cattle-raising, it is unthinkable for women to make the decision to sell a head of cattle without her husband's authorization. Since they are not entitled to make decisions, issues related to cattle do not figure among the problems to which women give priority. Moreover, men's constant denigration of women's productive work suggests that they do not like to publicize the fact that their wives are able to contribute to the household economy.

The links between women from the sierra and public institutions were minimal, since they have always been marginalized from government programs. The one exception has been health programs such as those provided by DIF. Until 5 years ago, with 'Progresa' (now 'Oportunidades'), which only operated in indigenous communities, the majority of women were not involved in meetings. This incorporation of women, in addition to being massive, has led to the greater visibility of women in this type of public spaces, which is the main difference between 'Oportunidades' and other previous programs. Despite the criticisms that this program has elicited, it has been positively rated by the women themselves.

Conversely, men have had a long history of meetings and negotiations with all kinds of government employees (from institutions involved in production, credit, agriculture and services), which are highly sought-after since they confer prestige and a higher position in the community and regional power structure. Moreover, these contacts create political clientelism and financial opportunities, either because they involve paid activities or because they create networks of corruption that produce financial gain.

The new social agents (NGOs) seeking alternatives for sustainable development are the only that provide the population, particularly women, with the possibility of

---

women to be seated and they accepted, the men said that they did not see why women should get involved in men's affairs. However, the women retorted that they were always up to date with their payments, while several fathers owed money. Faced with these arguments, the men lapsed into silence and the assembly began, in an extremely tense atmosphere.

interacting. But, if the technicians lack the necessary vision for including women, their actions will only have an effect on the adult males. It is not enough to change attitudes to women if these agents do not work in conjunction with men, realizing that these processes will build steps to enable women to assume new responsibilities and challenges in community projects.

Men defend their privileged status and authority in many ways, such as being able to handle official discourse with visiting technicians, controlling information and maintaining communication between themselves and external government officials. In many cases, men impose their authority through threats and physical violence against women. Commitments derived from *compadrazgo*, friendship or basic male alliances reproduce the unequal distribution of power between men and women within the community, making women extremely vulnerable to local political authorities.[12]

The population's social participation has been divided into spaces marked and restricted on the basis of gender. Indigenous and mestizo women participate and make decisions within their own spheres of action. As long as this happens, it does not create community conflicts. Problems begin when female activities involve spheres traditionally regarded by the population as unsuitable for their gender (such as assemblies, trade union organizations, political organizations, cattle-raising associations and even many school meetings). Thus, although women in Tatahuicapan can sometimes have a presence, they are excluded from regional policy.

Finally, neither indigenous nor mestizo men understand life without women. They recognize the importance of their work in the home and in the fields, provided they comply with the role expected of them in each culture. Any deviation from this norm drastically reduces a woman's value. Women's lack of recognition of their contribution to family and community life means that, when negotiating their demands, women begin from a much lower position than the one, men assign themselves. In this respect, the possibilities for women to wield power within their communities are extremely limited.

A Struggle: Ephemeral Moments of a Union During the Capture of the Water Reservoir 'Yuribia'

We plucked up our courage and just set off. We knew that if we were there, they wouldn't attack. About 300 policemen turned up and there we were, protecting the place and showing our faces, because we were determined (female participant in the capture of the dam named Yuribia).

The PRD supported the movement to make Tata an independent municipality. That's how people want things. Because we don't get any benefits from Mecayapan, the plans and

---

12 After several trips, women abandoned by their husbands and threatened with losing their land and their houses have finally managed to file a complaint in Tatahuicapan. However, it sometimes takes up to two years for a verdict to be reached. During this period, the husband may have already sold the land or the house. A woman from the community of López Arias had her appeal turned down after six years.

resources don't reach us. If you ask for something for Tata from Mecayapan, you don't get anything. (Doña Francisca)

In order to analyse women's political participation, it was interesting to explore Tatahuicapan's struggle to become a free municipality by the capture of the Yuribia reservoir. The Tatahuicapan authorities had been fighting for their political and economic independence from the municipality of Mecayapan. Although Tatahuicapan had a larger population than Mecayapan, its inhabitants depended on the budget assigned to the municipality of Mecayapan. The political groups in Tatahuicapan held the Mecayapan authorities responsible for the lack of social programs to benefit Tatahuicapan. Several attempts at turning Tatahuicapan into a free municipality had already failed.

The inhabitants of Tatahuicapan stressed the importance of becoming a municipality because of the size of the population, through which they justified having direct control over their budget and not depending on the political control of the adjacent community. The presence in their lands of the Yuribia reservoir, which satisfies most (nearly 80 per cent) of the water needs for the adjoining cities of Minatitlán and Coatzacoalcos, guaranteed, in its inhabitants' eyes, their economic and political independence.

During this struggle, they had received the support of certain government officials. Time went by, however, and nothing was solved. The villagers went back and forth, paying out large amounts of money to lawyers. The leaders of the movement, both PRI and PRD supporters, felt deceived by both the municipal president of Minatitlán and the governor of Veracruz. The assembly therefore decided to seize the reservoir facilities in order to exert political pressure.

Once the reservoir had been taken, a great deal of organization was required to keep all the participants within the reservoir. The women's participation covered various aspects: first, the organization and preparation of food; second, compliance with the surveillance shifts, which they attended punctually and thirdly, at the point when they were confronted with police agents, resistance and solidarity with their companions in the reservoir. The women organized voluntarily around a communal activity that was valued by the majority of the inhabitants, who were deeply concerned about the future of the community and their companions' safety. There was a mixture of women, with some old women and many adult women and very few young women. All in all, there were 80–100 women that supported the taking of the reservoir together with 150–250 men. Many of them had taken part at some stage in the church grass roots communities, several sympathized with the PRD, but few had all the information and even fewer had participated in the community assemblies where these matters were discussed. Of a total of 25 women interviewed, only three had attended the assemblies, because they had the right as ejidatarias. There were several reasons why they cooperated, such as the awareness of the importance of demanding that the state authorities grant them their economic and political independence and allow them to become a free municipality. At a more local level, others did not wish the municipal presidents of Mecayapan to decide the future of Tatahuicapan. Many of them thought that they would have a better education for their children, since more schools would be built, while others argued that under the statute of a free municipality, they would be able to receive assistance from programs. Finally, the husbands or sons of some of the other women had taken part and they supported them.

The women that were unable to be present had varying opinions. Some supported the women's collaboration and valued their bravery. In the words of Doña Pilar, 'Those women have really got guts, they are brave and they are not afraid, because they don't give in to the men.' An old woman said, 'I would have gone if I could, to show them that an old woman can still be of use, but I'm sick.' However, other women disapproved of the women's participation in the taking of the reservoir. 'Those are men's affairs. What can women do? They just get in the way,' added Doña Clemen.

These groups of women organized spontaneously around a common goal and struggle: some of them belong or at least sympathize with the PRD. Conversely, the men's participation in the capture of Yuribia was heavily influenced by political parties (PRD and PRI). The struggle was what they had in common, but the future of Tatahuicapan was a key issue that disunited them. The PRI supporters wanted power to be able to govern themselves. The alliances established and the external support were unclear, yet the result was a common struggle to demand the creation of a free municipality. The taking of the reservoir alerted the municipal authorities of Coatzacoalcos and Minatitlán. Approximately 500 policemen were sent in. Psychological rather than physical violence was used. The inhabitants were armed with sticks and arrows, but during the confrontation, they only used them to scare their opponents. The inhabitants of Tatahuicapan had not foreseen such a large deployment of police. This took them by surprise and there were hardly any people guarding the reservoir facilities, meaning that they withdrew without violence. However, one of the leaders, who was in the village, realized that one of the cars was carrying the under-general attorney from Minatitlán, and decided to kidnap him until he obtained an audience with the governor of Veracruz. After the audience, almost two years later, the free municipality was eventually created.

At that stage, the women's participation was highly valued by the men in the community. However, after the struggle had been won, their participation was scarcely remembered. The movement collapsed rapidly, and had no organizational continuity or regional political impact. Consequently, the women's political learning was minimal and their subsequent involvement in political movements has been virtually nil. In this respect, although it was a movement that involved several participants and despite the fact that they won, through the creation of the free municipality, the organization lack the social effervescence required to maintain the population's participation. The movement was co-opted by the official party at the time, the PRI, and its short duration meant that it failed to create a women's movement that could continue and be expressed in the struggle to meet other needs. There is no doubt that the factors that influenced the sierra women's possible participation in protest movements are similar to those present in urban movements. Besides the difficulties of the status of the private lives of the female participants, women's participation is influenced by regional culture, which does not permit the creation of shared spaces between men and women in decision making, the changes in productive activities that have displaced women in many communities, the lack of resources and economic alternatives for women, the high percentage of illiteracy among women and the lack of programs that actively involve the female sector of the population. Few women have a supportive family environment and enough personal and community tools to overcome obstacles and engage in collective action.

Potential for their Development

Given these limitations, what are the conditions that enable poor women, be they indigenous or mestizo, to open up spaces in community decision-making as regards access to land and the management of regional natural resources?

Women in the Sierra de Santa Martha live in extremely precarious conditions. The gender asymmetries constructed culturally and socially reinforce social inequalities and female poverty. How can one ensure that women can participate in political decisions and to engage in action based on this information?

Formally, community norms and institutions should be established to enable women to have legal equality and exercise their rights as human beings, such as access to land ownership, and control over what it produces. The shift from communal to ejido use of the land deprived women of this right. Nowadays, men not only decide on the sale of cattle but also of plots of land, without even telling their wives about these decisions. This situation makes the family's economic and social situation extremely vulnerable. Male authorities extend their original alliances and allow these operations to be carried out without the consent of either the wives. It is therefore vital to create mechanisms and institutions where women can go if these rights are violated and where they will be given clear, fair solutions immediately. Without these spaces, women have no real possibilities of action. Communicative spaces should be provided for women on their rights and possibilities. We have seen several cases of women who lose all of their access to land without ever finding an institution that could provide them with both information and support.[13]

Likewise, spaces should be created to enable rural, migrant and urban women to exchange experiences.[14] Creating these opportunities will enable women to see how other women solve their problems and therefore find ways of acquiring organizational training. However, without communication, these needs are not collectivized and there is not even a minimum form of organization. Maintaining this organization, however, requires a degree of social effervescence during which activists begin to see certain benefits from their struggle. Through their achievements, women realize

---

13 The judge's frivolous treatment of the women's legal case warrants accusations of corruption, non-compliance with obligations and lack of respect towards the constitutional rights of women from the sierra.

14 The experience of the participation of women in the popular urban movement can be extremely valuable if discussed in a rural setting. Women's participation in the organization led to changes that exacerbated power relations in the domestic and neighbourhood sphere and within the organization itself. The women demanded that the points as domestic violence and lack of nurseries be adopted as the organization's political demands. Consequently, the men feared losing control of their positions of leadership and were concerned that the movement would be divided (Mogrovejo, 1994 pp. 72–77.

that they are taken into account and that they are valued by the community they represent, which encourages them to continue.[15]

At the same time, we know of several welfare programs organized by DIF, in which, in the words of the indigenous women, 'they just come to tell us off, they tell us we live like pigs and that we'll always be poor if we live like that. Why should we go to the clinics if that's all they have to say and they don't help us when we need them?' Here we see how, even when a government budget exists, social policies fail to fulfil their role of offsetting social inequalities. Women's participation in this type of program is highly specific and they do not feel involved because they are not really taken into account in the design of their proposals in order to solve their problems.

In the processes promoted by non-governmental organizations or catholic organizations among Popoluca women on productive aspects, women have appropriated spaces that were once exclusive to men. Women's traditional exclusion from formal education and other areas of training means that when women are offered their own space, they are eager to participate. Moreover, experience has shown that when a woman participates, other members of the household are likely to participate.

These are populations where women have been formally and informally excluded from authority and the control of productive and credit resources, and the processes of communication, information, public action, and links with external institutions, which has created gender inequalities in access to opportunities for community participation. As long as these inequalities exist between men and women in access to family and institutional resources, women will be unable to create participatory spaces for decision-making regarding the management of natural resources in the region or community development. Unless authority and control are distributed between men and women in institutional structures, and there is fair, legal access to productive and credit resources and a clear assignment of activities and responsibilities within the family, without creating different skills and capacities, unequal gender relations will continue. Unless there are formal and informal spaces of information and communication where regional problems are discussed (that is on the right of access to land, the lack of jobs, migration in extremely precarious conditions) women will continue to be excluded from the decisions made for the region as whole. As the Nahua representative of the National Indigenous Congress said to the Chamber of Deputies, 'it doesn't just start here, it continues. (...) Recognition of the Cocopa initiative (...) will be the first step towards the government's recognition of the indigenous peoples of Mexico and from then onwards, we will begin to establish a new relationship between the government and indigenous peoples'.

References

Aranda, J. (1996), 'Las Mujeres Cafetaleras En Oaxaca', *Mujeres en el medio rural, Cuadernos Agrarios*, **13**, 129–151.

---

15 Continuing to participate in the movements, however, meant that the women had to be extremely well organized. Studies on urban movements show that women's participation involves a series of conflicting pressures due to the demands of their role as mothers, housewives, workers, wage earners, residents and party or community representatives.

Bonfil, P. (1996), Oficios, Conocimientos y Padecimientos: La Salud Como Práctica Política en el mundo Indígena Femenino', *Mujeres en el medio rural, Cuadernos Agrarios*, **13**, 43–62.

CEPAL (1999), *La Pobreza a Fines de los Años Noventa* (Santiago de Chile: CEPAL).

Cervigni, R. and Ramírez, F. (coords) (1996) 'Desarrollo sustentable y conservación de la biodiversidad: un estudio de caso en la Sierra de Santa Marta Veracruz, México', *PSSM*. A.C. Global Environment Facility and Centro Internacional para el Mejoramiento de Maíz y Trigo, Xalapa, Veracruz, 435 pp. (inédito).

Chambers, R. (1983), *Rural Development, Putting the Last First* (New York: Longman).

Chevalier, J. and Buckles, D. (1995), *A Land Without Gods: Process Theory, Maldevelopment and the Mexican Nahuas* (London: Zed Books).

Conapo (1998), *Índices de Marginación Municipal 1995* (Mexico: Conapo).

CRUO-UACH and PSSM. A. C. (1997), *Diagnóstico y propuesta del plan de desarrollo comunitario de San Fernando, Municipio De Soteapan, Veracruz*, Community Workshop *April 15th to 18th* (1997), Proders-Semarnap (unpublished document).

Duarte, I. (2006), 'Desde el sur organizado. Mujeres nahuas de Veracruz construyendo política' *Tesis de Doctorado en Antropología* (Mexico: CIESAS).

Foster, G. (1945), 'Sierra Popoluca Folklore and Beliefs', *American Archaeology and Ethnology*, **42**(2), 177–250 (Berkeley and Los Angeles: University of California Press).

Godínez Guevara, L. and Lazos Chavero, E. (2003), 'Sentir y percepciones de las mujeres sobre el deterioro ambiental: Retos Para Su empoderamiento' in *Género y medio ambiente*. Tuñón, E. (ed.) (Plaza y Valdés, México: Ecosur, SEMARNAT), 145–177.

González Montes, S. (1997), 'Mujeres, Trabajo y Pobreza En El Campo Mexicano: una Revisión Crítica de la Bibliografía Reciente,' in *Las mujeres en la pobreza*. Alatorre, J. et al. (eds) (Mexico: El Colegio de México), 179–214.

Hernández Castillo, A. (2004), 'Descentrando el Feminismo: Lecciones aprendidas de las Luchas de las Mujeres Indígenas', *Congreso Anual de la Asociación Latinoamericana de Ciencias Políticas* 29 Septiembre (México: Universidad Iberoamericana).

INEGI (2000), *XII Censo General De Población y Vivienda 2000, Resultados Preliminares, Aguascalientes, Ages*, 334–353.

INEGI (1995), 'Definite results', *Conteo de Población y Vivienda 1995*.

Kusnir, L. (1994), Consideraciones para la elaboración de un estado del arte sobre las políticas públicas y la mujer,' in *Las mujeres en la pobreza*. Alatorre, J. et al. (eds) (Mexico: Grupo Interdisciplinario sobre Mujer, Trabajo y Pobreza (Gimtrap)), 295–323.

Lazos Chavero, E. (1996) 'La ganaderización de dos comunidades veracruzanas: condiciones de la difusión de un modelo agrario', in *El Ropaje de la tierra. Naturaleza y cultura en cinco zonas rurales*. Paré, L. and Sánchez, M.J. (eds.), (Plaza y Valdés, México: IISUNAM), 177–242.

Lazos Chavero, E. and Godínez, L. (2004), 'Género en los procesos de sustentabilidad: potencialidades y límites', in *El amanecer del siglo y la población mexicana*. Lozano, F. (ed.) (Cuernavaca, México: CRIM-UNAM y SOMEDE), 621–649.

Lazos Chavero, E. and Paré, L. (2000), Miradas indígenas sobre una naturaleza entristecida (Plaza y Valdés, México: IISUNAM).

Mogrovejo, N. (1994), 'Movimiento urbano y feminismo popular en la ciudad de México', in *Mujeres y ciudades. Participación social, Vivienda y vida Cotidiana*. Massolo, A. (ed.) (México: El Colegio de México) 59–95.

Palma, R., Quesnel, A. and Delaunay, D. (2000), 'Una Nueva Dinámica Del Poblamiento Rural En México: El Caso Del Sur De Veracruz (1970–1995), Apuntes sustantivos y metodológicos,' in *El Sotavento veracruzano: procesos sociales y dinámicas territoriales*. Léonard, E. and Velázquez, E. (eds) (Mexico: CIESAS/IRD), 83–108.

Paré, L., Blanco, J.L., Buckles, D., Chevalier, J., Gutiérrez, R., Hernández, A., Perales, H., Ramírez, F. and Velázquez, E. (1992), 'La Sierra de Santa Marta: Hacia un desarrollo sustentable', Technical Report and Proyecto Sierra de Santa Marta. A. C, Instituto de Investigaciones Sociales de la UNAM, Carleton University, International Development Research Center, Xalapa.

Perales, H. (1992), 'El Autoconsumo en la Agricultura de los Popolucas de Soteapan, Veracruz', Master's thesis in Science, Col. de Posgraduados, Chapingo, México.

Reardon, T. and Vosti, S.A. (1995), 'Links between Rural Poverty and Environment in Developing Countries: Asset Categories and Investment Poverty', *World Development*, **23**(9), 1495–1506.

Salles, V. and Tuirán, R. (1999), '¿Cargan las Mujeres con el Peso de la Pobreza?, Puntos de Vista de un Debate', in *Mujer, género y población en México* García, B. (ed.) (Mexico: El Colegio de México/SOMEDE), 431–481.

Stuart, R.D. (1978), 'Subsistence Ecology of the Isthmus Nahuat Indians of Southern Veracruz, Mexico', Doctoral Thesis, University of California.

Tehuitzil, L. (2000), 'Estructura y composición de solares en una comunidad popoluca de la Sierra de Santa Marta, Veracruz, México'. Bachelor's thesis in Biology, Escuela de Biología de la Benemérita Universidad Autónoma de Puebla, Puebla.

Vázquez, V. (1996), 'Donde manda el hombre, no manda la Mujer, Género y tenencia de la tierra en el México rural', *Mujeres en el medio rural, Cuadernos Agrarios*, **13**, 63–83.

Velázquez Ortiz, F. (1990), *Información demográfica municipal del estado de Veracruz, 1900–1990*, IIESES–UV, Xalapa.

Velázquez, E. (1992), 'Política, Ganadería y Recursos Naturales En El Trópico Húmedo Veracruzano: El Caso Del Municipio De Mecayapan', *Relaciones Estudios de Historia y Sociedad*, **XII**(50), 23–63.

Velázquez, E. (1997) 'La Apropiación Del Espacio Entre Nahuas y popolucas de la Sierra Santa Marta, Veracruz', in *Nueve estudios sobre el espacio: representación y formas de apropiación*. Hoffmann, O. and Salmerón, F. (eds) (Mexico: CIESAS-ORSTROM).

PART 2
National Building and Identity

Chapter 4

Fashioning Indians or Beautiful Savages: The Case of Gaby Herbstein's Huellas[1]

Arnd Schneider

Introduction

In this chapter, I am exploring the complex ways in which indigenous people are visually represented in one particular instance in contemporary Argentina. Encounters between Europeans and their descendants and indigenous people in Argentina, in colonial and post-colonial times (before and after 1812), are the result of a historical process which I shall outline briefly in the first section of the paper. I shall then suggest how these encounters – which entailed visual representations – were framed within ideas about gender and the nation state. In the main section of the paper I shall analyse the calendar *Huellas* ('Traces') produced for the year 2000 by the Argentine fashion photographer Gaby Herbstein.

While stereotypes of indigenous people are constructed within Argentine society, they are never fixed, but in flux, and negotiated by different actors. Thus, in our example, indigenous people themselves (as political activists, consultants to the project, and artisans), the photographer and her production crew, as well as other commentators and consultants (for instance, anthropologists and non-governmental organizations) were all involved in the production of the calendar and, when interviewed, gave different interpretations to the process.

1   This chapter was first delivered as a paper to the Radical Anthropology Group's seminar in London in February 2001. I thank Chris Knight and Ana Lopes for having invited me, and the participants for their helpful suggestions in a vivid disussion. I recall an interesting discussion on the calendar with Amanda Hopkinson, and Norma Schenke kindly read a first draft of the paper. I am also grateful to Laura Malosetti Costa, Marta Penhos, Julio Sánchez, and again Norma Schenke in providing information on bibliographic sources. I also would like to thank all individuals and institutions mentioned in the text who generously made available interview time and helped locating resources for this project. A Spanish version of this paper was published in *Mujeres y Nacionalismo en America Latina, de la independencia a la nación del nuevo milenio*, ed. Natividad Gutiérrez, UNAM: Mexico City, 2004. In English this paper was first published in *Ethnoscripts*, 5(2), 2003, 2–33. A different version has appeared in Arnd Schneider, *Appropriation as Practice: Art and Identity in Argentina*, Palgrave Macmillan (Institute for the Study of the Americas): New York, 2006.

Hence the aim of this paper is to show that there are no simple ways of understanding representations of indigenous people in contemporary Argentina, for example, by opposing indigenous vs. non-indigenous representations. Rather, the important issues have to do with the political and gender perspectives of the participants, and how they conceive of the nation.

A first-hand look at the calendar probably would classify its images as sexist and idealized (in fact, as fabricated images of Indians), and that is exactly what some commentators did when I showed them the calendar. But such a critique would be stopping short of understanding why these images have been produced and set up in a particular way, and what their meaning is in contemporary Argentine society.

Extinction and Exoticism: Representing Indigenous People in Argentina

A comprehensive history of the visual representation of indigenous people in Argentina remains yet to be written, and would have to encompass both religious and secular art, as well photography since the second half of the nineteenth century.[2] Visual representations accompanied the growing marginalization of indigenous people on the territory that is now Argentina. Starting in the sixteenth century, the Spanish colonization subjugated indigenous populations of the Inca Empire in the North-West, and displaced many of them (for example, the Quilmes Indians of Tucumán).[3] Yet overall the Spaniards were not numerous and militarily strong enough to extinguish the mainly nomadic, hunter-gatherer aboriginal populations in the South and the North-East. From 1610, in Paraguay and Brazil, and in the north-eastern part of Argentina (today's province of Misiones) Jesuit missionaries were setting up *reducciones*, settling Guaraní Indians, converting them to Christianity and teaching them arts and sciences (these utopian projects came to an end with the expulsion of the Jesuits from Spain and Portugal in 1767–1768).

In the *Province* of Buenos Aires, Indians experienced raids into their territory (both for military and economic reasons, the South of the *Province* of Buenos Aires harbours important salt deposits), and responded with incursions into settled areas (so-called *malones*). After contact, Indians had adopted the horse from the Spaniards and large amounts of cattle. Thus, in some ways similar to what happened on the North American prairies, in the Pampas the livelihood and mode of subsistence changed. Hunter gatherers and horticulturalists turned into cattle nomads. Raids on Spanish farmsteads and frontier posts provided not only highly praised cattle and horses (which after first Spanish settlements had also multiplied in the wild), but occasionally also women.[4] In fact, the proverbial female captive (*la cautiva*) became an established motif in the literature and painting about this period.[5] As Laura Malosetti Costa has shown, the white defenceless woman 'raped' by the

---

2   cf. Malosetti Costa (1993); Penhos (1996).

3   cf. Rock (1987, p. 33); Sarasola (1992, p. 103), Bernand (1997, pp. 49–52).

4   cf. Quijada (2000, pp. 60–64), 2002).

5   Examples are Juan Cruz Varela's 'En el regreso de la expedición contra los indios bárbaros, mandada por el Coronel D. Federico Rauch' (1827), and the poem *La Cautiva* (1837) by Esteban Echeverría, cf. Malosetti Costa (1993); Penhos (1996)

dark and ferocious Indian on a horse symbolized the fight between 'civilization' and 'barbarism', promoted in letters and politics by D.F. Sarmiento, and in the arts by painters, such as Enrique Carlos Pellegrini and Johan Moritz Rugendas.[6] As Malosetti Costa rightly points out, the motif of *la cautiva* inverts the factual relations of power and politics in the Pampas: it is not the white man who take the Indian's land, but the Indian who takes the white man's most precious possession, his woman. Therefore, the white colonists are justified to wage war against the Indians.[7] The topos is, of course, much older and dates back to the seventeenth century and the chronicle *La Argentina Manuscrita* by Ruy Díaz de Guzmán, to the figure of Lucía Miranda, wife of the Capitán Sebastián Hurtado at the fortress of Sancti Spiritu, who is kidnapped ('raped' in the now obsolete sense of rapine or seizure) by the Timbú cacique Mangoré. Indians (not the whites) are portrayed as the real usurpers, and in turn retribution and the conquest itself are justified.[8] As Malosetti Costa highlights, the image of *la cautiva* was an erotic one. Two configurations dominate paintings and literature: the 'captured' woman, and the woman as prisoner, hostage to the desires of her new indigenous master. The question of 'race' of the indigenous other is linked to the stereotype of gender, a woman is only valued, when she is white (and Indians and whites are contrasted strongly in the paintings of the period).[9]

This pattern of partly friendly, partly hostile co-existence, marked both by treaties and commercial relations, as well as sporadic military engagement would continue even after Argentina's independence in 1812. Calfucurá, a powerful chief of the Mapuche Indians who had crossed into the Pampas since the eighteenth century,[10] was recognized as the real counterpart to established power in Buenos Aires, and as such was also represented in painting, for instance, when negotiating with the authorities.[11] The turning point came in the 1870s when the Argentine state, instigated by economic interests (read: greed for agricultural land on the fertile Pampas), decided to extend its internal frontier forward. The Campaign of the Desert (*Campaña del Desierto*) pushed the Mapuche Indians southwards onto marginal lands in Patagonia. Many were killed, others had to flee across the Andes to Chile, and others again survived precariously on Patagonian reservations, or in captivity and small settlements in the province of Buenos Aires. Though Argentine elites had

---

6   Johan Moritz Rugendas *El Malón* (dated 1835, Col. Yrarrázaval, Chile), another *Malón* (signed and dated in Munich, 1848), *El Rescate* (unfinished oil painting, ca. 1848–58, private collection, Buenos Aires), Angel Della Valle *La Vuelta del malón* (1892, Museo Nacional de Bellas Artes, Buenos Aires), Malosetti Costa (1993, pp. 6–18).

7   Malosetti Costa (1993, p. 1).

8   Malosetti Costa (1993, p. 2), following Iglesia (1992, p. 563).

9   Malosetti Costa (1993, p. 23).

10 The process has been called the araucanization of the Pampas, cf. Ortelli (1996) and Quijada (2000, p. 62).

11 cf. 'El presbítero Francisco Bibolini, Cura de 25 de Mayo, parlamenta con el cacique Calfucurá, 1859' or 'Invasión de 2.000 indios al Veinticinco de Mayo'lithograph 0,875 x 0,635 m. Museo de la Patagonia 'Perito Francisco P. Moreno' San Carlos de Bariloche (Inv. 1669). See Penhos (1999, note 1).

Figure 4.1   Antonio Pozzo, Linares y sus hombres (Linares and his men), 1870s
Museo Mitre, Buenos Aires. Shown as part of No entregar Carhue al Huinca, RES, 2000
Aires. Courtesy of the artist.

disputed the status of Indians before the Desert Campaign, after its conclusion, it was
clear that indigenous people would only occupy marginal positions in society.[12]

The Campaign of the Desert was documented by the photographer Pozzo who
accompanied the troops. Lithographs provided the conceptual basis for the composition
of portrait photographs of Indians, claiming a kind of authenticity when photographed
in groups, families or, more rarely, as individuals.[13] The majority were group or family
portraits, with generic titles such as 'Pampa Indians' or 'Toba Family' (Figure 4.1).
There are only few examples where individuals have been identified[14] – corresponding
to the Eurocentric stereotype of simple, socially undifferentiated tribal societies.

The Italian photographer Benito Panunzi, on the other hand, took photographs of
Indians who were visiting Buenos Aires between 1862 and 1864, that is before the
Campaign of the Desert. Among his works we find individual portraits, for example
of Casimiro Biguá and his son, yet these were carefully arranged studio photographs.
After the Desert Campaign it was Pozzo who photographed the defeated *cacique*
Pincén as a wild 'tiger of the Pampas'. More than a century later, coincidentally,
a descendant of the *cacique*, Luis Pincén, will be involved in the calendar project
'Huellas' (see below). To achieve this image of the Indian as 'wild beast', Pozzo asked

---

12 According to Quijada (2000, p. 69), the Argentine elites considered three options:
annihilation, settlement in reservations, and assimilation to the nation-state. Whilst the last options
found most favour in public opinion, de facto the Desert campaign resulted in a combination of
the first two, with small remnants of indigenous populations today surviving in Argentina.

13 cf. Penhos (1996).

14 cf. Penhos (1996).

Pincén to dress in the studio as he would have done with his Indians on the Pampas, that is with spear and *boleadoras* (the lassos with stone balls, later also adopted by the gauchos). As Marta Penhos points out, these paraphernalia were 'artificial and verosimil' objects at the same time.[15] It seems that two types of photographs prevailed: the ones that portrayed Indians out of context, and others which tried to artificially recreate or reenact the supposed 'natural' surroundings.

As we shall see further on, Gaby Herbstein's calendar stands in the tradition of the latter model of nineteenth century photography (see also Edwards, 1992).

There has been relatively little research on policies and attitudes towards indigenous people in twentieth century Argentina.[16] Genocidal campaigns against Indians continued into this century, and after the near extinction of Tierra del Fuego natives[17] it was only in 1936 that the last resistance of Toba and Pilagá Indians was broken in the Chaco.[18] By 1930 Argentine society had also experienced its first military coup, and military governments (interrupted by short civilian intervals) would dominate Argentine politics till the early 1980s. The last military government (*el proceso*, 1976–1983) made between 20,000 and 30,000 of its citizens disappear and was also particularly repressive towards Indians, slum dwellers and other marginal groups. During the current democratic period (Alfonsín, Menem, De la Rúa, Duhalde governments), Indian rights became more acknowledged (importantly, law 23.303 was passed in 1989 which aims to regulate land rights and set up a National Institute of Indigenous Affairs, INAI).[19] Since the 1980s there is also a resurgent cultural interest in indigenous cultures, their folklore, arts and crafts, coupled with more serious research in anthropology and archaeology (which had been closed during the military dictatorship). It is estimated that presently there are about 300,000–500,000 indigenous people in Argentina.[20]

In contemporary Argentina, democracy coupled with pronounced economic decline provided the framework for a revived interest in Latin American cultures and native peoples, further enhanced by growing international contacts with other Latin American countries, and more generally characterized by a now globalize exchange of ideas and artefacts. This configuration provides the background to the case study I shall now discuss in more detail.

---

15 cf. Penhos (1996, p. 5).

16 However, see Tessler (1989); Hernández (1992), Sarasola (1992, Chapters VII and VIII), Quijada (2000).

17 cf. Chapman (1982), and also the revealing photographic documents of a French scientific expedition to Cape Horn in 1882/3, *Cape Horn. Rencontre avec les indienes Yaghan*. Paris: Musée de l'Homme, 1995.

18 cf. Sarasola (1992, pp. 333–336).

19 cf. Sarasola (1992, pp. 483–489) for an overview on organizations occupied with indigenous people (state, private and indigenous organizations).

20 cf. Magrassi (1987), Lewis (1991), Sarasola (1992). The 2001 census counted so far 286, 510 indigenous people – but for some provinces as well as for the capital city, Buenos Aires, the results still have to be published. (INDEC. Encuesta Complementaria de Pueblos Indígenas 2004, www.indec.mecon.gov.ar.

Contentious Images

I have chosen the example of Gaby Herbstein's 'Huellas', because on the one hand it demonstrates well the controversial issues surrounding the contemporary representation of indigenous cultures. On the other hand, and beyond its strictly Argentine context, it also points to old (and new) white fantasies of 'playing' or staging Indians, ranging from white actors playing Indian characters in cinema, white novelists, such as the German Karl May, who never left Europe, writing countless novels with Indian heroes (with a fictional Apache called 'Winnetou', represented in film by a French actor Pierre Brice), European and North American children playing hide-and-seek varieties of Cowboys and Indians (often inspired by television serials, such as *Bonanza* in the 1960s and its many successors), and even anarchist leftists in German and Italian cities of the mid-1970s calling themselves 'urban Indians.'

During my fieldwork in Buenos Aires in 1999–2000, I had the opportunity to see the exhibition 'Huellas' accompanying the calendar in the shopping mall 'Abasto'. I interviewed the producers and other people involved, as well as outside commentators. I had first come across Herbstein's work through the Mapuche silversmith Silvia Rinque. She was one of the indigenous consultants to Herbstein's project, and provided silver jewellery for the model who was to represent the Mapuche woman in the calendar. I shall return to her opinion about the project later.

The socio-economic context of Herbstein's work, which is the commercial fashion and advertising world, makes it different from that of mainly non-commercial artistic photographers (though they might double occasionally in commercial projects, too). Each year the Herbstein studio produces a calendar around a particular theme (for example, in 1999 the zodiac was chosen), which then is distributed free to a specific and exclusive clientele. Thus, for the year 2000 calendar, the holders of Diners Card were selected.

The structure and lay-out of the calendar is straightforward: on large-format pages (48 × 64 cm images 42 × 56 cm), one fashion model represents one indigenous group for each month. Starting with January, the indigenous groups are, Toba, Wichí, Chané, Guaraní, Techuelche, Mapuche, Yámana, Kolla, Diaguita, Huarpe, Abipón, and Selk'nam. Small captions give a brief summary of the cosmovisión of the indigenous group. The front page depicts the same model used for the Toba, but with a different image. Photographs were shot with a professional still camera, and models and paraphernalia were arranged in a studio. The second page features historical photographs and drawings of indigenous people.[21] In the centre of the page a text, entitled 'Huellas', spells out the ideological programme of the calendar.

TRACES ("HUELLAS")

At the gateway of the year 2000
The traces are the essence of a search.
Not of the past. Not of history but of ourselves.
Of a culture. Of many cultures.
Of the same [culture]. That of our ancestors.

---

21 No individual sources for the archival photos are given, but a general bibliography is supplied in the acknowledgements section of the calendar.

Their traces remain.
Their way of thinking, of clothing themselves remains
To tell us how they were before the arrival of the *conquistadores*.
Their clothes are not a fig-leaf.
Nor a fruit of modesty,
But rather an aesthetic expression
Of the simple union with nature.
They noticed that the human body
Is little adorned
And took feathers from the birds,
From the trees fruits and flowers.
That's how they dressed, that's how they lived.
These are their traces.
We need to encounter them to encounter ourselves.
And begin again.

I shall return to this text later in the chapter. At the end of the calendar, four supplementary pages give information about the research and production of the calendar, credits to the collaborators, and the bibliography consulted. The first of these pages complements the display of archival photos at the beginning of the calendar, and shows small photographs documenting Gaby Herbstein and her crew's travel to various indigenous communities in Argentina, as well as backstage photos from the studio set. The central part of the page lists all the credit of this huge production (a video was also produced), as well as numerous sponsors for technical equipment, such as *Sony*, and the opening event of the exhibition of the photographs of the calendar in the shopping mall 'Abasto', including multinationals like *Coca-Cola*, *Bacardi*, *Fernet-Branca*, and *Johnny Walker*, and the Argentine brewery *Quilmes*.[22] A huge 'cast' of models, modelling agencies (those Gaby Herbstein works with usually), and support staff are mentioned for the calendar, exhibition and production of an accompanying video.

The indigenous consultants are thanked (with their tribal affiliation in brackets), as well as various anthropologists and NGOs who cooperated. The project also enlisted the support of the United Nations allowing the use of its emblem during the 'International Year of Peace' in 2000. Sergio Guzmán Castellano, the general co-coordinator of the Buenos Aires office of the United Nations explained the motivation for this move: 'the beautiful images revalorize the splendour of these [indigenous] peoples who understood peace as an art to live in harmony with the wisdom of nature'.[23]

The back page features a text, entitled *Presencias* ('Presences') by Carlos Martínez Sarasola, an Argentine anthropologist who was a consultant on the project, and is author of a standard work on Argentine Indians,[24] as well as director of an NGO Fundación *desde América*. The main message of the text is that despite ignorance, silence and willful obliteration by other Argentines (not least through repression and genocidal military campaigns), about half a million indigenous people in over 6,000

---

22 Named after the location in the south of Buenos Aires suburb where the vanquished Quilmes Indians where taken after their defeat by the Spaniards, and which was a Jesuit reduction, see also section 2.

23 B.A.E., Section 'Buenos Aires Cool' (7 December 1999).

24 cf. Sarasola (1992).

communities continue to exist, and are 'present' in Argentina. Maybe, this text rather than the mystical 'Huellas' (belying the somewhat naive approach of its authors) should have been placed at the beginning of the calendar.

Another NGO, 'Fundación Arte y Esperanza' (linked to the Catholic Church) which works on non-profit projects with indigenous artisans, is also credited. I interviewed both Martínez Sarasola, as well as Mercedes Homps of the Fundación Arte y Esperanza, who both said they had been initially supportive of the project but later found the idea of professional models rather than indigenous women being used disconcerting and inappropriate to the topic.

The lower part of that back-page shows a group photo of all the indigenous consultants on the project with their tribal affiliations. Amongst the indigenous consultants, I interviewed Luis Pincén (Tehuelche), Silvia Rinque (Mapuche) and Jorgelina Duarte (Mbyá-Guaraní).

The next of the supplementary pages presents small, contact-size photos for the 12 indigenous groups featured in the calendar, and short summaries of their history and present situation. The photos are a mixture of close-ups, and others from the same models and sets used for the main section of calendar. At the bottom of the page an extensive bibliography on indigenous people is quoted.[25] The back to this page features more publicity on Gaby Herbstein's photographic studio and the naked torso of a model painted and dressed up as an indigenous woman.

Intentions and Reactions

I interviewed Gaby Herbstein and her art director Julieta Garavaglia (who also runs a new art gallery Gara) in the modern Herbstein photographic studios in Buenos Aires' upper-middle class northern neighbourhood Palermo Viejo in February 2000.

In our conversation they explained their approach:

Gaby Herbstein:
Julieta and I had been working together on the previous calendar, and we fancied work on origins. We spent almost a year in doing the research, because this hadn't been done before.... We were not taught at school about indigenous people...We researched a lot in books, consulting reports of the *conquistadores*, as well as libraries, ethnographic museums, and private collections. Imagine, me doing that as a granddaughter of an English 'conqueror' who came here to build the railways.

Julieta Garavaglia:
Gaby is a fashion photographer – so it had to do with fashion, we were not going to photograph indigenous people. It's not documentary work. We also contacted indigenous people who told us about traditions transmitted by their grandparents. We contacted Silvia, on her silver work. And we travelled. We went to a Wichí community in Salta for a week and looked at how they lived and worked.

Also, most of the dresses and accessories were made by indigenous people. The idea was to show how they dressed before the arrival of the Spaniards. That was the purest

---

25 However, just title and author, not place and year of publication are indicated.

form. Then everything changed, the colonists came who clothed them, because before that the Indians were almost naked.

Basically, we wanted to retrieve the origin of the Argentines.

Gaby Herbstein:
This is really part of our history. The other thing is we wanted to give back to the Indians what they never obtained, dignity. They were always the *cabecitas negras*,[26] the disdained people. Theirs was a culture which was disdained.

What has fashion to do with the indigenous people? If only the indigenous people were fashionable! Well, to some degree we achieved this. There was a lot of press coverage, the people were interested in seeing the models. You know, beauty is something very important here in Argentina. So to show to the young people, attract their attention through the models so that they become interested in our culture is a way of entry, to get the topic across. The United Nations thought it was a good idea that through the calendar we could reach large numbers of young people, and that it was a good way to transmit our culture.

The people from the anthropology world were looking at us with suspicion: 'What do you have to do with it?' they asked us. For them, the world of advertising and fashion is frivolous and artificial. There was some resistance to our research, we had some trouble getting access to information.

The indigenous people asked us: 'Why not indigenous models?'

First, we only had selected two ethnic groups, not all of the present ones. For example, the Abipones and Yámanas already disappeared (so we *had* to use models for them). Also, it wasn't our idea... [to document indigenous cultures], but to show the link between fashion and indigenous people and their culture. This means that fashion gives back to the indigenous people their dignity and shows their culture. The idea was to find among the models those which resembled most indigenous people.

It was an indirect way to get the attention of young people. If I have a photograph of a Mapuche woman, it's just another photograph. But a model *representing* a Mapuche is different.

However, Silvia Rinque was opposed to this and said, 'I will find you a very beautiful Mapuche girl', yet when she saw our model she was very satisfied.

We invited the indigenous people on the set. They didn't understand much of the 'scenography' and the posture of the models but they helped us with telling us their myths. So every model we told a little bit of the story she was representing in the photo.

Gaby Herbstein's and Julieta Garavaglia's idea was to recreate the atmosphere of the turn-of-the-century photographs they had found in the archives. This was the reason that they used sepia tones, and studio set ups (for example, the jaguar). They also were inspired by the photographer of North American Indians Edward C. Curtis (who was famous for staged photography).[27]

---

26 *Cabecitas negras*, 'little blackheads', is the derogatory denomination applied by Argentines of supposed European descent (the majority) to those supposed to be of mixed, or indigenous descent, of the immigrants from the interior provinces, or more recently, from neighbouring countries (for ethnic and racial distinctions in Argentina, see Schneider, 2000a, 2000b).

27 cf. Theye (1989); Edwards (1992).

Gaby Herbstein:
We didn't shoot them as savages, but with the aesthetic of the era ... We didn't invent it, it existed [adornments, animals, tattoos]. We wanted to represent and reconstruct.

However, even in our conversation, there was no hint of taking these historical photographs critically for what they were: representations of vanquished savages taken by the victors, often for 'scientific' purposes, such as those of physical anthropology. Yet by adopting – even partially – the aesthetic of this era without any critical distance, one becomes complicit with its methods unknowingly or not. For instance, no attempt was made to enter the different discourses about Indians which were made in the photographic oeuvres of Panunzi and Pozzo, as was pointed out in the second section of the paper. Not only was the aura of historical photographs just artificially recreated (in fact, uncritically copied), but also the wealth of possible postures and gestures for the historical period was not taken into account.

But what were indigenous people themselves thinking about the production of the calendar and the final result?

I shall first turn to the testimony of Luis Pincén (a descendant of the Indian cacique Pincén, of the Tehuelche-Mapuche). In our interview, Pincén described to me the history of his family: the persecution and refuge of the cacique Pincén,[28] his ancestor, and then his own background as a biology teacher in Argentine schools and member of the *Fundación desde America*. Within the politically heterogeneous movement of indigenous people in Argentina Pincén occupied a moderate position. He thought that promoting the indigenous cause can be achieved through co-operation with whites, and was against what he called 'reverse racism' (that is the rejection of whites by Indians).

When we spoke about the calendar, Pincén was generally positive about it, as he saw this enterprise as a chance to promote the indigenous cause:

Gaby Herbstein came to us (that is *Fundación desde America*), investigating, searching for material, very respectfully. The idea was hers (and of her art director), and from the beginning I found it interesting to have a different viewpoint. We thought we had to co-operate and help. The idea was that the calendar would not be completely anthropological and would show some aesthetics, the glamour of indigenous women.

For me it was very important to re-evaluate, and vindicate the beauty of the dark indigenous woman (*morocha*). In Argentina and elsewhere, the stereotypes of beauty are very strong among women who are the most attached to fashion. We always criticize the fashion world as superficial... but for a work contrary to these stereotypes to speak about indigenous women, their dress, their beauty, to offer interesting elements which are never made public. So could this 'fashion machine' not be used in our favour?

Luis Pincén admitted that there was some criticism:

Some said it wasn't real, it did not truly represent our people – but nobody has the absolute truth.

For example, the lizard on top of the head of the Toba was put there because it has to do with the cosmology of the Toba (Figure 4.2). What happens, is that 98 per cent of Toba

---

28 On the historical figure of cacique Pincén, see Sarasola (1992).

Figure 4.2   Exhibition *Huellas*, Buenos Aires, 2000
By permission of Gaby Herbstein. Photograph by Gaby Herbstein.

are actually converted to evangelical Pentecostal churches – so what can these Toba say on their mythology, even if they live in their community? With the new religion they will negate their culture.

I really would have liked the models to be indigenous girls, there are beautiful ones. However, when I observed the shooting from the 'backstage' I had to realize, they had to use models.

Somebody professional had to do this, because to prepare the photos takes a lot of time. The girl representing the Diaguita stayed for six hours till they finished the make up and then four or five hours to pose. Such a thing a professional has to do not a common woman. When the Colla woman posed, they prepared her for four hours, and then she spent another four hours on the photographic set in uncomfortable positions. Also, Herbstein assured us that she would choose models with 'indigenous' features.

One wonders, however, why Luis Pincén emphasized the beauty and the glamour of indigenous women, and yet justified Herbstein's decision to use fashion models. Was this beauty something indigenous women could achieve on their own, or only through being represented by non-indigenous models, imbued with the aesthetic ideals of Western advertising?

Silvia Rinque, a Mapuche silversmith, who also cooperated with the production of the calendar, did not agree with Pincén's position and felt that he had betrayed the indigenous cause. Rinque made all the silver jewellery for the Mapuche 'model', advised on the dress, and insisted on the way she would appear (the reader will recall that Herbstein and Garavaglia had to convince her of a white model being used). But she still had substantial reservations, especially about the other photographs which she found sexually too explicit (such as the Yámana model, holding a red bream on her head). However, she was very happy – as she said, 'at least 90 per cent' –,with her work and the representation of the Mapuche woman 'I did not want that one sees the legs and the arms', but strongly disagreed with the choice of professional models.

We asked for, in fact we demanded, indigenous models, but she responded, 'So, for the Abipones (an extinct indigenous group) whom shall I select?' Well, she should have selected another indigenous group. But these are all professional, very fashionable models (*sumamente fashion*).

Another significant point Silvia Rinque was making had to do with the issues of indigenous rights and the appropriation of indigenous crafts and artefacts (and by extension, symbols, myths, and traditions).[29] While she was paid for her work and could adorn the model representing the 'Mapuche' woman with her silver jewellery (which, however, she just lent to Gaby Herbstein), she was not credited as 'Silvia Rinque, Mapuche silversmith & jeweller', but just as 'Silvia Rinque, Mapuche'. As she emphasized, crediting her profession would have helped her get more commissions and enhance the diffusion of her work. Her resigned summary comment was: 'The calendar went half way of what we indigenous people wanted.'

Finally, I also met Jorgelina Duarte of the Guaraní-Mbyá. My diary entry for that meeting gives an idea of the mixed attitude of Jorgelina towards the calendar.

In the morning I meet Jorgelina Duarte, Silvia Rinque's Guaraní friend and collaborator on the 'Huellas' catalogue by Gaby Herbstein. She lives in Entre Ríos Street and I have to travel two stops by the Metro and then walk down Entre Ríos about four blocks. I am not quite sure which neighbourhood this is but it gets very 'popular' and quite ugly, opposite her block I see large buildings, *Obras Sanitarias de la Nación* (the state waterworks),

---

29 On appropriation, see Schneider (2003), (2006).

Figure 4.3   Exhibition *Huellas*, Buenos Aires, 2000
By permission of Gaby Herbstein. Photograph by Arnd Schneider.

and Colegio Carlos Pellegrini (the once famous high school – now it looks more like an evening school). I arrive at the building and have to take the elevator, and then, at end of a dark and dirty corridor, I find the apartment. Very small, it is laid out across two levels. Jorgelina welcomes me, her sister visiting with her brother from Misiones province, and her young boy, are also there. We talk about the calendar. She says it was controversial, since the indigenous people didn't have full say, and the photographer (Gaby Herbstein) did not choose indigenous models. At the same time, Jorgelina is somehow proud of the calendar and has hung it up on the wall of her flat. She likes the Mapuche, Guaraní, Colla pictures, but disagrees with the juicier, exotic, erotic images of Toba, Wichí (Figure 4.3) 'This is a woman like an animal, they would not have dressed like this for hunting and gathering!' she says, and Yámana, Apibón (Figure 4.4) 'This is against the sense of decency of indigenous women', she comments.

She likes the Guaraní picture, but says that the facial painting is Guaraní-Tupí (that is of the Brazilian group), not of the Argentine Mbyá-Guaraní. In contrast, she shows me pictures from a German calendar made about 10 years ago, which a friend had copied for her and which she shows in school projects. The calendar depicts members of the Guaraní community, their houses, and some activity, a mixture of ethnographic documentation and 'happy' smiling indigenous people.

Promotion of the Guaraní cause is her main activity in Buenos Aires. She has just come back from some holidays in the comunidad to promote awareness about the Guaraní, and to sell craft. Her grandfather is the cacique of the *comunidad*. She shows me some documents on how they have been trying for some time to promote clean drinking water for the community. It costs about 200, 000 pesos (the Peso is worth US$1), but maybe less, a construction firm working for the provincial government, will take its slice. She goes over and over the file again and can't understand where it's being blocked. They don't yet know the new local members of the provincial assembly, for which there had been

Figure 4.4   Exhibition *Huellas*, Buenos Aires, 2000
By permission of Gaby Herbstein. Photograph by Arnd Schneider.

recent elections. Also, there are competing indigenous organizations in Misiones, and foundations who receive money from Luxembourg. 'But', she says, 'the money doesn't reach the indigenous community!' We then have *tereré*, the cold maté with ice cubes and fruit juice, drunk in Misiones and Paraguay where it is also offered with herbs.

Her husband comes back; he works as a cleaner and maintenance guy far away in the province of Buenos Aires, and in the northern suburb of Belgrano. But the money is not enough, rent is $250[30] – a lot of money. They have the telephone barred for outgoing calls, and his mother is helping them with money, 'si no, no alcanza'. I make a photocopy from an article of the *El Territorio* paper from Misiones, reporting on Guaraní protests. Jorgelina wants me to phone Silvia Rinque to ask her to call her back.

Conclusion: Conquering New Ancestors

In order to understand the full context of Gaby Herbstein's and Julieta Garavaglia's intentions when planning, researching and producing the calendar, it is useful to return to an assertion which they made in the 'Huellas' text (see above) and also in the interview. Their main interest is in 'origins', that is wanting to show how indigenous people lived before the arrival of the Spaniards, in short, showing the 'origins of the Argentines'. Here we find the key to their motivations, and in fact those of much current indigenist discourse in Argentina, that is by people in the arts who appropriate and interpret indigenous cultures. Basically, this line of thought claims that indigenous pre-conquest populations are the ancestors of contemporary

---

30 Equivalent to US$250.

Argentines, when in fact at the time no nation-state existed and since then most of the indigenous people have been extinguished. Moreover, reference is made to pre-historic Indians not contemporary ones, whose existence both as representers (in this case as models) and represented is denied – except for the small format photographs on the supplementary pages. One might also ask: ancestors to whom? Most Argentines are descendants of Europeans, and constructing such a 'new', but in fact, very old, ancestry to indigenous people albeit as historical fossils, is obviously different from the dominant nationalist projects, which would establish identity of the nation state on two quite different pillars. The first of these being independence, including a glorious colonial past for the upper-class Spanish 'Creole' families, but obliterating the indigenous and African contribution to the lower class *criollos*.[31] The second pillar of the nation state consisted in the later modernization through European migration, though this concept was stratified according to the provenance of immigrants, Northerners were eventually preferred over Southerners. It seems that indigenist discourse almost achieves to invert the old proverb (often retold to me by *porteños*), according to which Mexicans descended from the Aztecs, Peruvians from the Incas, and Argentines from the ships, that is by actually substituting Mapuche –or other indigenous populations – for 'ships'. The original proverb and the new 'indigenism' also point to a kind of envy at other Latin American countries' ancestral culture, and the lack of it is seen as the main reason why Argentines would have such a fragile national identity. In fact, already in the late nineteenth and early twentieth centuries some sectors of the Argentine literary and political elite constructed (and construed) Indians as ancestors of the nation-state; one example for this is the writer Ricardo Rojas.[32]

A second part in Herbstein's and Garavaglia's explication concerns their artistic ideals and concepts of beauty, such as those gained from working with professional models (rather than indigenous women) and keeping apparently to an 'aesthetic of the era'. The explicit aim is to make indigenous people fashionable, and thereby 'sell' them to a young white fashion-oriented public. The ideal of beauty is that promoted by the international fashion world: young, slim, almost anorexic, long-legged girls. However, Pincén shared this ideal, and was delighted to see beautiful fashion models dressed up as Indians, thus giving 'glamour' and 'beauty' to indigenous women. One wonders, however, whether the blonde ideal of Argentine society which is ubiquitous in advertising and on the streets with many women wearing dyed blonde hair (*platinizada* 'platinized', being the popular euphemism for it), has not just been replaced by darker colours through the sepia tinting, but no aesthetic specific to or originated by indigenous people is promoted, with the exception of the Mapuche representation, perhaps. Finally, the short texts accompanying the images offering mythological extracts, often are not matched by the actual depictions. Thus, the

---

31 cf. Schneider (1998, 2000); Bernand (2000), Quijada (2000).

32 cf. Penhos (1996b); the important works by Rojas in this respect are *La Restauración Nacionalista* (Buenos Aires, 1909), *Blasón de Plata. Meditaciones y evocaciones de Ricardo Rojas sobre el abolengo de los argentinos* (Buenos Aires, Martín García, 1912), and *Eurindia* (in *obras de Ricardo Rojas*, Vol.5, Buenos Aires: La Facultad, 1924), cf. also Quijada (1996, 1997).

Selk'nam woman is too obviously a 'white' fashion model, where the text speaks of 'There was a time in which *krech*, the moon, and the women dominated the world. They terrorized men representing different spirits till one day the men rebelled and there was a big fight …' . Other texts are more revealing, such as the quote from Charles Darwin who despised of the Yámana since they knew no property, but are mismatched by the accompanying photo showing a nude model with a fish.

What kind of indigenous women are represented in the calendar? Using fashion models, undoubtedly sends a strong message about beauty and eroticism on the one hand which corresponds to stereotypes in Argentine society. On the other hand, dressing models up as imagined turn-of-the-century Indians, and producing sepia prints has two effects: first, Indians are once more portrayed as museum pieces, pertaining to a pristine past before the arrival of Europeans. Thus, the photographs become complicit with turn-of-the-century ideas about savage Indians. Secondly, as women they become objects of desire for a white public.

There seems to operate a double negation in the work of Herbstein and Garavaglia. Indians not only are not shown in their present conditions (except for some small photos on the trip to indigenous communities), but contemporary Indians are also denied representing their own past, because indigenous models were not used employed. As such the photos correspond to a 'white' and widespread Argentine phantasy about Indians as extinct, living mostly as savages in the past. They also correspond to a reverse perception of indigenous women as more sensual, closer to nature and sexually less inhibited than their European counterparts. Somehow, here the indigenous women curiously occupy the position their male companions (who are absent in the calendar) had in the phantasies and actual encounters of Europeans: as Amazon-like warriors who capture and spellbind the male and female gaze, while at the same time being the *cautivas* of male desires.[33]

That these desires are not the exclusive domain of white *porteños* is shown by the statement of Pincén who emphasized the concept of beauty in indigenous women. But has the fashion industry and the beauty ideal (or rather ideology) it promotes really been used to the advantage of indigenous people, as Pincén hoped it would? Most of the reactions from the press seem to speak a different language. There, very little understanding of the presumed political and cultural message to rehabilitate Indians in the minds of Argentine mainstream society is to be found. Rather, one finds platitudes about fashion, beauty, exotic stereotypes, with titles such as 'Sexy Almanac',[34] 'The presenter of Petete (a television character and a fashion model) is a tigress',[35] 'María, a VIP Indian',[36] and one paper even asking 'Which were the most elegant tribes?' Other papers, of the 'light' variety, were obviously more interested in reporting on the presence of the rich and famous at the launch of the calendar, than on the content 'The Sabatinis at a photographic show' – accompanied by photos of former tennis star Gabriela Sabatini, her brother Osvaldo, and his wife, the

---

33 Cf. section 2 and Malosetti Costa (1993).
34 *Crónica*, 2 November 1999.
35 *Clarín*, 21 November 1999.
36 *Revista Noticias*, 6 November 1999.

actress Catherine Fulop:[37] 'Let's go for a walk'[38] (on Catherine Fulop and Osvaldo Sabatini attending the exhibition launching the calendar), 'How beautiful are you, Cathy!' (on Catherine Fulop attending the event).[39] A few other papers did some more serious reporting, mentioning the idea and intentions of the calendar, archival research and visit to indigenous communities, support by the United Nations, the work of Mapuche silversmith Silvia Rinque, and the controversy about using white professional models rather than indigenous women.[40] *La Nación* was probably the only paper which ironically lamented '…pity that they (the indigenous people) were not shown in the photos, because they are not as fashionable as the models.'[41]

The authors of the calendar maintained that they were faithful to the archival photographs they located through their research. Yet it was precisely in the historical context of extinction and subjugation, anthropological research and experiments, that the original photographs were shot, reflecting the evolutionist and racist ideology of their era.[42] Thus, shooting studio photographs today with reference to archival photos without criticizing and contextualizing them for what they are, the contemporary photographs become complicit with the historical intentions, as pointed out earlier in the paper. This is not to say that Herbstein and her team shared the ideology of the end of the nineteenth and twentieth century about Indians. To the contrary, they were led, in their own words, by intentions of 'vindicating Indians', of conferring 'dignity' to them, and of making them 'fashionable'. For instance, in the exhibition in the 'Abasto' shopping mall, the central display at the entrance, showed the images from the calendar in smaller format, accompanied by a statement from the cacique Cangapol:

The earth nourishes us, and provides for us. She raises us and she eats us. To whom belongs the air? To whom the water, salt, wood and the animals? To somebody? To all? What would happen if an Indian would demand all this for himself? Cacique Cangapol (Figure 4.5).

However, in the calendar, their intentions remain far from being unequivocal, to the point of being open to misinterpretation, and thus serving the opposite purpose, which is clearly evidenced by the reception in the press. In fact, quite different approaches are explored by Argentine artists, and I can only mention here in passing the work of contemporary photographers and artists, such as Res (Figure 4.6) and Lionel Luna.

---

37 *Crónica*, 14 December 1999.

38 *Revista Pronto*, 15 December 1999.

39 *Revista TV Guía*, 19 December 1999.

40 *Revista Para Ti, 26 November 1999*; 'The traces of the past illustrate the New Year', *B.A.E.*, 7 December 1999; 'Ethnic Calendar', *La Razón*, 7 December 1999; 'Models to photograph the past', *La Prensa*, 8 December 1999; 'The photographer Gaby Herbstein renders tribute to the indigenous people', *El Cronista*, 10 December 1999; 'Twelve Ethnic Groups and as many months', *La Nación*, 23 December 1999.

41 *La Nación*, 21 November 1999.

42 cf. Stocking (1982); Theye (1989), Edwards (1992), Penhos (forthcoming).

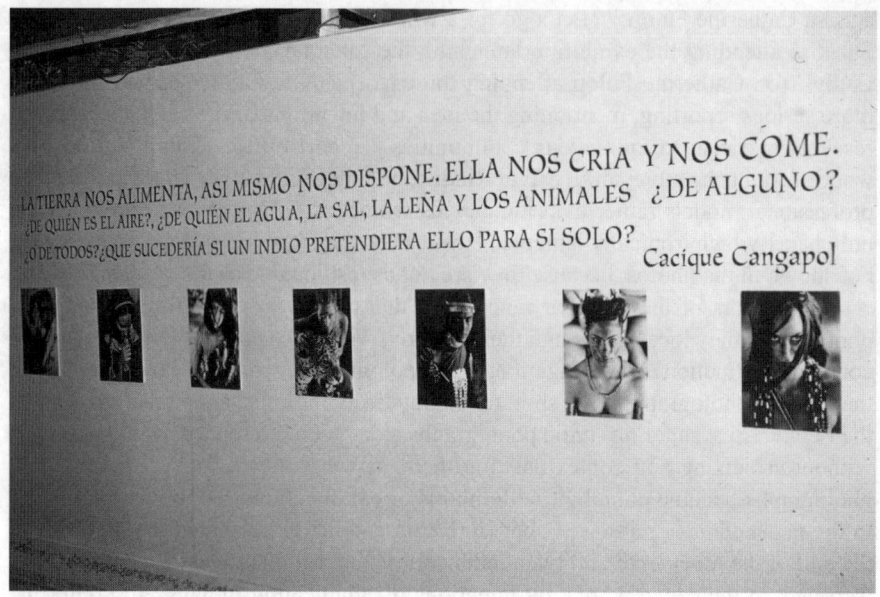

Figure 4.5   Exhibition *Huellas*, Buenos Aires, 2000
By permission of Gaby Herbstein. Photograph by Arnd Schneider.

Figure 4.6   No entregar Carhue al Huinca, RES, Buenos Aires
Courtesy of the artist.

Indigenous people, obviously, have to speak for themselves. Yet it is noteworthy that in the statements by Luis Pincén and Silvia Rinque, while the latter was critical of the project, the enhanced publicity for the Indian cause in Argentina was valued as positive.

When I showed the calendar to Argentine friends, I obtained mixed reactions. On the one hand, there were those who would quickly identify it as a superficial enterprise of the fashion world, while acknowledging the technical and aesthetic quality of the photos. Others would say, 'These are just fashion photos, they have nothing to do with Indians'. There were also those who were immediately impressed by the quality of the images, and put them in their context as studio photos by a fashion photographer, using famous models without having any documentary pretensions about contemporary Indians.

From observing visitors on several visits to the 'Huellas' exhibition in the Abasto shopping mall, I could discern that they were all white middle or upper middle class *porteños*, some of them reacting with surprise to the pictures, others with curiosity and being intrigued by the topic. One has to add that it is not a common sight to see in Buenos Aires large displays of indigenous people, even if they are of an artificial nature. Usually, the large billboards on the central *Avenida 9 de Julio* and other downtown avenues, are used for advertising airlines, computers, and fashion, or during election periods by political parties.

In some way, it is therefore commercially courageous to bring indigenous people into the public sphere, in what is the political, economic, and cultural centre of the country which has always marginalized indigenous people. But such a move also pays off commercially. As Herbstein mentioned in the interview, once companies had heard of the calendar project and had seen the successful launch, they too wanted to use indigenous people for their advertising campaigns. Hence Herbstein studios designed an advertising campaign for a cigarette company, featuring the members of the only indigenous Rugby team of the country, Guaraní players from the Chaco. In November 1999, there had been a conference on indigenous people (the second of its kind) at the San Martín cultural centre. However, in terms of public display, that is the part visible to outside by-passers, there were only a few handicraft stalls, confirming probably the image *porteños* had of indigenous people anyway. That is to say, people dressed in folkloric costumes, selling arts and crafts such as flutes, wrist bands, and little statues.

The discussion of the 'Huellas' exhibition and calendar also illuminates issues of the public perception of the other in Buenos Aires. While this issue merits further research, towns in the province of Buenos Aires, and more so in Patagonia, often seem to have monuments commemorating the 'past' indigenous population, but there are to my knowledge no such public places of remembrance in the city of Buenos Aires.

Certainly, the calendar also represents an appropriation of the indigenous body. By posing as indigenous women, the models actually get into the skin of an imaginary indigenous other who is not allowed to represent herself (other than to decorate the skin of white women with their accessories). Thus, these images occupy a public space in Buenos Aires which has been left vacant since the Spanish conquest. Only captive

Indians, Creole descendants and more recently indigenous immigrants from Peru, Bolivia, and Paraguay would represent this conceptual space at the bottom of society.

There is yet another form of appropriation, when Gaby Herbstein and Julieta Garavaglia speak of Indians as the origin of 'us' Argentines. Here, the idea (or ideology) of the nation-state subsumes Indians as its ancestors. This is problematic, both historically, because it was the Argentine nation-state which defeated the last indigenous resistance, and politically in the present, because indigenous communities in Argentina are seeking their right to self-determination. Similar to what has been achieved in the North American context, some indigenous leaders conceive of their communities as 'nations' and want autonomy from Buenos Aires coupled with far-reaching rights over their territories, if not independence.

Having returned to London from fieldwork in Argentina, I showed the calendar to Norma Schenke, an Argentine artist working in London, and doing research into the representation of indigenous people in Argentine photography of the nineteenth century. In our discussion, she made the valid point that despite the noble intentions of the producers, the calendar results again in the discrimination of indigenous people by imposing European models (sic!) of beauty.

Thus, it could be questioned whether the production of the calendar does not stem from a patronizing attitude, when Herbstein and Garavaglia pretend to return to indigenous people their dignity. The issue is whether such dignity would not have been achieved better through their more active participation.

Herbstein's work is possibly best described as an aestheticizing and idealizing approach to the representation of the indigenous, dictated by the presumed parameters of the fashion world, which are primarily commercial ones. A different kind of approach probably would take a second step, in order to achieve a more aesthetically fragmented representation (including notions of the 'ugly', and 'realist', according to fashion ideals), and express a reflexive critique of the status quo of indigenous people in Argentina (both past and present). In different contexts, the fashion house *Benetton* has been an example for an aesthetically more complex proposition, challenging traditional concepts of beauty and taking up politically controversial issues. However, *Benetton* too has aroused controversy with its approach and practices; for instance, in Argentina its policy of enclosing large areas of land for sheep farms in Patagonia is contested by the local Mapuche.

Returning to our opening remarks, we can conclude that in this calendar, stereotypes of beauty of the urban Argentine society, and *porteño* society in particular, are transposed to staged indigenous women (by white fashion models). The nation-state (or Gaby Herbstein's understanding of it) has now not only appropriated indigenous space of the present, but also indigenous people of past generations, thus achieving a colonization of the others' history. People who in Eric Wolf's terms were, from the Western vantage point, 'People without history'[43] (in fact had their own history, though this was denied by the West), now become inextricably part of *our* history.

---

43 cf. Wolf (1982).

References

Bernand, C. (1998) 'Esclaves et affranchis d'origine Africaine', *Cahiers Internationaux de Sociologie*, CV, 325–340.

Bernand, C. (2000) 'La Población Negra De Buenos Aires (1777–1862)', *Homogeneidad y nación: Con un Estudio De Caso: Argentina, Siglos XIX y X.X.* Quijada, M., Bernand, C. and Schneider, A. (Madrid: Consejo Superior de Investigaciones Cientificas).

Chapman, A. (1982), *Drama and Power in a Hunting Society: The Selk'nam of Tierra del Fuego* (Cambridge: Cambridge University Press).

Edwards, E., ed. (1992), *Anthropology and Photography 1860 – 1920* (New Haven: Yale University Press).

Hernández, I. (1992), *Los Indios en la Argentina* (Madrid: MAPFRE).

Iglesia, C. (1992) 'La Mujer Cautiva: Cuerpo, mito y Frontera', *In Historia de las Mujeres en Occidente: Del Renacimiento a la Edad Moderna*. Duby, G. and Perrot, M. (eds) (Madrid: Taurus).

Magrassi, G.E. (1987) *Los Aborígenes de la Argentina: Ensayo Socio-Histórico-Cultural* (Buenos Aires: Ediciones Búsqueda).

Malosetti Costa, L. (1993), 'El Rapto De Cautivas Blancas: un Aspecto Erótico de la Barbarie En la Plástica Rioplatense Del Siglo XIX'. Paper presented at the XVII Coloquio Internacional de Historia del Arte; Arte, Historia e Identidad en América Visiones comparativas Instituto de Investigaciones Estéticas de la Universidad Nacional Autónoma De Mexico and Comité International d'Histoire de l'Art, Zacatecas, Mexico, 22–27 September.

Maybury-Lewis, D. (1991) 'Becoming Indian in Lowland South America', *Nation-States and Indians in Latin America*, Urban, G. and Sherzer, J. (eds) (Austin: University of Texas Press).

Ortelli, S. (1996) 'La araucanización de las pampas: ¿ Realidad Histórica o Construcción De Los Etnólogos?', *Anuario del IEHS (Tandil)*, 208–225.

Penhos, M. (1996a) 'Retratos de indios y actos de representación', *Memoria del 4° Congreso De Historia de la Fotografía En la Argentina* (Buenos Aires: CEP).

Penhos, M. (1996b) 'Actores de una historia sin conflictos, Acerca de los indios en pinturas del Museo Histórico Nacional' in *Estudios e Investigaciones: Instituto de Teoría e Historia Del Arte 'Julio E. Payró'*, 6 (Buenos Aires: F. de Filosofía y Letras, U.B.A.).

Penhos, M. (1999) 'Representación e identidad comunitaria. Calfucurá y Bibolini frente a 25 de Mayo', *Epílogos y Prólogos Para Un Fin De Siglo*, Buenos Aires: Caia.

Quijada, M. (1996) 'Los "Incas arios": Historia, Lengua y Raza En la Construcción Nacional Hispanoamericana', *Histórica*, **XX**(2), 243–269.

Quijada, M. (1997) 'Ancestros, Ciudadanos, Piezas De Museo: Modelos Antropológicos y Construcción Nacional En la Argentina Decimononica' *Modèles Européenes en Amérique Latine XIXème siècle*. Lamparière, A. et al. (eds.) (Paris: Editions du CNRS).

Quijada, M. (2000) 'Indígenas, Tierras y Ciudadanía', *Homogeneidad y Nación: Con un Estudio De Caso: Argentina, Siglos XIX y X.X.* Quijada, M., Bernand, C. and Schneider, A. (Madrid: Consejo Superior de Investigaciones Científicas).

Quijada, M. (2002) 'Repensando la frontera sur argentina: concepto, contenido, continuidades y discontinuidades de una realidad espacial y Étnica (Siglos XVII –XIX)', *Revista de Indias*, **LXII**(224), 103–142.

Rock, D. (1987) *Argentina 1516–1987: From Spanish Colonization to the Falklands War and Alfonsín* (London: I.B.Tauris).

Sarasola, C.M. (1992), *Nuestros paisanos los indios* (Buenos Aires: Emecé).

Schneider, A. (1998) 'Discours sur l'altérité dans l'Argentine moderne', *Cahiers Internationaux de Sociologie*, CV, 341–360.

Schneider, A. (2000a) 'Discourses of Ethnic Distinctions in Contemporary Argentina' in *Ideology and Discursive Practices: Spain and Latin America*. Domínguez, F. (ed.) (Berne/New York: Peter Lang).

Schneider, A. (2000b) 'Immigrantes Europeos y De Otros Orígenes', *Homogeneidad y nación: Con un Estudio De Caso: Argentina, Siglos XIX y X.X. Mónica Quijada, Carmen Bernand and Arnd Schneider* (Madrid: Consejo Superior de Investigaciones Cientificas).

Schneider, A. (2003) 'On "appropriation": A Critical Reappraisal of the Concept and its Application in Global Art Practices', *Social Anthropology*, **11**(2), 215–219.

Schneider, A. (2006), 'Appropriations', in *Contemporary Art and Anthropology*, Schneider, A and Wright, C. (eds.) (Oxford: Berg).

Serbín, A. 'Las Organizaciones Indígenas de la Argentina', *América Indígena*, **XLI**(3), 407–437.

Serbín, A. (forthcoming) 'Frente y Perfil, Imagen Fotográfica e Identificación En Las Prácticas Antropológicas y Criminológicas De Fin De Siglo XIX', in *Usar las imágenes. Representaciones y sociedad en la Argentina*. Munilla Lacasa, L. and Penhos, M. (eds.).

Stocking, G. (1982), *Race, Culture and Evolution: Essays in the History of Anthropology* (Chicago: University of Chicago Press).

Tessler, M. (1989), *Los Aborígenes Durante El peronismo y Los Gobiernos Militares* (Buenos Aires: Centro Editor América Latina).

Theye, T., ed. (1989), *Der geraubte Schatten* (Munich: Münchener Stadtmuseum).

Wolf, E. (1982), *Europe and the People without History* (Berkeley: University of California Press).

Chapter 5

Mimí Derba and Azteca Films: The Rise of Nationalism and the First Mexican Woman Film-Maker[1]

Irene García
Translated by Nattie Gulubov

The Beginnings

In 1905, 10 years after the birth of the cinema, Mexican photographers began to create their own cinematographic style: a unique perspective of scenes from everyday life that privileged an urban and bourgeois culture and a festive mood, but neglected the countryside, the dispossessed and the tragic. The armed uprising of 1910 was a watershed in film production because it stimulated the emergence of the documentary about the Revolution, and so became the origin of Mexican cinema, because it generated its own aesthetics and also shaped a distinctive notion of 'Mexicanness'.

Unlike documentary, fiction silent films did not appear in Mexico until 1917, although the first attempts to produce 'vistas of art of great interest and actuality, which will rival those from abroad'[2] were made in 1907[3] and 1915. Revolutionary

---

1   An early version of this article was first a section from my master's dissertation in Media Studies, researched with funding from the *Programa Interdisciplinario de Estudios de la Mujer*, El Colegio de México and by Conacyt as part of a project called 'Etnia o nación: los intelectuales indígenas de México', coordinated by Natividad Gutiérrez, and later a conference paper read at the Latin American Studies Associaton congress held in Miami, March 2000.

2   'Nueva industria del cine en México', *El Monitor* (8 April 1915), 4; Quoted in Aurelio De Los Reyes, *Cine y Sociedad En México. 1986–1930*, vol.I. *Vivir de sueños.1896–1920*, UNAM-Cineteca Nacional, Mexico, 1981, p. 202.

3   See *Aventuras de Tip-Top en Chapultepec* and *El, Grito de Dolores in Aurelio de los Reyes, Filmografía del cine mudo mexicano (1896–1929)*, UNAM-Filmoteca, Mexico, 1986, pp. 41–43. On the other hand, according to the historian Ángel Miquel, the interest shown by producers was also due to a change in the attitudes of distributors, who began to lease films instead of selling them, allowing both the producers and exhibitors the possibility of increasing their earnings. See "Cines y públicos en el México de principios de siglo", *Dicine*, 44, March 1992, and "El público en los cines de la ciudad de México (1896–1917)" in Eduardo de la Vega Alfaro and Enrique E. Sánchez Ruiz (eds), *Bye bye Lumiére.... Investigación sobre cine en México*, Universidad de Guadalajara, 1994, p. 144.

documentaries had practically disappeared from view by 1916 and gave way to a 'new' type of cinema, which transformed cinematographic rhetoric and the people involved in its production.[4]

The most serious and noteworthy effort to launch the Mexican film industry came from Mimí Derba, a young woman of the middle class with an extensive education in the arts who, from the age of eighteen, was a successful actress and singer of *zarzuelas* (light opera) in the main theatres of Mexico City. Mimí also contributed to various Porfirian publications, in which she very clearly and sensitively acknowledged the condition of women at the time. When she was 24 she decided to become a prominent figure in cinema, although to achieve her goal she would have to found the industry, a task which she accomplished when she suggested the creation of a film production company to Enrique Rosas, an important photographer and film impresario. In Azteca Films Mimí headed a team that in 1917 produced, edited and promoted five films; she acted in four, wrote two scripts and was the production designer on one, work for which she became the first woman film-maker in Mexico.

But Mimí deserves merit not only for her pioneering role in the creation of a national cinema, but also because she had the imagination to think of film not as a reflection of reality but as an art form with its own expressive possibilities. Inspired by the *zeitgeist* of the age, this would have to be a nationalist art, thus Derba contributed to the creation of a nationalist discourse, which would later be consolidated during the golden age of Mexican cinema.

The Background

A nationalist art, which sought to describe the local customs and landscapes of the country, prevailed in Mexico from the end of the nineteenth century. The ideal aesthetic to achieve this goal was naturalism, and the documentary form was best suited to the task. This trend was further nourished by the Revolution, which was recorded by the documentary, believed to be the most truthful testimony of events because of its capacity to depict reality 'faithfully'. These conditions were necessary for the subsequent interest in the development of a cinema, which would not only be national but nationalist.

Another motive drove this concern: by 1917 the Revolution had been front-page news for seven years in the North American press, and producers had taken advantage of this interest by presenting the 'vortex of the Mexican war',[5] whose attraction was even greater than that of the previously popular Edenic landscapes. This depiction of the Revolution was plagued by stereotypes and prejudice against which Mexicans began to rebel, they instead looked forward to the rise of a new industry, which would vindicate their culture abroad.[6]

---

4   cf. Aurelio de los Reyes, 'El Cine en México (1896–1930)' in Aurelio de los Reyes et al. (eds.) *80 años de cine en México*, UNAM (Imágenes 2), Mexico, 1977, p. 57.

5   See Margarita de Orellana, *La Mirada CircularEl Cine Norteamericano de la Revolución Mexicana* (1911–1917), Joaquín Mortiz (Cuadernos de Joaquín Mortiz), Mexico, 1991, pp. 22–33.

6   Idem.

The historian Aurelio de los Reyes has offered additional reasons to explain the creation of fiction films in 1917. The first, and perhaps the most important, was the fall in European production during the First World War. The second is that the United States of America did not promote commerce with Mexico because of its generalized instability, and the Mexican audience continued to reject their cinema probably because it deliberately degraded Mexican culture. The third reason was the widespread unemployment of actors, brought about when film impresarios put a stop to variety shows in cinemas in response to threats of unionization made by theatrical actors. The fourth and last reason was the pressing demand of an audience hungry for fiction that would alleviate its own starvation and provide distraction from the political catastrophes experienced on a daily basis.[7]

Yet another reason may be suggested: the cult of the film star had risen and the North American, French and Italian industries began to exploit this phenomenon. Female spectators became consumers of the fashions established by actresses and of the gossip surrounding them.[8] The 'new' Mexican cinema did not escape this trend, since from 1916 Lydia Borelli, Francesca Bertini, Pina Minichelli, among others, had already become celebrities, so Mexican actresses began to imitate the style of their acting. Eva Padilla very openly imitated Meninchelli, and Mimí mimicked Bertini, whom she greatly admired. Others would take it upon themselves to write and read the gossip columns.

Nationalist sentiment was the main source of inspiration for the widespread desire for a Mexican film industry. Nationalism had already influenced other art forms throughout the country and, in the eyes of its viewers, compensated for the offences committed by North American filmmakers. More importantly, nationalism was a necessary sentiment for the constitutionalist reconstruction of a national identity with which to ward off foreign intrusions. Thus, arose the 'dream of a powerful and prosperous Mexican film industry'.[9] 'National production experienced a radical break between the old and the new; the unconsciously national cinema was left behind to be replaced by a consciously nationalist cinema'.[10]

But nationalist propaganda was expressed in different ways in fiction films. According to Aurelio de los Reyes, it is possible to identify three types of film: influenced by the aesthetics of Romanticism and Mexican 'zarzuela', the *costumbristas* focused on landscapes and national types, depicting regional customs and manners. Historical films were based upon the pre-hispanic past or the Colonial period and, lastly, cosmopolitan films, clearly influenced by the Italian films of divas, though shot on location in Mexico.[11]

Several artists experimented with the new art form: Jacobo Granat attempted to make a film with the famous Mexican actress 'La Gatita Blanca'; Carranza asked the *Dirección General de Bellas Artes* to produce newsreels and the unfortunate Manual

7   cf. Aurelio de los Reyes, Cine y Sociedad…. (op. cit., p. 204).
8   Ibid., pp. 199–200.
9   Ibid., p. 202.
10 Idem.
11 Aurelio de los Reyes, *Medio siglo de cine Mexicano (1896–1947)*, Trillas (Linterna Mágica 10), Mexico, 1998 (1987), p. 68.

de la Bandera tried to establish a film school.[12] The task of bringing this dream to fruition fell to Mimí Derba and Enrique Rosas.

The Actors and Actresses

In March 1916 Francisco Villa invaded Columbus, Ohio; he had not yet been vanquished by Obregón. The American Government reacted immediately by invading Mexican territory. Carranza resisted the invasion while simultaneously attempting to impose some unity on the country.

In October 1916, Mimí Derba, for the first time, expressed her wish to act in films:

> Mimí wants to go to the movies. She feels the magnetic pull to live a life of rhythmic attitudes and delicate gestures on the screen.... The *zarzuelas* may bore her a little. The vulgarity of the environment behind the scenes is torture to her, She dreams with the cinema. To live the life bursting with the *sprit* and charm which we admire in scenes from *La mujer desnuda*, in which Lydia Borelli experiences the tortuous path from love to pain.... This is Mimí's dream.[13]

Derba was not a typical woman of her time: her stoicism and devotion to her career at a time when women only had two choices, her refusal to have a partner who would not respect her life-style and financial independence, her passion for writing and reading, are all evidence that she was a persevering woman who faced challenges gladly irrespective of the risks and consequences. At the age of 24 she could dispose of her father's inheritance and made use of the 100 thousand pesos that came to her.[14] This was a significant sum of money if we take into account that, according to the columnist Gil Braltar, 'a movie costs 50 thousand pesos'.[15] She was obviously in a position to make her dream come true if and when she could find another investor, and Enrique Rosas was best suited to this role because of his long career as an

---

12 'Manuel de la Bandera was the first actor to conceive the idea of a national film industry, and to this end in September 1917 founded a small academy to train the future actors of Mexican cinema .... *De la Bandera* did not accomplish his plans and very soon another company with more capital (Azteca Films) pre-empted him' in Reyes de la Maza, L. (ed.), *Salón Rojo (Programas y crónicas del cine mudo en México)*, Vol. I (UNAM), 1895–1920-Dirección General de Difusión Cultural (Cuadernos de Cine), Mexico, 1968, p. 158. See also Gabriel Ramírez, *Crónica del cine mudo mexicano*, Cineteca Nacional, Mexico, 1989, pp. 53–56.

13 Hugo Sol, 'Mimí Derba, Artista deliciosa que adora el cinematógrafo', 'Instantáneas' in *El Nacional. Diario Libre de la Noche*, 7 October 1916. It must be said that during the interview we discover, for the first time, some of her personal fancies: she wears a comfortable kimono, her dressing room is decorated with photographs of her colleagues and, curiously, at the centre there is a portrait of the German kaiser; she adores a Parisian porcelain doll called Rodolfo and expresses her admiration and enthusiasm for the playwrights Jacinto Benavente, Alfred de Musset and Eduardo Marquina. Additionally, she dreams of travelling to New York.

14 This she stated in an interview given before her death in 1953. See 'Sale del sanatorio la artista que fundó uno de los primeros estudios de México', *Excélsior*, 10 July 1953, p. 4–b.

15 'Escenarios y Pantallas' in Excélsior, 13 November 1917, p. 3.

exhibitor and photographer of the most important events in the political life of the country. He became interested in fiction films when he realized that the age of the documentary was drawing to a close.

Thus, more than a dream it was a fait accompli, because at the beginning of November Mimí Derba bid farewell to the stage with a performance in her honour at the Catedral de la Tanda[16] and at the end of the month, already in touch with Enrique Rosas, formally announced that she would be making films. In this reporter's enthusiasm we again come across the idea that film could be a pedagogical tool used to inspire nationalism:

> The idea that the unique artist Mimí Derba is creating a film-production company which will develop matters of national interest inspired by truly historical subjects, showing the real Mexican customs and lift the audience's spirits by introducing it to the social tendencies that our civilization requires cannot be overlooked, given the scope of its possibilities which, in time, may be of use in the education of the public... especially if it is a matter of encouraging a social class, such as our middle and lower class. Mimí Derba's idea must be a source of great satisfaction for her and may be the first step in a very important area of our culture.[17]

That December, when the theatre season was over, she travelled to Los Angeles on a visit to Universal City and possibly to take acting lessons.[18] She also made a note of everything that was necessary to establish a film company and realized that her own, whatever her efforts, would always be lacking; however, upon her return in an interview she reiterated her desire to make films 'to demonstrate abroad just how capable we are. Let them know our middle classes, our upper class, the clean audience, instead of the ragged, filthy outcasts who are always in the spotlight and clear the way for denigrating opinions'. She had, undoubtedly, seen films in which 'a Mexican is always a traitor, deceitful, while the American is a type brimming with virtue'.[19]

Azteca Films was formally created in March – its name was Sociedad Cinematográfica Mexicana Rosas, Derba y Cia.[20] According to some accounts the premises were at the corner of Balderas and Juárez on a large plot of land whose only standing building had been a hospice and a fire station, although there was also a large pavillion, and all the necessary departments for film production: developing and printing, props and offices. The premises also included several laboratories, an exhibition room, dressing rooms, and of course a large piece of land to be used for

---

16 'Teatros', *El Nacional*, 3 November 1916. The earnings from benefit performances were given to the person who was been honoured.

17 Henry, 'Mimí Derba hará películas, El cine nacional como medio de enseñanza público', *El Universal*, 27 November 1916, quoted in Luis Reyes de la Maza, *Salón Rojo* (op. cit., pp. 160–161).

18 'Progresa en México el complicado arte de la cinematografía', quoted in Ángel Miquel, *Mimí Derba*, Archivo Fílmico Agrasánchez/Filmoteca de la UNAM (Mujeres del Cine Mexicano), Mexico (2000).

19 Idem.

20 *El entreacto*, n/d (circa October 1917), quoted in Gabriel Ramírez, op. cit., pp. 63–64. See also Ángel Miquel, *Mimí Derba*, op. cit.

the sets. According to one reporter, 'it was all taken very seriously... the creation of film with artists and Mexican themes.'[21] That month 'the first scenes were shot as practice and to scout the talent available for future roles..... The audience, a motley crowd, applauded every scene'.[22]

Another reporter wrote that Azteca Films began to work 'with enough capital, good technical and artistic resources and plenty of enthusiasm'. And again we encounter the nationalist impulse: the creation of the company was very satisfying because it 'provides a practical and effective means for Mexico to gain prestige abroad, promoting our customs and our splendour, our current civilization, unique and stable, our cultural treasures, etc'.[23]

Salustiano, the pseudonym used by José Manuel Ramos, in a review published in *Mefistófeles* on 7 April 1917 said that while the artists auditioned 'it was obvious that they had absolutely no idea of what they were trying to do',[24] so their failure was to be expected since:

> One can perceive in them a very particular tendency to overact and gesticulate outrageously [and] when on screen those marked movements come across as grotesque and remind us of the films made fifteen years ago when the art was in diapers and had not yet felt the presence of those models of discretion and sobriety Nepitti, Collo, Carminatti, to name only the most famous Italian actors.[25]

Italian cinema was the most influential at the time, and the actors continued to use a technique best suited to the theatre. Mimí, however, was 'truly filmic' and doubtlessly would become a 'leading actress'.

Additionally, the reporter said that the company would begin to work on a film called *Los Aguiluchos*, reminiscent of 'the glorious event of the defense of the Castillo de Chapultepec in 1947'.[26] From other accounts we know that this film would later be called *Chapultepec*, though in the end, after several setbacks in production, it was never filmed. Several years later José María Sánchez García explained why the film was never made. His explanation may not be all that far-fetched:

---

21 'Impresiones de un cronista de cines: "El sueño de Mimí"', *El Universal*, 19 March 1917, reproduced in Helena Almoina, *Notas para la Historia Del Cine en México (1896–1925)*, Filmoteca-UNAM, Mexico, vol.I, p. 115.

22 Idem.

23 Alfa y Omega y Dufilm, 'Escenarios y Pantallas', *Excélsior*, 27 March 1917.

24 The writer's visit to the Azteca Films premises was probably due to the fact that he was working on the second script filmed by the company, *Alma de sacrificio*. According to the reporter Silvestre Bonard (alias Carlos Noriega Hope), Ramos was a 'poet who plunged into film with the force of all his optimism, his shock of hair and temperament'. After this incursion into film, Ramos directed and acted in *Confesión trágica* (1919), adapted *La Banda del automóvil gris*(1919) and directed *Viaje redondo* (1920). See Carlos Noriega Hope (Silvestre Bonard), *El teatro de las sombras. El cine por fuera y por dentro*, Botas, Mexico, n/d, pp. 164–165, and Aurelio de los Reyes, *Filmografía...*, op. cit.

25 Quoted in José María Sánchez García, 'Historia del cine Mexicano', *Cinema Reporter* 691, 13 October 1951, pp. 39 and 40.

26 Idem.

But the fear that the public, used to the tragic melodramas which arrived from Europe, would not react to an educational piece with approval explains why in practice Azteca Films gave preference to social themes of a more international style, copied from the passionate tragedies which arrived from France and Italy.[27]

Aside from the rehearsals, and while the *atellier* was under construction, Azteca Films conducted public readings of the scripts they would produce. Eduardo Gómez Haro read his own *Entre la vida y la muerte* and *En defensa propia* by Mimí. At the time 'Enrique Rosas was at the Museo Nacional de Arqueología filming the company's emblem: the Aztec calendar, revealed by a China Poblana, with the words "Azteca Films" at its centre'.[28]

The Films

At the beginning of May the company began to film the script by Mimí Derba *En defensa propia* (In self-defense), a melodrama that tried to imitate Italian films. It was first screened on Saturday 14 July at the Arbeu theatre. It consisted of 10 reels, Joaquín Coss was the art director, Mimí played the leading role as Enriqueta, María Carballé was her antagonist, Eva, and the source of their conflict was Julio Taboada (Julio Mancera).

The plot was simple. Enriqueta starts off as a new governess working in the house of the young Julio Mancera; soon after they fall in love and marry, but cousin Eva arrives from Europe and gradually draws him away from Enriqueta, who does not surrender and instead reveals Eva's duplicity during a masked ball, when Eva is in the midst of a love scene with one of her suitors, thus resolving the conflict. Enriqueta has acted in *self-defense*.

The mood before the screening was charged with expectation, intensified by those members of the press who had been asked to the press screening. Salustiano was among them and he wrote the following about the film:-

> It is a social comedy in which Mimí gives us a sample of her talent, since it is upon a very simple plot that she has created a magnificent character, showing details of feminine psychology which are truly admirable. The acting, and the fact that the protagonist is also the writer, guarantee the success of her interpretation.
>
> [The films by Azteca Films] will be proof that we are capable of competing with an advantage, on beautiful locations, or in elegant avenues, or in magnificent palaces such as those found in European films. *En defensa propia* has scenes in Xochimilco which will surely be captivating, especially the full shot at dusk which is a veritable ode to beauty and photographic perfection.[29]

---

27 Idem.

28 'Impresiones de nuestro cronista de cines: los primeros esfuerzos', 'Por la pantalla', *El Universal*, 28 April 1917, reproduced in Helena Almoina, op. cit., p. 128.

29 Salustiano, *Mefistófeles*, reproduced in José María Sánchez García, 'Historia del cine Mexicano', op. cit., and 'Apuntes para la historia de nuestro cine', *Novedades*, 1 April 1945.

The reporters from *El Universal* predicted that the movie would inaugurate 'a significant and prestigious phase in the annals of Mexican *silent drama*'. About the photography they said that it on occasion reached perfection, the scenic movement is admirable, the *mise-en-scene* is correct and elegant, the costume design and the accessories are of impeccable propriety. In sum, '*En defensa propia* will not disgrace itself if it were to be shown in any foreign cinemas'.[30]

In his review for *Mefistófeles* Salustiano described the mood of the premiere as follows:

> The Arbeu Theatre was full of intellectual types on Saturday when the first film edited by the workshop on Juárez Street was screened. The audience's curiosity was transformed after the first scenes into unabashed enthusiasm expressed through the most spontaneous and warm applause. Mimí, extremely moved, thanked the audience from the stage, grateful for their show of approval.... . Just before the end of the screening, in response to an ovation from the audience, Mimí and Enrique Rosas appeared on stage, the gifted directors of this company which is well on its way to success and which will be the first to champion Mexican cinematography abroad.... . There has been no lack of detractors, such as the Gothic children of the type who only accept as good whatever comes from beyond our borders and choose to purchase home products only when they are foreign counterfeits, who speak ill of Mimí's workshop and prefer to trade in forgeries.[31]

The following Monday, on 16 July 1917, in the new section of *Excélsior* 'Escenarios y Pantallas', Zeta reviewed the first Azteca Films production film. The review claimed that it was, without a doubt, the best film ever made in Mexico, the photography, the sets, and Mimí's wardrobe were greatly admired, but the review also found fault with the production design, because the depiction of the lifestyle of the metropolitan upper class was lacking, the plot was so naive that it bordered on the infantile, but what was important about the film was that 'it is brilliant proof that in the country a little enthusiasm and perseverance are enough to gain independence in the industrial production of works of film'.[32]

Less than a week later, as promised, the second film by Azteca Films was screened at the Arbeu Theatre on 20 July. *Alma de Sacrificio* (Soul of Sacrifice), a melodrama in seven parts, was written by José Manual Ramos, and the production design and photography were by the same crew that had worked on the previous film. On this occasion Mimí only contributed as the protagonist (she played the role of Rosa) and

---

30 '*En defensa propia*. Hermosa película mexicana de arte', *El Universal*, 13 July 1917, reproduced in Helena Almoina, op. cit., p. 169.

31 Salustiano, quoted in José María Sánchez García, 'Historia del cine Mexicano', *Cinema Reporter*, 10 November 1951. Hipólito Seijas mentioned that the 'spectators gave a standing ovation to the artists and urged Mimí and Enrique Rosas onto the stage to enjoy the voluptuous applause', in Helena Almoina, op. cit., p. 171.

32 Aurelio de los Reyes has mentioned that interest in the Revolutionary documentary had waned. But this neglect was justified in Zeta's case; his real name was Francisco Zamora and he was of Nicaraguan origin, probably recently arrived in Mexico. See Ángel Miquel, 'El público en los cines de la ciudad de México (1896–1917)', in Eduardo de la Vega Alfaro and Enrique E. Sánchez Ruiz (eds), *Bye bye Lumiére... Investigación sobre cine en México*, Universidad Autónoma de Guadalajara (Ensayos 2), Guadalajara, 1992, p. 151.

was cast along Emilia Castillo (Catalina). The music, specially written for the film, was by Miguel Lerdo de Tejada and was played live during the screening.

The plot was, again, very simple, and also melodramatic: Rosa and Catalina are orphaned sisters. Catalina is seduced by Ramiro (Manuel Campa Siliceo) and gives birth to a son, who cannot be recognized by his father because he is married. So Catalina has no choice but to return to her sister's home with an illegitimate child in her arms. Some time later Catalina falls in love with Luciano del Moral (Julio Taboada) but to keep him she says that the child is Rosa's. She, *Alma de Sacrificio*, publicly accepts the lie and presents the child as a product of her sinful youth.

José María Sánchez García wrote one of the reviews and, in his view, 'the positive reception of this film was even more enthusiastic than the first'.[33]

On the 26th the film was shown at the Casino cinema and then at the Hipólito. By 15 August 1917 Seijas noted that *En defensa propia* had been shown in more than 50 exhibition outlets and had made a profit of over 20,000 pesos.[34]

On 23 August 1917 the premiere of *La tigresa* (The Tigress) was advertised at the Arbeu theatre. The film would be screened three times on a single day. The slogan with which the film was advertised stated that it was a passionate drama and slightly sentimental, like the previous films: "'I would like to be the heroine of a cruel poem... a burning and painful poem", says the protagonist, and dies tragically of a broken heart'.[35] The script was by Teresa Farías de Isassi, a 'distinguished lady from our best social circles who is already noteworthy for her play *Cerebro y corazón*'.[36] The photography was, again, in the hands of the experienced Enrique Rosas, but on this occasion the newspapers did not identify the scene director, perhaps because it had been Mimí Derba and she, with typical modesty, or simply because she chose not to draw attention to one of the many tasks which she performed in the company, did not make a fuss. The fact is that Mimí, without Joaquín Coss who was on a tour in San Luis Potosí, and without the responsibility of acting, took it upon herself to be the scene director. This is what Hipólito Seijas believed, who interviewed her in those days about the crisis in the theatre and found her 'exhausted, eager, giving orders, *directing* the scenes from *La tigresa*'.[37]

The direction of the actors was acknowledged in this instance. Salustiano highlighted Fernando Navarro in the role of Bruno, because 'with better scene direction his work excelled'.[38] Hipólito Seijas also mentioned the acting:-

The protagonists are Mrs. Uthoff, who in rehearsal comes across as very elegant, and the exceptional "mime" Fernando Navarro, who is truly masterly in his interpretation of his

33 José María Sánchez García, 'Historia del cine Mexicano', *Cinema Reporter* **696**, 17 November 1951, pp. 49–50.

34 *El Universal*, 'Por la pantalla'.

35 See the advertisements in *El Universal* and *Excélsior*, 23 August 1917.

36 José María Sánchez García, 'Historia del cine Mexicano', *Cinema Reporter* **701**, 22 December 1951.

37 'Sí puede existir la producción dramática mexicana', *El Universal Ilustrado*, 17 August 1917. Emphasis added.

38 Quoted in José María Sánchez García, 'Historia del cine Mexicano', *Cinema Reporter*, 22 December 1951.

character, a humble labourer who, as a result of *la tigresa*'s rejection, becomes a furious madman. The scene has been put together no expenses spared and will be a new triumph for national cinematography.[39]

The argument, again, was simple, almost implausible, according to reviewers at the time: Eva (Sara Uthoff) fantasies about becoming the protagonist in a cruel and painful poem and to this end wins the love of Bruno (Fernando Navarro), her social inferior, which makes the relationship impossible. Some time later Eva marries a wealthy youth of her own class and makes this known to Bruno to drive him mad with jealousy. The unfortunate man ends up in a mental hospital. One day, Eva pays a charitable visit to the hospital and out of curiosity approaches Bruno's cell. When he sees her he breaks through he bars and throws himself upon her, thus stifling her to death. The *tigresa* dies a victim of her own whims.

The film was screened on 27 August 1917 in the *Salón Casino* and was reviewed the following day by Hipólito Seijas in *El Universal*. What comes as a surprise in this review is the fact that the original film had been censored after the first screening:

> The scenes in the asylum, and the parade of lunatics which aroused a feeling of bitterness among the spectators, were suppressed from the second screening. The same happened to a parade of two or three poor children bearing their enormous 'chambergos de petate' (traditional Mexican hats). So all attempts to depict what was conceived as truly Mexican were excluded for the sake of a 'Mexicanness' specifically identified with the Mexican middle class.

On the same day, in the 'Escenarios y Pantallas' section of *Excélsior*, Zeta is more disillusioned than Seijas, and very critical of the script:

> The women in the film are, for the scriptwriters, people of pointless cruelty and impossible to compare to normal people..... . I do not understand why Azteca Films adapts scripts in such a precipitated manner. I also ignore the reasons why they do not find someone with a modicum of literary taste and an elementary understanding of reality, to help them assess these bland dramas to which they are devoted. The plot crafted by Mrs. Farías de Isassi does not deserve the expenses made to bring the project to fruition or the time invested in it, nor the work which it required.

Obviously, reviewers continued to expect films that would perfect the naturalist aesthetic and depict reality with greater precision.

In any event, the critics did not take to the film as they had to previous productions, and Lázaro P. Fel said that the first 'hit the screen with greater tranquility, blessed by benevolent *croniqueurs*, who were deliberately optimistic so as to stimulate the burgeoning art'. *La tigresa*, he continues, 'has not ceased to knit the brows of the critics'.[40] Nevertheless, on 30 August *La tigresa* was screened in the Rivera Theatre.

---

39 'Nuevo estreno de película nacional' in 'Por la Pantalla', *El Universal*, 23 August 1917.

40 'Películas nacionales', *Revista de Revistas*, 2 September 1917, reproduced in Helena Almoina, op. cit., p. 194.

The next feature film, filmed at the beginning of September, was *La soñadora* (The Dreamer):

> Directed and played by Eduardo Arozamena, the famous Nanche... who, legend has it (and one should believe it), also wrote the script in a single night at one sitting. The next day he appeared before Rosas and Derba with the script and a quick browse was enough to convince them of its worth. Rosas decided to buy it for 900 pesos, but Derba, always generous, gave him another 100 which, frankly, was a splendid offer at the time.[41]

Although reviewers had complained of the simplicity of the previous plots on this occasion they were not given the opportunity because they had difficulties in understanding it, perhaps because they were used to linear plots and this certainly was not one of them. Emma (Mimí Derba) is a model who inspires Ernesto (Eduardo Arozamena) to finish a painting called *La soñadora*. After a brief romance they part. Some years later Ernesto is on duty at a prison and encounters Emma. He tells the story behind their separation using flashback: he had to go to war. After, Emma, visibly down-trodden, tells him her own story, also through flashback: she had fallen into the hands of a scoundrel who drove her into prostitution, then found love again until Juana Nery (again played by the evil Sara Uthoff) had disrupted the relationship. Emma murders her and is rejected by her lover, goes to prison and upon her release looks for Ernesto. While distracted by her, a prisoner escapes so Ernesto is accused of treason. He dies at the hands of a captain and Emma is driven to insanity by bitterness when she sees that her former lover is dead.

According to Hipólito Seijas, the film is brimming with beautiful details such as the landing strip, the Louis XVI ball with authentic costumes – each valued at 500 pesos, the cabaret and the statuesque poses adopted by Mimí in Ernesto's workshop. The details were highly criticized in other accounts: 'the minuet, awkwardly performed, all the dancers ending as best they can, comes across as old-fashioned in our violent times of danzón and the foxtrot'.[42] In fact, an argument broke out in the newspapers about the position of critics towards national films. One reporter said that reviewers 'forget the brutal anachronisms of foreign films; but when it comes to our own they pay attention to whether the protagonist has clean fingernails'.[43] Others believed that it was up to them to point out errors, because this attitude would encourage the film industry to progress. But Mimí's work was always acknowledged, especially in this film: 'she has moments of pleasant and moving spontaneity, for example in the ninth part when she finds herself in prison and the expression on her face reflects her overwhelming sadness and sense of failure; without grand displays of feeling or ridiculous gestures, she communicates with delicate eloquence the entire tragedy of her life'.[44]

---

41 Gabriel Ramírez, op. cit., p. 71.

42 'Juicios ingenuos', *El Pueblo*, 27 September 1917, r in Luis Reyes de la Maza (op. cit., p. 124).

43 'Impresiones de un cronista de cines: La soñadora fue un gran triunfo' in 'Por la Pantalla', *El Universal*, 25 September 1917, quoted in Helena Almoina, op. cit., p. 206.

44 'Juicios ingenuos', *art. cit.*

On Thursday 15 November 1917, in 'Escenarios y Pantallas', there was an anonymous review of *End la sombra* (In the Shadows), played by Mimí Derba and Segurola. The reporters did not review the film, tired perhaps of the same plots.

The film, however, is a comedy of errors. The opera singer Segurola receives a note in his dressing room in which he is propositioned, though on condition that he disguise himself. He goes to the meeting, which is repeated once again, yet is unable to discover the identity of the woman until the third occasion when he knocks her out with chloroform. However, when he discovers that she is the wife of a friend he tries to bring her around only to realize that he has murdered her. At the end he discovers that he has only dreamed these encounters, but the incident leads him to tear up the invitation and forget the entire matter.

It has been argued that the plot was merely a pretext to show off the Italian company that was on tour at the Arbeu theatre. It was believed that, although they could not sing on scene, 'their popularity would suffice to drag the insolvent audience to the film and keep it running'.[45]

At the end of the year the company closed its books at a profit for the investors Rosas and Derba: 'We have made several films, using only national resources, and we are happy with our work', Mimí stated in an interview with Liedo Fumilla from *Cine Mundial* at the Hotel McAlpin on 6th Avenue and 34th Street in New York. Among many things the reporter pointed out the following: 'these initiatives are unusual for women in Latin America'. For the interviewer Mimí's appearance was worth noting, though he points out that on very few occasions had other reporters commented upon it: 'She is not loquacious, she says exactly the right things and says them with delicious precision'.

By then Mimí remained convinced that

> My aspirations go beyond my own lifetime and are inextricably bound to a sincerely patriotic ideal. In Mexico cinematographic production is unexplored territory, completely virgin soil. Why should we not map and explore it if we have the necessary resources, the will, intelligence and culture? The Mexican Revolution and all that it has subverted forces us to build upon the ruins of the old a vast and extensive civilization, and peace, which has given hope to all, encourages all kinds of initiatives. Ours consists in turning Mexico into a country which produces films comparable to those from North America, Italy or France.[46]

The artist, the dominant voice in the interview – although Enrique Rosas also expressed his views – explained the reason for her journey:

> [We have come to New York] to speak the truth about Mexico and to look for the resources necessary to expand our industry, just like those industrialists who come from other countries for the same reason; to spread the truth about a cultured Mexico, social and progressive; to erase the deeply embedded prejudice that Mexico is uncivil, always rebellious, increasingly backward; the Mexico, in short, of the "peal". To achieve this and convince the Yankees that we are different, that Mexico is more than a horde of savages,

---

45 Ibid., p. 72.

46 Liedo Fumilla, 'La Escena Muda En México: Opinión de Mimí Derba', *Cine Mundial*, January 1918.

we have brought our own films and when the audience sees them it will surely change its views.[47]

But it was not long before Rosas and Derba awoke from the dream of consolidating a national cinematographic industry. According to Gabriel Ramírez, it was much too late when they realized that their production company would have an uncertain future given the absolute control that foreign companies held over distribution, creating a relationship of dependence against which nothing could be done.[48]

Rosas and Derba were unable to 'sell' the films to American distributors, and the market they had won over in Mexico was already saturated. Additionally, they came across many problems upon their return, some were financial and they found no official support, and then a series of intrigues which to date remain obscure.[49]

Azteca Films left behind many unfinished projects, such as the above-mentioned *Chapultepec*, *Entre la vida y la muerte* and any number of scripts which were indeed about national subjects such as *Yólotl*, *El periquillo sarniento*, and *La leyenda de don Juan Manuel*.[50] Rosas decided to keep the company, or what was left of it, and the actors and actresses, much against their will, returned to the theatre, Mimí included.

The Credits

Although it is possible to blame Azteca Films for promising to deliver subjects of national interest but had instead developed international, cosmopolitan subjects which were of interest only to the Mexican middle class, the importance of these pioneers resides in their almost heroic attempt to launch the Mexican film industry in earnest. They were inspired not only by commercial interests or a nationalist ideal, but by something even more praiseworthy: both saw film as an important artistic form of expression for humanity. Mimí introduced archetypes such as the *femme fatale* and the submissive woman, and brought to the cinema dramatic genres such as the melodrama and comedy which were rescued and consolidated during the golden age of Mexican film of the 1940s and 1950s, and are still very much alive in the mass media.

---

47 Idem.

48 cf. Ramírez, G. op. cit.

49 cf. Aldebarán, 'Por qué no prosperó el cine en México', *El Universal Ilustrado*, 17 March 1924, quoted in Ángel Miquel, *Mimí Derba* (op. cit.). See also "Confidencias e indiscreciones", *Jueves de Excélsior*, 17 November 1927, and "Sale del sanatorio la artista que fundó uno de los primeros estudios en México", *Excélsior*, 10 July 1953, p. 4-b.

50 See Ramírez, G., op. cit., p. 73.

Chapter 6

Eréndira on Horseback: Variations on a Tale of Conquest and Resistance[1]

Ana Cristina Ramírez Barreto

...the body is the focus of strategic narratives established in the visual arts, as it is the seat of sensory experience that permits the construction and reconstruction of meanings in these works. (Karen Cordero Reiman, 2004, p. 61)

Several important studies deal with female figures associated with Mexican nationalism, but most of them have centered on the binomial Malinche-Guadalupe, 'our original besmirched mother' (Glantz, 1994, p. 16) and the Holy Virgin. Very little is known about Eréndira, a heroine who, in all probability, existed only as one of the fictional characters with which Eduardo Ruiz – a liberal soldier, lawyer and writer from the state of Michoacán (México)[2] – adorned his collection of historical tales entitled *Michoacán: Paisajes, tradiciones y leyendas* (1891–1900) ('Michoacán: Landscapes, Traditions, and Legends') that he based on sixteenth-century document entitled *Relación de Michoacán* or *Códice Escorial*. It seems like Ruiz conceived Eréndira as the positive image of doña Marina (la Malinche), Hernán Cortés' famous lengua or translator. Eréndira is a fiercely independent woman, a patriot with her own ideas, a woman chaste and childless who contrasts sharply to *la Malinche*, whom nineteenth-century liberal historiography vilified as a traitress to her race, as a mother of two *mestizo* children, and as a whore or *la chingada* ('the raped one', as Octavio Paz wrote in 1950). At the same time, however, conservative historiography depicted her as nothing less than an angel sent by God to protect the Catholic Conquest (Manrique, 1994, p. 248; González Hernández, 2002). In this version, Eréndira appears as an exceptional figure: a heroine beyond reproach, impeccable, perhaps even beyond belief.

---

1 An earlier version of this text was discussed at K'waniskhuyarani, Grupo de Estudiosos del Pueblo Purépecha (Pátzcuaro, 30/07/05) and published in *e-misférica. Performance and Politics in the Americas*. Electronic Journal of the Hemispheric Institute for Performance and Politics (New York University). 2005, 2, 2, pp. 1–19. Access: http://www.hemisphericinstitute. org/journal/2_2/ramirez.html. Thanks to Paul Kersey for his translation. This work is part of the project 'Eréndira. La leyenda tras el nombre', funded by the *Programa de Mejoramiento al Profesorado* (Promep), 2006.
2 Eduardo Ruiz was born in Paracho, Michoacán in 1839 and died in Uruapan, Michoacán in 1902. See biographies by Romero (1960), Talavera (1985) and Hernández (1987); see also García (1998).

It is not my purpose here, though, to delve more deeply into the idea of Eréndira as a mirrored reflection of doña Marina/la Malinche, nor is it my intention to present an explanation of the origins of this name, which might be attributed – though erroneously – to García Márquez (1972). Rather, I wish to examine part of the literary background of this 'first anti-colonialist heroine', for whom a personage as important as General Lázaro Cárdenas del Río[3] demonstrated a fervent admiration. This was revealed, among other acts, by his penchant for bestowing the name 'Eréndira' upon places that were especially dear to him and by the presence of several murals that show Eréndira mounted on horseback. I also remark the meanings of these images, or visual narratives, which tell us different stories: in one, Eréndira, perhaps unconscious, lies upon a horse in full gallop. In another, she is shown riding skilfully, confronting a group of Spanish soldiers. A third mural shows Eréndira escaping from her enemies, mounted side-saddle, like a lady. I argue that these visual representations show us such a variety of narratives because of the convergence of three elements: 1) a lack of information, as the 'original' text does not describe exactly how she mounted upon her horse; 2) the complexity of the very action that is represented, that is the body of an indigenous woman juxtaposed with that of a beast brought to the American continent by those same Spaniards she is pictured resisting; and, 3) the very broad understanding of how a 'perfect' native heroine must ride.

The Textual Tale: Eréndira According to Eduardo Ruiz

Today in Michoacán, Eréndira is by no means an unusual name for women. As far as we know now, the first written reference to the use of Eréndira as a woman's name comes from the writings of Eduardo Ruiz himself, where it appears as the title of one of the stories he published in *Michoacán. Paisajes, tradiciones y leyendas*.[4] Ruiz

---

3   Lázaro Cárdenas del Río was born in Jiquilpan, Michoacán in 1895 and died in Mexico City in 1970. He began his military career as a revolutionary soldier and in 1920 rose to the rank of general. He was elected governor of Michoacán (1928–1932) and president of Mexico (1934–1940). In 1938, he nationalized Mexico's petroleum reserves and expropriated the equipment of the foreign oil companies in the country. After his term as president, he served as Mexico's Secretary of Defense through 1945. The political system and civic nationalism that dominated Mexico for over half a century was consolidated during his regime. His son, Cuauhtémoc Cárdenas Solórzano (b. 1934), was a senator for the state of Michoacán from 1974 to 1980 and governor there from 1980 to 1986. He was a founder of the *Partido de la Revolución Democrática* (Party of the Democratic Revolution, PRD) and is considered the 'moral leader' of that party. Cuauhtémoc Cárdenas has been a candidate in presidential elections on three occasions (1988, 1994, 2000). His son, Lázaro Cárdenas Batel (an anthropologist, Jiquilpan, 1962), is currently governor of Michoacán (2002–2008). There are several studies on cardenismo and the Cárdenas era: see Spenser and Levinson (1999); Knight (2000), Nava (2004), and Oikión (2005); and, on women in the Cárdenas era, Tuñón (1992) and Olcott (2005).

4   Volume 1 appeared in 1891, received excellent reviews from contemporary experts (except Nicolás León) and sold out quickly. Volume 2 was published in 1900. Ruiz wrote tales basing his imagination on historical sources such as *La Relación de Michoacán*, and Rea's *La Crónica de las Provincias de San Pedro y San Pablo Michoacán*, and on what his father

was a leading liberal politician of his time, a Magistrate on Mexico's Supreme Court, a historian, a writer and also a partisan (guerrillero) who fought against the French intervention in the period often called Mexico's 'Second Independence' (1864–1867). His writings on domination and rebellion in the face of an earlier European invader in the sixteenth century – which serves as the setting for the heroine that interests us here – was thus filtered through his own experience as a rebel who battled both the nineteenth-century European invader and the 'traitors' who acclaimed him. He was part of the wide intellectual movement which strove to develop a national literature nurtured by the realities of the country (Giron, 1976; Glantz, 2005).

In more recent times, this narrative was rescue, projected and amplified by a post-revolutionary ideological impulse. In this later stage, the literary image of Eréndira is still present, both in public art (certain murals in Michoacán) and as a first name of many more women than those who ever bore it before the 1930s. The name Eréndira has appeared, subsisted and reappeared in times of distress and periods of conflict, destruction and proposals for reconstruction. The legend of Eréndira on horseback is a story of rebellion, passion, treason and alliances among antagonistic forces that at some point in time seemed utterly irreconcilable.[5] Old tales are often re-told and re-invented as pre-set challenges are faced, but this political use of narratives does not impugn their original arguments. Yet, some pieces are still missing and scant attention has been paid to the ways in which the bodies of heroine and horse have been represented.

Let us now consider the text that inspired these varied plastic representations: Eréndira on horseback by Eduardo Ruiz.[6] The chapter entitled 'Eréndira' is divided into six parts: 1) The Beginning of the Conquest; 2) War; 3) Humiliation and Vengeance; 4) Preaching the Gospel; 5) Sacrifice; and, 6) Apotheosis. It recounts the story of a group of warriors that repudiated the surrender of their *irecha* (the monarch of the indigenous P'urhépecha people) to the Spanish conquerors. At a fort in Pátzcuaro, these rebels confronted a P'urhépecha army sent by the new *irecha*, named Tzimtzicha, that was reinforced by five Spanish cavalrymen under the command of Cristóbal de Olid. In this story, the rebels win the battle and capture a horse that they intended to offer up as a sacrifice to the gods.

However, Eréndira, the daughter of Timas – a rebel warrior and one-time adviser to the monarch – impeded the sacrifice and asked that the horse be gave to her. She soon learned to mount the animal in the town of Capacuaro on the eastern shore of Lake Pátzcuaro (sic). Sometime later, Nanuma, a general in Tzimtzicha's army

---

and his friends enjoyed recounting during leisurely afternoons in their hometown of Paracho (Ruiz, 1891–1900, pp. 18–20. However, he makes no reference to the fictional literature that undoubtedly also influenced his work.

5   See Vázquez (2001, pp. 384–386) on the role of aesthetics and imagination in the social construction of intercultural reality, with specific reference to the legend of Eréndira as a story whose content includes cultural confrontation, encounter and exchange.

6   The chapter on Eréndira did not appear until the second volume, in 1900. However, in the *Prologue* to that tome, the author informs us that it includes a compilation of '...some unpublished legends and others that have been published in diverse newspapers' (Ruiz, 1981–1900, p. 449). Unfortunately, this does not make it clear into which category the legend of Eréndira falls (Talavera, 1985, pp. 131–148; Hernández, 1987, pp. 292–311).

who yearned to subdue Eréndira and make her his wife – or slave – led a surprise attack on Timas' manor in Capacuaro. His soldiers murdered Timas and divided up his possessions and women. To the wonderment of the attackers, Eréndira suddenly burst upon the scene on horseback, fought for her life and escaped into the forest. Part 3 of the tale ends with these words:

> Nanuma chose as his part of the spoils, Eréndira, who if she refused to become his wife would then become his slave. Having divided up the booty [he] hurried into the master bedroom to take possession of [his] prey.
>
> But at that precise moment, a dazzling vision of white, like some divine image from a dream, appeared upon the threshold. It was the beautiful maiden herself, mounted upon a magnificent steed that opened a breach among the murderers, throwing Nanuma himself to the ground.
>
> As light as the wind, she then disappeared into the thick vegetation of the pine forest.
>
> The night bird flapped its wings, leapt from branch to branch and twittered chirps of gladness.
>
> At that moment the sun burst out in the East, filling the world with luminous effluvia.
>
> (Ruiz, 1891–1900, p. 529)

The story continues with the spiritual conquest of the rest of the people and an incendiary discourse delivered by Eréndira:

> The people were still [gathered] in the large town square, acclaiming their saviors [Franciscan friars, recently arrived from Mexico City], when upon the summit of the [pyramid] appeared Eréndira, purple-faced with indignation, but of virginal appearance.
>
> '*P'urhépechas*!' she exclaimed in a tremulous voice, yet one [imbued] with a powerful tone, 'we have seen the Spaniards who came to carry away our treasures and seize our lands [yet] today we just look on as these men who appear in the guise of beggars come to take away our children as if they were orphans, to destroy our gods, and to impose upon us a strange religion. What then shall be left to us?' (Ruiz, 1891–1900: 535–536).

Following this impassioned speech, the next section of Ruiz' account tells us that Eréndira intervened at a critical moment in the evangelization process as the interpreter of the words of a Franciscan missionary named Friar Martín de la Coruña. In this scene, she first intercedes to prevent the crowd from lynching the clergyman after he had profaned one of their temples (Ruiz, 1891–1900, pp. 483–552). Just as Hernán Cortés had found *la Malinche* among his slaves – 'the tongue' that would allow him to discover the secrets of those lands (Glantz, 1994, pp. 91–114) – so Friar Martín was found and saved by another such 'tongue', one that interceded freely for him, first out of a sense of mercy and then out of passion. In a few cryptic lines, Ruiz describes how the two became enamoured almost to the point of delirium. According to the author, Friar Martín achieved sainthood upon refusing to have sexual relations with the naked Eréndira, who was lying at his side impassioned, and recently baptized:[7]

---

7   Textually, this passage reads as follows: "Father – Eréndira said to him – I have followed you everywhere; my soul searched for you, and my eyes could not find you. You

Unexpectedly, the friar releases Eréndira, falls to his knees in the middle of the bedroom, forms a cross with his arms and, bowing his forehead, raises to the heavens a prayer so fervent that it distanced his soul from earthly delights; and so God crowns his temples with the diadem of his love and showers him with blessings: 'removing from him all carnal appetites [and] making him so pure that though he was still of flesh and blood he acted as if he were not' [cited in La Rea, *Crónica de la provincial de San Pedro y San Pablo de Michoacán*].

Upon raising himself from the ground, Friar Martín finds that he is no longer a man but that he has been converted into an angel.

Eréndira, prostrate on the bed, sheds abundant tears and sobs miserably, as if her heart were breaking into pieces.

At that moment, the dome of the heavens fills with stars, and the moon rises on the horizon like a host (hostia) of chastity. (Ruiz, 1891–1900, p. 549)

Friar Martín's decision to choose chastity affects Eréndira, whom Ruiz portrays as a woman who was passionate and free in her erotic desires. For her, chastity is an effect – not sought, but accepted – of the friar's self-imposed restrictions (his vow of celibacy). Thus, Ruiz elevates Eréndira to what seems to be an impeccable plane of erotic emancipation; obliged by respect for the religious beliefs of her beloved, she is neither a hussy nor a prude. She is free, but impeded by circumstance from obtaining sexual satisfaction with her lover, and thus from bearing mestizo children.

The version of Eréndira that Jesús Romero Flores included in his *Diccionario Michoacano de Historia y Geografía* (1960) is much briefer and laconic, an account that ends with Eréndira's flight on horseback:

Shortly thereafter, the fort was attacked by surprise once again and the valiant warrior, Timas, was slain. When the battle was at fever pitch, the maiden Eréndira appeared there, mounted upon a spirited white steed. She opened a breach with her weapon that she wielded with great dexterity and killed the leader of the traitors, Nanuma who wished to possess her because for some time he had felt a violent passion for her. Riding like the wind, Eréndira vanished into the thick vegetation of the forests around Pátzcuaro, and nothing more was ever known of this valiant woman, who preferred death to falling into the hands of those who had invaded her country. (Romero Flores, 1960, p. 186)

Curiously, as we review successive accounts of Eréndira, the portrait they paint is a much more intrepid one than that presented by Ruiz: not only does she escape on horseback and knock Nanuma to the ground, but now she is armed and actually slays him! There are other contemporary literary narratives that recount this episode, and some of them go so far as to speak of a continuous, sustained *guerrilla* war against the invaders and

---

have baptized my brothers, why have you abandoned only me? – It is true Eréndira, you remind me that you have not yet received the baptismal waters: May God send you through them the grace that you so greatly need! – That I also need so greatly, thought the priest… as he wet the young woman's forehead and, lifting up his own heart to the heavens, murmured: – I baptize you in the name of the Father, the Son, and the Holy Spirit! – Ah! Now I am a Christian – cried Eréndira – Now you can love me. No longer shall you flee from me; now we share the same God' (Ruiz, 1891–1900, p. 545). Note that Ruiz does not say which Christian name was given to Eréndira by the friar. It is odd that once baptized she should still be called by her pagan name.

their allies (Salas Léon, 1968; Santillán Aguilar, 1972; Huerta Ruiz, 2000), but all of those tales find their primary source of inspiration either in Ruiz' original story or in the images painted on certain walls in Jiquilpan and Pátzcuaro in the 1940s.

The Painted Version: Eréndira in the Shade of Cárdenas' Houses

Cardenismo was no simple political phenomenon, nor does it have one unique form of expression. Some authors emphasize Cárdenas' responsiveness to popular aspirations, while others underline the mythical character of presidential power and the absence of justice and democracy that pervaded the post-revolutionary regimes (Spenser and Levinson, 1999). Jocelyn Olcott has recently elucidated how women in the Cárdenas era were encouraged to organize and how they reached the most visible political spaces and almost attained citizenship, though she then goes on to describe how their efforts were co-opted and transformed into just another way of reaffirming patriarchy:

> Seeing women as imbued with natural morality, Cárdenas enlisted their support in rooting out vice and corruption… . By 1936, the national *cardenista* project had eclipsed its roots in Michoacán. National mass organization overshadowed and eventually obviated their state-level counterparts…The changing national political climate moved the center of women's activism in Michoacán from temperance and anti-clerical leagues to mass organizations and labour unions… In short, despite the fact that the cardenistas linked these activities [grassroots organizing, leadership training and experience in negotiations] with an essentialized femininity, the leagues drew women into the masculinized realm of political praxis. (Olcott, 2005, pp. 72–91)

Early in the 1950s, Victoriano Anguiano Equihua (a P'urhépecha lawyer and politician who helped young General Cárdenas in his campaign for governor by opening meetings and translating from, or to, P'urhépecha), wrote of cardenismo as a Janus-faced enterprise: revolutionary, but at the same time feudal and authoritarian. Anguiano Equihua (1951) criticized certain aspects of *cardenista* politics, such as its co-optation of popular organizations, its paternalism and its lack of democracy. His book was published by his own company: *Editorial Eréndira*; and when his daughter was born in 1935, he named her Eréndira. Clearly, Anguiano was well aware of Eduardo Ruiz' tale and its epic meaning.[8]

Images of Eréndira on horseback are available to us by virtue of the fact that they form part of Mexico's 'public art'. The post-revolutionary state needed to instill among its citizens a unified, triumphal history, and visual aesthetics played a central role in their efforts (Paz 198, Acevedo and Ramírez, 1986; Tibol and Alanís, 1986, Azuela de la Cueva, 2001, Reyes Palma, 2002: 36, Alonso, 2004). However, most of the images of Eréndira were originally painted on private property, especially at homes owned by Lázaro Cárdenas, though these were later opened to the public.

The iconography of Eréndira on horseback spans a rich range of variations made possible only by the fact that her legend narrates the actions of a woman

---

8   Gloria Cáceres, interview with María Eréndira Anguiano Roch, Morelia, Michoacán, 17 November 2004.

mounted on a horse in circumstances of great peril. In contrast to the depiction of masculine equestrian images, the task of representing a female body mounted on horseback offered enormous challenges to those plastic artists who, in their different interpretations, had to decide just how to portray the exact nature of that historical moment: was she to be painted sitting astride her mount like a man on horseback, or in side-saddle fashion ('a mujeriegas')?[9] Should she be depicted in full attack mode or in flight? Was she to be seen as a *caballera*[10] (cavalrywoman) or as a lady? The variations among these different interpretations reveal the tension of the symbolisms and meanings that each version presents, and bestows greater political, historical and cultural density upon an apparently simple interpretation of the juxtaposition of an indigenous female body and the form of a beast recently arrived from another world and introduced by a conquering people.

The tale of Eréndira is not so much about a woman who finds herself in the midst of the Conquest; rather, it centers upon the image of a woman on horseback. The beast must be seen, because the horse is the critical element in this act of intentional martial domination,[11] for it places its astonishing combination of speed, strength and will at the service of the rider who is capable of summoning them, making no distinction for sex, geographical origin, religion or political ideals.

The trail of the plastic narrative that Cárdenas' devotion left behind in, at least, the cities of Pátzcuaro and Jiquilpan, is not a simple reiteration of this event because, in fact, it reveals the interest he had while contemplating these images, this most decisive organic and technical juxtaposition of civilization: horse and rider, especially in the setting of this narrative of resistance and appropriation, and in spite of its marked ambiguity.

Not Quite a Rider, Perhaps a Package

Probably the earliest painted version of Eréndira is the one at the Interdisciplinary Center for Research on Integral Regional Development (*Centro Interdisciplinario de Investigaciones para el Desarrollo Integral Regional*, CIIDIR, Instituto Politécnico Nacional) in Jiquilpan, Michoacán, Lázaro Cárdenas' birthplace (Figure 6.1). According to Álvaro Ochoa Serrano, the author of this sketch was Revueltas (1902–1935), who depicted the violent episode from Ruiz' tale in which Nanuma attacks and

---

9   This is an ancient expression that refers to mounting 'like a woman' by placing both legs on the same side of the horse. We find it written this way in Quijote when it is suggested to Sancho Panza that he mount this way on the rump of Clavileño, the wooden horse that would supposedly carry both men to heaven.

10   Both the *Diccionario de Autoridades* (1729) and the earliest editions of the *Diccionario de la Real Academia de la Lengua Española* record masculine and feminine forms of the word *caballero*, *caballera* (one who goes on horseback). By the 4th edn (1803), *caballera* is classified only as an adjective and must be accompanied by a verb, as in *ir caballera* or *montar caballera*. These examples lead us to think that *ir caballero o caballera* means not only mounting the horse, but necessarily includes exercising dominion over the mount, be it a broomstick or the actual animal.

11   I use the word 'intentional' to distinguish the horse from other terrible weapons brought from Europe that decimated the aboriginal population, such as infections and plagues.

Figure 6.1   *Eréndira*, **sketch by Fermín Revueltas painted in a house**
at Jiquilpan, Michoacán owned by Cárdenas-Fernández
family, which now serves as the Centro Interdisciplinario de
Investigaciones para el Desarrollo Integral Regional (CIIDIR),
Instituto Politécnico Nacional
Interview with Álvaro Ochoa, 21/11/2002. Photograph by Jesús Ernesto López.

kills Eréndira's father, Timas. Eréndira then escapes from the cruel fate of becoming
the wife or slave of Nanuma, the coward who first surrendered to the invaders and
then murdered her father, by mounting upon the very horse that she had earlier saved
from sacrifice. But in this image she is not actually seen riding the horse: apparently
she is lying unconscious on its back with her hands locked around its neck. Her skirt
is hidden from view, so we cannot see how she is mounted, whether astride the horse
or side-saddle. Here, Eréndira seems to be more a dead weight or a package, than
some kind of Amazon warrior.

A Brave and Skilled Horsewoman

La historia de Michoacán ('The History of Michoacán') is a mural painted by
O'Gorman (1905–1982) between 1941 and 1942, which is on display at the *Gertrudis
Bocanegra* Public Library in Pátzcuaro, Michoacán,[12] a building that was originally

_____

12 Several texts have been written on Juan O'Gorman, his work and life and the mural
housed at the Gertrudis Bocanegra Public Library in Pátzcuaro. See: Cervantes (1945); Luna

a sixteenth-century church. O'Gorman's murals reflect the historical narrative style and didactic Marxism of his mentor, Diego Rivera. Shortly before painting this particular piece, O'Gorman had painted a mural he entitled 'The Conquest of Air by Man' in the Mexico City Airport. His best known piece of public art is the mural at the library of Mexico City's National Autonomous University.

The fresco in the Public Library portrays the epic history of the P'urhépecha people. The starting point of O'Gorman's visual narrative is the origin of the world as told in P'urhépecha mythology (based on Ruiz' book). It then continues through a series of descending scenes that speak of that culture's pre-Hispanic history. Towards the middle of this mural, the conquerors burst upon the scene mounted on horseback, depicted in a manner that emphasizes their violent, rapacious nature. But there as well, on the left margin and at the beginning of that same line, there emerges another figure, also mounted on horseback, to confront them. It is Eréndira, mounted upon a smallish, dappled horse fitted with a bridle and ready to leap wherever she orders, which seems to be almost a caricature of the massive, serene, poised steeds of the conquerors. Beside Eréndira, an eagle warrior advances. This figure would seem to represent a *mexica* soldier, though that seems out of place, given that the people involved are *P'urhépechas*.

Eréndira – as O'Gorman painted her – is semi-naked, her chest and legs exposed (Figure 6.2). She gallops along apparently with no need to cling to her mount. Her left hand is raised in a defiant fist while her right hand is pointing toward Tanganxuan II, the last of the *irechas*, who is being tortured by the invaders (another conqueror, sitting symmetrically opposite Eréndira, is also pointing toward this figure). This arrangement allows the artist to emphasize the equestrian dexterity of this emboldened Eréndira who controls the horse using only her legs, and thus frees her hands. This is precisely the skill that one can – indeed must – master in order to fight while on horseback, and the image portrays an astonishing union of heterogeneous bodies and wills. This is clearly a combative Eréndira.[13]

A Lady in Flight

In 1943, a year after O'Gorman finished *La historia de Michoacán*, Roberto Cueva del Río painted another mural also inspired by Ruiz' legend. On this occasion, the site chosen was the library at the so-called *Quinta Eréndira* ('the Eréndira country house', also in Pátzcuaro), another home that belonged to Lázaro Cárdenas. According to Cárdenas himself, the *Quinta Eréndira* was a 'sanctuary in which to spend pleasant days and bitter moments' (Vargas Tentory, 2005, p. 95).[14]

(1973), Rodríguez (1982) and Masters (2005). The Eréndira that appears in the mural is barely mentioned, though.

13 Salas (1990, pp. 36–37), links the two greatest 'patriots' of the Conquest: Cuauhtémoc and this painted heroine –Eréndira – and contrasts both of them with la Malinche.

14 Cárdenas gave this name to another of his properties, *Playa Eréndira*, located on the Pacific coast not far from the port city in Michoacán that bears his name: *Puerto Lázaro Cárdenas*.

Figure 6.2 *Historia de Michoacán* (*Eréndira* **fragment), Juan O'Gorman,
fresco 14 x 12 m. mural in the Gertrudis Bocanegra Library (ex-
Augustine convent) Pátzcuaro, 1941–1942**
Source: CD by Tracy Novinger © 2005, reproduced here with her kind permission. See also:
'Biblioteca Pública Federal Gertrudis Bocanegra', http://perso.orange.fr/patzcuaro/mx/03/
mx/03cubg02.htm.

In 1950, Cárdenas donated this property to the UNESCO so that it could
establish on that site its first 'Regional Center for Basic Education in Latin America'
(*Centro Regional de Educación Fundamental para América Latina*, CREFAL).
The objective of this Center was to train teachers and researchers in the area of
primary school instruction with special emphasis on the educational problems of
marginalized groups in a regional perspective. Since 1951, this Center has hosted
researchers, rural schoolteachers and literacy instructors from Latin America and
the Caribbean. The mural there thus ceased to be a simple adornment on a piece of
private property and its nationalistic and didactic message passed into the public
domain. Located in an international center devoted to education, the library where

Figure 6.3 *Eréndira*, **Roberto Cueva del Río, mural in the Library at the**
Quinta Eréndira, now the CREFAL Flag Room, Pátzcuaro, 1943
Courtesy of CREFAL.

Figure 6.4 *Eréndira* **(fragment), Roberto Cueva del Río, mural in the**
Library at the *Quinta Eréndira*, now the CREFAL Flag Room,
Pátzcuaro, 1943
Courtesy of CREFAL.

the mural was painted now serves as CREFAL's Flag Room. At this meeting place for individuals and organizations that share the mission of 'constructing a more just and humane world through education',[15] it is difficult indeed for the eye not to come to rest upon images of Eréndira: it is there in the name of the *Quinta* itself, in the mural painted in the Flag Room, in a carving in the limestone of the fountain at the main entrance to the complex, and even on one of the benches in the garden. The name is almost everywhere, and it may well be that its popularity among the common people disseminated from this very site.

Cueva del Río used only a narrow range of his palette (Figures 6.3 and 6.4). In his work, Eréndira is portrayed riding not astride the horse, but side-saddle, very feminine and ladylike. Also, in this mural she is literally draped in clothes that cover her from her shoulders all the way down to her ankles. Far from presenting a combative attitude, she is depicted in flight, tightly clutching the mane of her unbridled mount and galloping quickly towards the group of allies. Right behind her, their faces threatening and dehumanized in grey-green tones, come the Indian and Spanish enemies, some on foot, others on horseback. There is no question here as to the active sense of the appropriation of the horse, but on this occasion it is not as a weapon of war but as a blessed angel of speed, provided to assure her salvation. Moreover, as if this did not suffice, Cueva's Eréndira is burdened with all manner of constraints that limit her body's ability to dominate the horse: the long skirt, the side-saddle posture, the struggle to maintain her balance, her limited manoeuvrability with both hands occupied in clinging to the animal. But what we cannot see clearly is whether her eyes are closed, or if is she looking at the ground with her gaze fixed upon her father's lifeless body. It may even be the case that she is looking out at us with the blank stare of the blind.[16]

In Common People's Houses: A Patriotic Amazon as Calendar Icon

Between 1930 and 1960, a publishing house called *Galas de México* created a striking series of illustrated calendars. These images circulated as gifts given by stores, breweries and tequila or cigarette companies to adorn the homes and workshops of their customers (both rich and poor). In Carlos Monsiváis' words (1995, pp. 65–71), they were examples of 'The charm of utopia hanging on the wall'. These decorative calendars portrayed and glorified in a nostalgic way several motifs associated with Mexico, including nationalism, historical events and patriotic heroes. Women are also often the central figures in these popular visual expressions of Mexican national identity, though their images tend to reflect common feminine stereotypes of self-

---

15 CREFAL, 'Solidez institucional'. Available at http://tariacuri.crefal.edu.mx/crefal/crefal/solidez_institucional.htm. For background on this topic and the letter in which General Cárdenas offers to donate the *Quinta Eréndira* for this purpose, see: http://tariacuri.crefal.edu.mx/crefal/crefal/guia_visitante_completo.htm.

16 Others murals by Cueva del Río are in the Cultural Institute of Mexico (Washington D.C.), Museo Regional de Guerrero (Chilpancingo), Palacio Municipal and Casino de la Selva, Cuernavaca, México.

Figure 6.5 *Eréndira*, **Alfredo González, Oil on canvas. 125 x 100 cm. Galas de México Collection**
Courtesy of Museo Soumaya. Photograph by Javier Hinojosa.

sacrifice and devotion, or to portray sleeping beauties (or perhaps captured in death), and coquettes with alluring bodies and always-smiling faces.

While these comments hold true for most of Galas' work, the *Eréndira* by Alfredo González (Figure 6.5) is a notable exception. Here, Eréndira is portrayed in a battle scene, an armed and fearless woman who charges directly towards her enemies, riding with her legs spread astride. She is staring at a fallen Indian and shouting or calling to the warriors around her, while several astonished Spaniards and Indians look up towards her. The unbridled horse rises on its haunches to elevate her beyond the reach of enemy swords, seemingly obeying Eréndira commands but never taking its eyes off the waiting Spaniards.

Of course, half-naked torsos of Indian women could not be missing from these aesthetic calendars, but what is exceptional here is the narrative portrayed in the image. The entire scene revolves around the depiction of an Indian woman fighting on horseback. It is extremely rare to find this kind of violence and these particular figures or personages in Galas' collections, which were much more inclined to present cheerful, optimistic, commercial, visual images.

While words can express with great clarity some of the attributes and values that this episode suggests, other meanings cannot be found in documents of literary discourse. Though they may be omitted from written records, it is impossible to pass over certain details in these visual representations. We must ask, for example, how exactly did Eréndira mount her steed? None of the written accounts describes in detail the position of the heroine's body upon the horse. In spite of their ingeniousness and variations, all of the literary versions based on Ruiz' original work include this 'blind spot' and none of them tell the reader whether she rode side-saddle like a woman – and why – or if she sat astride the saddle like a man. Nor do they attempt to tell us what the implications of this might be.

Artists, on the other hand, have no choice but to illustrate this aspect of the tale. The chaste Eréndira – a woman almost completely cloaked by clothing who does not expose her genitalia to contact with the horse's back – is part of a nuanced history that is clearly distinct from that other version, which reveals no difference between the way in which the male conquerors mount their steeds and Eréndira's position upon her horse. Here, Eréndira is clearly portrayed as a cavalrywoman. We see before us a phallic Eréndira, a figure who appears to exercise domination over the beast (phallus-horse) that she holds between her thighs.

Despite a certain thematic unity the representations of Eréndira demonstrate extreme variations of interpretation at even the most elemental level, where we capture the real or expressive meaning (the pre-iconographic level, to use Panofsky's characterization, 1962, pp. 13–15). What is it exactly that we perceive in these images of Eréndira? Do they all tell the same story? How does the fact that we are dealing with the juxtaposition of an indigenous female body and the body of a beast from another world make it more complex or difficult to achieve a univocal representation? All four of these paintings of Eréndira represent the same situation. They were based on the same textual source of inspiration, and were separated by just a few years, yet despite these similarities they seem to portray four very different heroines from four quite different histories.

Conclusion: Retelling Old Tales

One particularly suitable place to invent, construct and project ethnic and national identities is in historical-literary narratives, but visual aesthetics also play a major role in such national imaginaries. The cult of the hero/heroine justifies historical work and gives meaning to the political labours of a powerful nation that searches doggedly for such figures. Francisco Reyes refers to the post-revolutionary mural as a device of power, a technology that operates in the order of visibility and obliges the onlooker to read it pedagogically, at the level of the common sense attributed to the normal viewer:

The mural, seen as a stratagem for reordering the past, is the scheming, the unity of synthesis, in which a contradictory totality of ancient memories and modern experiences finds accommodation, a reconfiguration of the specter of sentiments, including those most traumatic, staunched there through recourse to aestheticism or symbolization. (Reyes Palma, 2002: 36)

It was through a late nineteenth-century liberal narrative that Eréndira on horseback came to be iconographically invented and re-interpreted in the first half of the twentieth century and again at the beginning of the 21st. The iconography of an indigenous woman on horseback in a situation of peril unfolds before us through a whole range of nuances that narrate histories that are just as varied. We may consider this a disquieting visual richness that arose from the challenge that awaited those plastic artists who attempted to place an indigenous woman on horseback in the midst of battle.

However, this rich variety of distinct versions emerges not only from the gaps left in the written narratives, but also from a fundamental aspect of the story itself. When portrayed as a dead weight on the back of a horse, Eréndira becomes an emblem of autonomy and free will; not one that is blind to the threats these face but, rather, one capable of achieving an understanding of them. She carefully observes how the danger is transported and how this agent of the invader – the horse – can be re-directed and thus transformed into an ally. The richness of the story of Eréndira resides not only in the fact that certain individuals have embellished to some degree those parts that remain unknown to us, but also in that at one and the same time it represents the value of will and understanding, of resistance and aperture, of tenacity and of the capacity to make alliances.

Eréndira was born as a figure of nationalist fiction, a daughter of liberal thinkers who were attempting to elaborate a feminist and indigenous tale worthy of their times: the post-French intervention period in the nineteenth century, the post-revolutionary epoch in the twentieth, and the twenty-first century's era of 'political correctness'.[17] Thus, even though she was a woman characterized by great bravery, Eréndira cannot escape from the logic of an andocentric patriarchate: after all, she was invented by men, painted by men and promoted by men, though today she is evoked by the

---

17 In the early twenty-first century, during his term as governor of Michoacán, Lázaro Cárdenas Batel (grandson of Lázaro Cárdenas del Río), further sponsored the diffusion of the figure of Eréndira and endowed it with an epic, indigenist ideology, and a feminist, anti-colonialist nature. This occurred when the Michoacán Women's Institute (Instituto Michoacano de la Mujer) promoted the creation of the 'Eréndira Award' (Presea *Eréndira*) to honour distinguished women and, apparently, also men, for their work in favour of greater equality. Also. the Ministry of Culture of his government instituted the 'State Award for the Arts' (Premio Estatal de las Artes), which was similarly named after Eréndira.

women who share her name. Eréndira was a male fantasy that involved newborn daughters.

Although this personage fascinated even such an influential statesman as Lázaro Cárdenas, and in the shade of his houses achieved a surprising degree of diffusion, it is clear to us that her name travelled much more readily than did the contents of her legend, which is to be narrated in an upcoming motion picture. Though not without certain reservations, we can affirm that even the most chauvinistic and ethnically-essentialist version of Eréndira would fail in its attempt to propose the establishment of a 'heroine cult' capable of crystallizing into a new 'nationalist' emblem. The impossibility of this is not to be attributed only to the circumstance that this heroic figure lurks in the most shadowy of all the dark corners of our field of social and historical knowledge. Rather, there is a much more radical reason: with all of its variations, the visual narrative of an indigenous woman on horseback focuses our attention on the basic aperture that negates not only all essentialist separatism but also all fixation on naturalized differences, whether they be attributed to indigenous people, to woman, or to beasts.

References

Acevedo, E. and Ramírez, M.C. (commentators) (1986), 'Decoraciones que pasaron a ser revolucionarias', in *El Nacionalismo y el Arte Mexicano (1900–1940)*. IIE-UNAM (México: Universidad Nacional Autónoma de México), 171–216.

Alonso, A.M. (2004), 'Conforming Disconformity: "Mestizaje", Hybridity, and the Aesthetics of Mexican Nationalism', *Cultural Anthropology*, **19**, 459–490.

Anguiano Equihua, V. (1951), *Lázaro Cárdenas: su feudo y la política nacional / Con un Juicio De José Vasconcelos y prólogo de Manuel Moreno Sánchez* (México: Eréndira).

Azuela de la Cueva, A. (2001), 'Arte y poder: La Revolución Pictórica de la Revolución Mexicana y su Influencia En la Construcción De una Imagen'. PhD thesis in Social Science, Zamora, Michoacán: El Colegio de Michoacán.

Cervantes, E.A. (1945), *Pintura de Juan O'Gorman en la Biblioteca 'Gertrudis Bocanegra' de Pátzcuaro*, Michoacán, México.

Cordero Reiman, K. (2004), 'La Invención de las neoidentidades mexicanas: estrategias modernas y posmodernas' in *Hacia otra historia del arte en México, tomo IV: Disolvencias (1960–2000)*. Benítez Dueñas, I.M. (ed.) (México: Consejo Nacional para la Cultura y las Artes/CURARE).

García, C.G. (1998), *Las mujeres de Ruiz: la participación femenina durante la intervención francesa en Michoacán, en la obra de Eduardo Ruiz* (México: Centro de Estudios Históricos del Porfiriato).

García Márquez, G. (1972), *La increíble y triste historia de la cándida Eréndira y de su abuela desalmada; siete cuentos* (Barcelona: Barral Editores).

Giron, N. (1976), 'La Idea de "cultura nacional" en el Siglo XIX: Altamirano y Ramírez' in *En Torno a la Cultura Nacional*. Aguilar Camín, H. (ed.) (México: Instituto Nacional Indigenista), 51–83.

Glantz, M. (1994) 2001, *La Malinche, Sues Padres y Sues Hijos* (México: Taurus).

Glantz, M. (2005), 'El proyecto cultural nacionalista de Ignacio M. Altamirano', *Fractal 31*. http://www.fractal.com.mx/F31Glantz.html.

González Hernández, C. (2002), *Doña Marina (la Malinche) y la Formación de la Identidad Mexicana* (Madrid: Encuentro Ediciones).

Hernández, P. (1987), 'Eduardo Ruiz, su obra y su tiempo'. B.A. thesis in History, Universidad Michoacana de San Nicolás de Hidalgo.

Knight, A. (2000), 'El Cardenismo, ¿Culminación de la Revolución Mexicana?' in *Cinco miradas británicas a la historia de México*. Brading, D.A. (ed.) (México: CONACULTA, INAH).

Manrique, J.A. (1994) '2001, 'Malinche'' in *La Malinche, Sues Padres y Sues Hijos*. Glantz, M. (ed.) (México: Taurus), 247–249.

Masters, H. (2005), *Shadows on a Wall: Juan O'Gorman and the Mural in Pátzcuaro* (Pittsburgh: University of Pittsburgh Press).

Monsiváis, C. (1995), *Los rituales del caos* (México: Ediciones Era).

Nava, E. (2004), 'El cardenismo en Michoacán (1910–1990)'. Doctoral dissertation, Faculty of Political Science, Universidad Nacional Autonoma de Mexico, México.

Oikión, V. (2004), *Los Hombres Del Poder en Michoacán, 1924–1962* (Zamora: El Colegio de Michoacán/Universidad Michoacana de San Nicolás de Hidalgo).

Olcott, J. (2005), *Revolutionary Women in Postrevolutionary Mexico* (Durham: Duke University Press).

Panofsky, E. (1962, 1998) *Estudios sobre iconología* (Madrid: Alianza).

Paz, O. (1950), *El laberinto de la soledad* (México: Cuadernos Americanos).

Paz, O. (1986), 'Visión e ideología, Sobre el Muralismo Mexicano', *Vuelta*, **11**(121), 14–21.

Reyes Palma, F. (2002), 'Otras modernidades, Otros Modernismos' in *Hacia otra historia del arte en México, vol. III, La Fabricación Del Arte Nacional a Debate, 1920–1950*. Acevedo, E. (ed.) (México: Consejo Nacional para la Cultura y las Artes/CURARE), 17–38.

Rodríguez Prampolini, I. and O'Gorman, J. (1982), *Juan O'Gorman: Arquitecto y Pintor* (México: Universidad Nacional Autonoma de Mexico).

Romero Flores, J. (1960), *Diccionario Michoacano de Historia y Geografía* (Morelia: Talleres Tipográficos de la Escuela Técnica Industrial 'Álvaro Obregón').

Ruiz, E. (1891–1900) (1971), *Michoacán: Paisajes, Tradiciones y Leyendas* México: Balsal Editores.

Ruiz, J.L.H. -Un purhépecha pues..., (2000), *Patamban prehispánico*, http://www. monarcaonline.com.mx/patambanpre.html, sección histórica -no la de leyenda y ficción- del sitio *Monarca. Expresión de lo nuestro*, © 2000, Librería de la Huerta.

Salas, E. (1990, 1995) *Soldaderas en los Ejércitos Mexicanos: Mitos e Historia* (México: Diana).

Salas León, A. (1968), *Pátzcuaro: Cosas de Antaño y Hogaño* (Morelia: author's edition).

Santillán Aguilar, R. (1972), *Eréndira* (Zitácuaro, Michoacán).

Spenser, D. and Levinson, B.A. (1999), 'Linking State and Society in Discourse and Action: Political and Cultural Studies of the Cárdenas Era in Mexico', *Latin American Research Review*, **34**, 227–245.

Talavera Ibarra, P.L. and Ruiz, E. (1985), *Eduardo Ruiz, o, El Fausto de la Ciudad del Progreso* (Morelia, Michoacán; Universidad Michoacana de San Nicolás de Hidalgo, Coordinación de la Investigación Científica).

Tibol, R. and Alanís, J. (commentator) (1986), 'El nacionalismo en la plástica durante el cardenismo' in *El Nacionalismo y el Arte Mexicano*. IIE-UNAM (México: Universidad Nacional Autónoma de México), 235–255.

Tuñón, J. (1992), *Mujeres que se organizan: El Frente Único Pro Derechos de la Mujer, 1935–1938* (México: Universidad Nacional Autonoma de Mexico/Miguel Ángel Porrúa).

Vargas Tentory, F. (2005), *Lucas Ortiz Benítez. Un Autorretrato y Cinco Bocetos* (Morelia: Ayuntamiento Constitucional de Taretan, 2005–2007/Unión Local de productores de caña de azúcar/Libros EDDI S.A. de C.V.).

Vázquez León, L. (2001), 'Noche de muertos en Xanichu, Estética del claroscuro cinematográfico, teatralidad ritual y construcción social de una realidad intercultural en Michoacán' in *Estudios michoacanos IX*. Sánchez Rodríguez, M. and Bautista, C. (eds.) (Zamora, Michoacán: El Colegio de Michoacán/IMC), 335–400.

Chapter 7

The Role of the Mayan Woman Inside the Revolutionary Institutional Party (PRI)

Leticia Paredes Guerrero[1]

My dad was prijista (priísta), that's why I am prijista.   (Doña Emiliana)

Until the presidential election of July 2000, the *Partido Revolucionario Institucional* (PRI) was the dominant political party in Mexico. This article will demonstrate the political participation of Yucatecan Mayan women in this party. To achieve this objective a rural, female leader from Yucatan will be used as a model to exemplify types of involvement. Miguel Bartolomé's work on the social dynamism acquired by the Mayan culture from a subaltern condition will be used to explain female participation in local politics and Angelo Panebianco's assessments of power and incentives for political participation will also be taken into consideration.

Social Dynamism and the Subaltern Condition

According to Bartolomé (1992) '[Social] dynamics are inherent to all other social structures, and its activity does not stop, in spite of the onslaught of modifications caused by external factors that determine the fast-paced transformations of the social structures' (Bartolomé, 1992, p. 21). Thus, two types of transforming forces are found: firstly, one that imposes itself on society as a result of external factors (in this case, the Conquest of Mexico by Spain, the Spanish Colony, an economy based on agriculture, the political system that governs Mexico today, and so on); and secondly, the indigenous dynamics, inherent to all social formation, based on its own structural tensions (Bartolomé, 1992, p. 21).

This depicts societies with a double dynamism: on the one hand, colonized societies are not a reflection of the world that is imposed on them, whereas on the other, the internal dynamism of collective life is valued. These parallel views form part of a multiple and interconnected system in which the dominant group

1   I wish to thank Doña Emiliana for letting me recount the story of her life, from which I have taken some fragments for this essay. I also want to thank Efrain Eric Poot for his advice. I am grateful to León Castellanos Jankiewicz and Margaret Shrimpton for their translation skills.

imposes a process that permeates down through all the structures of the dominated society; which in turn reacts according to its own group's internal dynamics, thereby revealing an implicit desire for survival inherent to the interior structures of its own colonized society (Bartolomé, 1992, pp. 22–23).

This differentiated dynamics imposes a subaltern condition on the Maya culture as a result of domination that might have led to a process of extinction; however, the Maya ethnic group have their own strategies, which have enabled them to build up survival mechanisms that allow them both to adapt, and to use the dominant socio-political conditions to their favour.

From this perspective, the relationship established between the Mayan group and Mexico's major political structure today, is explained, on the one hand, beginning with the external pressure that is exerted by the formal political structure. The system imposes its political entourage in the rural community with the *Confederación Nacional Campesina* (National Rural Confederation, known as CNC), which is one of the three sectors that sustain the PRI. This situation leads the Mayan ethnical group to assume identities, which are formally or legally recognized, and allows them access to certain benefits (lands, credits, material, and so on) that are basic for its survival as a group.

On the other hand, indigenous dynamics allows us to identify elements with an organizational character that transform themselves according to general conditions without losing their essential role as perpetrators of Mayan identity, such as: the identity of the community and the social organization based on family and ritualistic relationships (such as the kinship bonding that exists between parents and godparents, known as *compadres*).

These observations are exemplified by the situation of Doña Emiliana, a Mayan leader, born into a peasant family dedicated to the production of henequen in the municipality of Hunucmá, in Yucatan. Her father, Don Nicolás, was a worker of the land sponsored by the State (ejidatario), who cultivated henequen. Under these working conditions Emiliana's father established a vertical relationship with the Mexican State, since the government controlled the production of henequen, and his status as an *ejidatario* tied him to the corporate structure of the CNC, as well as to a collaboration with the PRI. This situation led Don Nicolás to participate in the political activities of both the CNC and the PRI, so as not to lose his land and his work.

Being a henequen *ejidatario*, as in the case of Emiliana's father, has been an important element for the preservation of ethnic identity, as it is through this that community structures, family organization, traditions and customs in the Mayan society have been able to be maintained.

The vertical relationship established between the Mexican State and the henequen *ejidatarios*, both in the production processes and in corporate forms through its organizations, shows that community reproduction cannot be understood in any other terms, and it is therefore logical to believe in the importance of the transmission – from one generation to another – of the forms in which the Mayan ethic group participates in activities related to the *Partido Revolucionario Institucional*. As an example of this, there is Emiliana's conception of her own political participation in the PRI, when she remarks:

I am *prijista* because my father was *prijista*. They raised us since we were small as *prijistas*, that's the way our father taught us, that's why we know we are *prijistas*. When elections come, we go and vote for the PRI, and I won't change. It's like religion: I am Catholic, and that's the way my religion is, and that's the way my party is.

These concepts of ethnic subalternity, social dynamics, exterior pressure, and indigenous dynamics are useful to explain the structural context in which the relationships between the Mayan ethnic group and the dominating apparatus of the Mexican State came to be.

Power and its Incentives

However, to identify the subjective elements that allow the individual to decide whether to continue to cooperate with the PRI or not, it is useful to look again at Angelo Panebianco's definition of power and the numerous incentives for political participation that various members of an organization are given.

Panebianco defines power as 'an asymmetric but reciprocal relationship, which manifests itself in an unbalanced negotiation. It is an unequal exchange in which one side earns more than the other.' Conceiving it as an exchange relationship, power cannot be viewed as absolute, for its limits are given by its own interaction. Therefore, the relationship between leaders and their followers must be conceived as one of unequal exchange, where the former earns more than the latter, although the leader must give something to his followers (Panebianco, 1995, p. 64).

The success of the leaders depends on the control that is held by them upon certain resources that are related to the areas of organizational uncertainty, or rather, to those elements that, if not adequately controlled, could threaten the internal stability and survival of the organizations. These resources, controlled by the leaders, give them the possibility for internal negotiating within the power games that can be unbalanced in their favour. But the leader's power comes to an end when his capacity for convening is diminished (Panebianco, 1995, p. 65).

Negotiations in the game of power are made on two different levels; the first one takes place between the leaders themselves, originating a horizontal relationship; whereas the second deals with negotiations that are established between leaders and their followers, forming a vertical relationship. The second level is understood on the basis of the exchange of collective or selective incentives for participation. The first kinds of incentives are linked to organizational purposes, and are defined as identity incentives. There are two types of selective incentives: material and status incentives (Panebianco, 1995, p. 65).

In every political party, the leaders' supporters must be people who are useful to the functionality of the party as a whole, and who express themselves in similar ways. To ensure participation, the leaders distribute incentives. Therefore, all of the members of the organization enjoy some of these benefits, or profit from some of them. It is important to point out that one of the functions of organizational ideology is to conceal the selective incentives, since excessive visibility compromises the image of the party as an organization dedicated to fighting for a cause (Panebianco, 1995, p. 68).

This relationship of power, along with the incentives, aimed at greater participation allow us to understand the way negotiations have been made in the circles of power between Emiliana and the PRI. Based on the work that Emiliana carries out for the party, with the purpose of acquiring more followers, the organizational leaders provide Emiliana with selective, as well as collective incentives. This consideration leads to the following description of Emiliana's participation within the PRI.

Who is Emiliana?

Previously, reference was made to Emiliana in order to illustrate some of the reasons that explain the presence of the Mayan woman in the PRI. To understand these reasons, it is necessary to know about Emiliana and her way of life.

Emiliana was born in a town named Hunucmá, in the State of Yucatan, which is situated in the northwester part of the State. Her parents were Don Nicolás and Doña Cristina, both of whom were of Mayan origin, and came from poverty-stricken families. Don Nicolás was an *ejidatario* who cultivated henequen, but his earnings were insufficient to cover his family's expenses and so Doña Cristina worked as a domestic worker in the city of Mérida. Emiliana's birth put Doña Cristina's reproductive period to an end, after having had six children. Emiliana is the youngest of two brothers and four sisters.

Her position as the youngest child brought her a series of benefits, such as going to school. Her brothers and sisters did not have the opportunity to receive an education, since they were busy incorporating themselves into the work force inside and outside their home so that the family could sustain itself. Emiliana's opportunity for an education made Don Nicolás hope that by having a learned daughter, she could somehow escape his condition of poverty. For this reason, he wanted his daughter to study to become a nurse, since it was a career very highly regarded in the community; Emiliana's interests, however were quite different, because she wanted to become a lawyer.

At the age of 13, when Emiliana was starting her sixth grade of elementary school, her aspirations for becoming a professional were destroyed with the death of her father, because the already poor family was affected economically. This situation forced her to abandon her studies so that she could help out in supporting the family. Through her mother, she obtained a job in a home as a domestic worker. This situation was not pleasant for Emiliana, who did not like receiving orders from her employers, but she could not abandon her job, firstly because that would have meant disobeying her mother, and secondly, the money she received from working was a considerable sum that helped sustain the fatherless family.

Emiliana worked as a household maid until she was 17, when she married Luis, known as Licho,[2] whose place of origin was also Hunucmá, and who was employed as a police officer in the same community. The marriage did not improve Emiliana's economical condition, but it did cause her to initiate her reproductive stage in life at the age of 18: one year into the marriage, her first daughter was born, and a year later,

---

2   Luis is a name that is commonly known as Licho in Yucatan.

she gave birth to a second girl. The consecutive birth of their daughters made the young couple's needs even more demanding, which prompted Luis to start working in the *Instituto Mexicano del Seguro Social* (Mexican Institute of Social Security, known as IMSS), in the Services department.

The fact that Luis had to work outside the community was an inconvenience, often causing long absences from home. The family's economical decline continued, however, mainly due to the birth of a third child, which forced Emiliana to move into her mother's house and become a worker once again. She made sure her new job would not mean working away from the village, because although she had her husband's permission to work, his consent did not include employment outside the community. It is under these circumstances, in which Emiliana says, 'I had to work in something I knew how to do', so she started selling homemade cakes, *tamales*, panuchos and sweets on the streets of Hunucmá.

The sixth year of marriage proved to be a very hard one for Emiliana. She suffered from the loss of her fourth daughter, who was only two months old. Two months later, her mother passed away as well. These circumstances brought certain changes: her husband returned to work within the community, and she stopped selling food in the streets.

Motives for a visible participation in the PRI

A short time after the death of her two-month-old baby girl, Doña Emiliana became pregnant once more, hoping to replace her great loss. This attempt proved to be made in vain: her pregnancy represented high risks, and she was forced to have an abortion. The following year, she put her efforts into having another baby, but with fruitless results. Due to her constant failures at becoming pregnant, her husband told her that during her last pregnancy, fearing that he might lose her, he authorized the doctors to tie her fallopian tubes. The doctors decided not to inform her of her sterile condition, so as 'not to make her feel bad and sad'. Her reaction was the following:

> When I heard that I had been sterilized, I became very frustrated, because I thought that I was no longer useful as a woman anymore. My mind thought that a woman's sole purpose was to have children. I thought that I wasn't worth anything because I couldn't have any more children, but this disappointment made me look for other activities to do.

During the time Emiliana was depressed, one of her sisters was very helpful in making her overcome her sad situation by constantly inviting her to political gatherings: at first to the ones organized by the CNC, and later to events planned by the PRI that were held inside the town as well as in other communities. All this with the pretext of accompanying a *comadre* of her sister, who was a priísta.

It was not rare for Emiliana to attend these events organized by political parties, since she had been educated as a partisan: 'I am prijista (priísta), because my father was prijista.' It was precisely her presence at these gatherings, which led her to understand that a woman's role in life is not exclusively destined to reproduction. She convinced herself that 'women are able to do more things'. It was from this time on that she started to visualize her political participation, and her incursion into the working world once more.

Rise of a Leader

The event that confirmed Emiliana as a community leader took place during the post-electoral social mobilizations organized by the PRI in 1987, in which she and her sister decided to fight for the recognition of the victory of the party in the municipal elections that were held that same year. They did this by organizing their supporters, and they asked the governor of the State to help put an end to the conflict.

Two circumstantial facts were decisive in her recognition as a leader of the PRI in her community. The first was having accompanied the governor himself in the same vehicle, when he went to Hunucmá with the purpose of solving the conflict. This was confirmed as she was the first person to descend from the vehicle the governor was in, when the committee arrived in the municipality. The second incident consisted in her participation as a speaker in the gathering that the *priístas* prepared that same day in the town square, which she describes as follows: '...and they recognized us as leaders, because when we said we won because we had to win, since then the PRI calls us to talk about anything.'

Emiliana's Activities Inside the PRI

After these events had taken place, the work of the new leader in the *Partido Revolucionario Institucional* was ever more visible and was widely recognized by her community. One of her activities, and the most important one that she has been doing since, consists in promoting votes for the PRI, which heightens during pre-election periods. Also, one of her main functions as a member of the party is to go to all the towns that belong to the municipality of Hunucmá and make door-to-door visits. It is during these visits that she tries to convince people to vote for the PRI, with arguments that are similar to the ones that she expresses in the following paragraph:

> Do you know how to vote? – When they answer – no, I don't know how to vote –, we tell them – you are going to vote here (and we show them an electoral ballot). This is the PRI, because if you vote for the PAN, ask something from the PAN, but if you vote PRI, ask the PRI – When they ask us – Do they give? – we tell them – yes they do!, if they don't give you today, they will give you some other day.

These activities in favour of her political institution have made her a political intermediary; her duties are not limited to the electoral scene, since she also intervenes in other community activities. It is not rare for her to be organizing parties, such as those for Children's Day, Mother's Day or Christmas, and many others. To finance the parties, she goes to different government dependencies in search of articles to hand out during the gatherings: toys, fruit juices, candy and presents.

She also organizes the women of the town, and mobilizes them to attend any political event organized by the CNC, the PRI or by any other government institution. When these political rallies take place in the municipality, invitations are sent out with the specification that food will be offered, which often consists of *cochinita* tacos or sandwiches along with soft drinks. If the event is held in the city of Mérida, transportation is offered to those who do not have a vehicle, so that they can attend.

With the purpose of organizing the women in the town, Emiliana, with the help of her sister and her *comadre* founded an association called 'Artisans of the Mayab', which has approximately 100 members and belongs to the Social Solidarity Society (SSS). The initial set-up meeting to plan the organization of this group was attended by representatives of the PRI, and some of the advice they gave them was that the Board of Directors should be made up entirely of family members 'to prevent problems'. With this in mind, Emiliana's sister was named President, her *comadre* was made Secretary and she was elected as Treasurer. This organization not only allows women to mobilize themselves politically, but it also has a say in certain economical circumstances. One of these economical advantages consists in having access to benefits from social programs (such as credits, machinery, kitchen utensils, and so on) with which they organize the women in different units: agricultural, sewing and kitchen workshops. They also assemble the women so that they attend certain events of economic importance that are organized by the government, such as the Xmatkuil State Agricultural Fair, exhibitions in Mérida or fairs in other municipalities of Yucatan.

During the periods when there are no active electoral processes, Emiliana's activities consist of attending events organized by the PRI or the CNC, for which she can be summoned at any time without previous notice by the political institution or by the national organization as well, if any of these are in need of her presence. She comments on this situation as follows:

> One day my food was ready (she sells food among employees of different government dependencies in the city of Merida) and a lawyer came to tell me that Dr Berlín (state leader of the CNC) needed me to go to the meeting of the CNC that day, which was going to be held in the *Casa del Pueblo* (the PRI's headquarters in Yucatan, known as House of the People). I started wondering what I was going to do with my food, so I told Licho and he told me – Too bad. If they sent for you, you must go. I will sell the food here – so I left.

All of the things she does for her party inside her community have demonstrated to the Party that she is important as a leader. That is why the PRI was interested in training her in the political ways of the party, with the objective of including her in their training programmes. The purpose of the programme is to teach a selected group of party militants the main statutes of the party and ways of defending these ideals and actions under any circumstances. Emiliana has outlined her own opinion about this training, and affirms that she has been taught to defend herself against the *Partido de Acción Nacional* (National Action Party, known as PAN):[3]

> In the training programme they teach us to defend ourselves, because with time they will beat us. That's why they teach us to defend ourselves from the PAN, but we do not insult the PAN, but he PAN insults us. We don't insult them because we have to act according to

---

3   There is a certain rivalry between the PRI and the PAN in Yucatan. These parties are the ones with the most significant presence in the State.

the rules of politics, so when they tell me that we steal, I tell them that everyone steals, and that the PRI steals, but it gives you something, but when the Pan steals it doesn't give you anything. When they say that the PRI sold Mexico, I tell them that they shouldn't care, since they didn't get affected, because they weren't sold.

Emiliana's political role highlights her as a leader: as an organizational agent with her own supporters, but who is also an ideal follower of the organizational leaders of the PRI. She is of great use to the functioning of this political institution in the municipality of Hunucmá, for she is a militant who participates actively in all the activities in which the political leaders need her to be in. She does not have a work schedule nor established working hours or dates. The only thing that is needed is a request from one of the leaders of the party, so that she can respond to the calling.

Her work becomes more visible and intense during election periods because she has to persuade as many people as possible to vote for the PRI. Thus, she visits homes, organizes events, accompanies the candidates on tours throughout the towns, translates their speeches into Mayan, if they don't know how to speak the language, takes people to political gatherings, talks as an orator in the reunions, gives away hats, shirts, bags, food rations, rice, beans and cornmeal exclusively to women, and attends all of the events that the political party organizes in the city of Mérida.

Given the fact that Emiliana has acquired a part of the social status that she enjoys within her family and her community from the PRI, she does not question her participation, nor does she doubt her party's undertakings. She supports it and does everything that is necessary to make the PRI stay in the circles of power. This situation makes Emiliana form part of a group of people that legitimize the PRI without flinching, and as a consequence, this makes her an ideal follower of this political institution. In Panebianco's terms, she is a believer of the organization.

In the game of power, there are unbalanced negotiations, in which the leaders gain more benefits than the followers, but it is in these relationships that incentives are present, which are necessary to maintain the support of the followers. In Emiliana's case, incentives are also present in different forms: collective incentives and selective ones, which can be material or can refer to status. These incentives also branch into two types: one is where she, as a leader, hands out incentives to her followers. These are material most of the time. On another level, there are those incentives that she obtains for being a leading supporter of the party.

From Emiliana's experiences of the relationship between party leaders and supporters we can observe that women's roles take two different positions: we find her as a leader, but we also see her as a supporter. This demonstrates that a woman can maintain, simultaneously, two different courses of action. However, one can also see her through only one aspect, when she carries out her role as a follower, as in the case of the women she organizes and rallies.

Material Incentives

Emiliana's role as a political mediator allows us to see the way material incentives are used to maintain the relationships between leaders and supporters of any particular organization. In this relationship, the leaders benefit from the support and political legitimacy that is given to them by their followers, since this allows them to continue to exercise their power. Meanwhile, the supporters are given incentives in the form of material benefits. In this case, they benefit from the gifts that Emiliana gives them in certain moments, or from the advantages of governmental programmes. This same relationship is established between Emiliana and the influential section of the party, but always in a discreet way, given that she also receives a series of incentives that consist of family benefits.

Emiliana herself describes the benefits that she receives from her participation in the political scene, which are an incentive to her continued participation in political activities and are strengthened by the network of social relationships that she establishes with certain political leaders, government workers and public service employees:

> They don't pay us for the work we do. That's right. We don't get paid. One simply has to take advantage of certain situations to find out where the money is going to come from. When my children were small and were sick, I went to the PRI and told them what was happening, and they gave me money to take them to the doctor and for medicine. I also got them scholarships: For secondary school they gave $100.00 pesos and for high school they gave $150.00 pesos. When my youngest daughter entered high school, I went there to ask for a scholarship for her and they didn't want to give her one. So I asked them if all the work I did for them was in vain, and they said – all right *gordita*, we are going to give you the scholarship. So there is my daughter studying with a scholarship. It is not much, but it helps.
>
> My son is studying to be a business administrator, so I got him a job with a friend of mine in the Commission for the Regulation of the use of the Ground (CUSEI), and they gave him the job, so now he is earning his own money. My daughter is studying psychology, and since they are going to open a Children's Development Centre (CENDI) in Hunucmá, I've already been to talk to the woman in charge so that she gives my daughter a job, and she told me that she'll see what she can do.

Her dealings have also helped her get incorporated into the working world, for she has permission to sell the food that she prepares in certain government dependencies in Merida. This made her stop selling food in the town she lives in, as she used to do:

> I prepare my food to sell and go to *Desarrollo* (Main Offices of Rural Development, which is a dependency of the State government) and I sell my candies, tamales, empanadas and bread to the employees who work there. Sometimes they tell me – Doña Emiliana, this is too expensive! – and I tell them to go downtown in Mérida and buy a pie that is cheap, but it's not tasty. Then they tell me, – You're right Doña Emiliana, this is really good – and they even give me a tip.

Her condition as a Mayan woman has helped Emiliana more in the political field than in the working one because she has had access to the different social programmes that the government promotes. On the other hand, if she applied for a job in a governmental agency or in the PRI, her condition as a Mayan would not allow her obtain a good job, because it is widely believed that Mayan women do not have the capacity to assume those responsibilities, mainly as they do not have university studies. Emiliana talks about this as follows:

One day I went to see the President of Mexico. I asked my husband: ¿what if we ask the President? ¿Don't they say he gives? So I wrote him a letter and told him that if he gave me a job making pastries, which I learned because I am poor, I would give work to the women of Hunucmá. Ten days later, they gave me access to $15,000 pesos to buy an oven and a beater.

The Yucatecan government has also helped us a lot. They gave us a credit, and when they gave it to me I told the women that I had put their names in and that they had given us the money. I told them that I was going to show them how to make cakes and that we were to pay $800.00 pesos monthly for two years. When they heard that we had to pay, they didn't want to join so I started paying it myself, but six months later, the governor told me – You don't have to continue paying it. It's a gift.

According to Emiliana, when she goes to apply for a job:

They see you are a peasant, and they don't give you any work unless it has to do with cleaning, and this is worse if you do not have any studies to back you up. And to wear an *hipil* (traditional woman's attire in Yucatan) without anything else it's not the same as wearing it with a *rebozo*". (to wear the *hipil* with a crossed shawl is a sign of ethnicity.)

Election periods are the times when material incentives are more visible in the rural communities, because gifts are given in the name of the candidates who are running for a political position. It is in this way that Emiliana has obtained various handouts, sewing machines, mills, and so on. In her own words:

We already know that when politics (elections) are close they give you more so that is when we take advantage of the situation. They tell us that it is not much, but since they give it to us for free, we don't have any problems with that.

When the elections of 2001 came near, Emiliana was hoping to have a candidature, since she had been working for the party for a number of years and because of a comment that a State leader had made to her. That's why she indicates:

I have been working for fifteen years in the party, and they say that with that experience you can be a candidate in the PRI. That's why a representative told me, my *comadre* and my sister to get registered to see if one of us could be made a candidate. He also said that if they did not choose us to run for office, then they had to choose one of us as part of a committee. That's the way the game is played there.

Emiliana's goal was to have a business of her own so that she could ensure her family's economical well-being. To fulfil this objective, she thought of using her friendly relationship with the governor of the State, so as to acquire the necessary resources:

I want to have my own restaurant. I hope that I can do this before the governor in turn leaves office, because he likes me a lot. Anything I ask him, he will give me. He's already introduced me to the man in charge of Industrial Development, so that I can go and talk to him and tell him what I need. I hope that it works out for me. (She accomplished this goal).

Emiliana considers the time that she has spent as a militant for the PRI, gratifying, mainly because her active participation in the political scene has not represented significant sacrifices nor has it generated family problems in her home, given that she has all the approval of her family members in what she does. Besides, her tasks give her a certain social recognition within the community she lives in. She describes this situation as follows:

> I live politics and I like politics. I like to clap in the gatherings. Everybody says hello and everyone knows you there. Even the ones who come from Mexico City acknowledge you. It is nice, and that's what I like, and Licho supports me.

Status Incentives

Political participation has permitted Emiliana to enjoy not only material incentives, but status incentives as well. These incentives are related to the fact of being recognized as a public leader of the women in the town, and with social and economical increase, as well as ethnic status.

As a leader of women, Emiliana is known in Hunucmá as someone who helps the people of the town through the material goods that she distributes. She is also taken into high regard by the population because of the negotiations she carries out with her political relationships to procure medical assistance, medicines, scholarships and jobs for the members of her community.

The social and economical increase that Emiliana has is reflected in concrete facts, such as: the re-building of her house made out of hay and adobe by one made of concrete blocks and cement, the access that her three children had to a university education and the acquisition of new habits of everyday life, such as the use of a knife and fork to eat with, and the learning of proper manners for certain circumstances. Her social position is identified in the way people address themselves to her. Before she became recognized as a leader of the *Partido Revolucionario Institucional*, the members of her community simply called her 'Emiliana', but ever since her formal participation in the party and her incorporation to the working sector, people refer to her as 'Doña Emiliana'.

Her ethnic status is perceived by the way she dresses. The typical *huipil* dress that woman wear in Yucatan is used along with a complementary garment that goes under it called *huastan*. Rural women at mid-calf length usually use this item of clothing, but Emiliana, her sister and her *comadre*, use it down to their ankle. That detail gives them a different position in contrast to the other women who live in the town.

All the years that Emiliana has participated in the political scene, have made her change her perception about women. She now realizes that reproduction is not the only function of women, and that they can perform more tasks than those are determined by biology. But she also understands that the changes that a woman makes in her life are made by personal and individual willpower. These modifications cannot be made in a collective way, but they are possible on an individual basis despite the various kinds of subordination a woman may encounter, such as generical, class and ethnic subordination.

All of the above is expressed when she says:

Women don't have the opportunity of getting out, because they are poor and peasants, and don't have the permission of their husbands to do what they want. Even if they wanted to participate in politics, they can't because of this. There are others who say that they don't want to be a part of it, and let themselves be carried away by their husband's opinions. They say that they are happy like that.

Conclusion

The experiences of Emiliana's political participation inside the *Partido Revolucionario Institucional*, allow us to point out that, in the case of Yucatan, the presence of the Mayan woman inside the party can be explained as a part of the social dynamic that was established in the rural part of Yucatan, and as part of the corporate forms of political participation that were established by the PRI. This is because the political institution of the PRI was the only party with presence in the 106 municipalities that form the State, which is partly due to the corporative structure of the CNC. In the peasant's mind this generated, a conception that consisted in believing the PRI to be the only political option that existed in the State. This situation was favoured by relationships of negotiation, because the reproduction of the worker's corporative did not concentrate itself solely in the interior of the workforce stations. On the contrary: it broke those barriers, and penetrated the family sphere.

If the presence of the Mayan woman inside the PRI can be explained according to Bartolomé with external and indigenous pressures, her permanence within the system is related to the existence of a series of material and status incentives, which allow the party to have intermediary actors (leaders) and political clientele that legitimize it as a political institution.

Emiliana's experiences also show that in order for a woman's presence to become visible in the political arena, it is necessary to take into account a series of factors relating both to the female condition and to the social and political dynamics of the context. We therefore observe how Emiliana moves into the political arena in the precise moment when she breaks her ties to her condition as a reproductive woman and assumes her role as a political woman

Also, through her political activity, we can perceive that women can occupy a series of different positions within one same context, as in this case we observed Emiliana as a leader, and/or as a supporter. This situation can be explained from an organizational perspective, based on the need for organizing a particular sector of society. Another view that can be taken is the fact that women can be present in diverse positions of society to influence their own reality.

References

Bartolomé, M.A. (1992), *La Dinámica social de los mayas en Yucatán* (México: CNCA/INI).
Guerrero, L.P. (1999 and 2002) Interview with Doña Emiliana, July 18th, July 19th, August 15th, August 24th 1999 and September, 2002 (Merida Yucatan).
Panebianco, A. (1995), *Modelos de Partido* (Madrid, Spain: Alianza Universidad).

PART 3
Multiculturalism and the Revival of Ethnicity

Chapter 8

Women Who Know How to Talk: Gender, Women, Political Participation and Multiculturalism in Mexico

Margarita Zárate Vidal

This chapter examines the complex subject of women's political participation and their contribution to the debate on the construction of a multicultural nation in Mexico.[1] Gender and multiculturalism are the main concerns of this article. My departure point is that the opposition cultures-nation is not enough to solve the problem of inequality. If we confront the nation state against the multiple views and experiences of subaltern cultures, it is quite clear that the fairer alternative is to establish a new multicultural model of nation. Besides, within the construction of both, cultures and nation, there prevails a deep gender inequality; also women have been seen as the ultimate bearer of culture in many societies, and because of this it is important to look at the relation between multicultural citizenship and their implication for women's positionality. Three other reasons are central to this issue: the discussion of the close association of woman and nation, woman and customs, and the social construction of gender and the 'feminine'. The discussion of liberal notions of citizenship and the topic of differential rights addressed to different type of women. Finally we should realize that achieving a multicultural society does not guarantee a better positioning for women, unless we take into account the various concepts concerning a good life from a gender perspective, challenging the association between women and/or custom, culture, nation. Despite the advantage of analysing cultures in the plural, not culture in the singular, we have to realize that the states have promoted the idea of a specific type of multiculturalism, a state multiculturalism; one not challenged, but strengthened, by the idea of cultures.

In seeking to discuss this last premise, I first want to suggest the idea, following Eriksen's (1997) point, that 'cultures' are neither clearly bounded, tightly integrated, nor unchanging. Moreover, as Gupta and Ferguson have rightly pointed out, the isomorphism of space, place and culture creates a fiction that mapped cultures onto specific places and with specific peoples. However, paradoxically, the issue of territoriality is even more salient as shown by the case of Chiapas and the

1 I would like to thank Federico Besserer's thoughtful commentary on a earlier version. Thanks also to Lucia Rayas and Gillian Turner for their careful English review of this article.

Ley Indígena. Furthermore, despite sharing Gupta's and Ferguson's criticism of essentialism and naturalism in the relationship between 'people' and 'its' territory, and citizens of states and territories, we must acknowledge that we are presently dealing, on the side of the agents or protagonists – with 'ideas of localized culture'. On the other side we are witnessing claims on 'our own place' 'nuestro territorio' as empowering on unequal national contexts.[2]

Currently, the issue of the construction of a truly multicultural nation, the kind of autonomy to be sought, and the place of women within this process has been a polemical and rather complex political project in Mexico. Chiapas and Oaxaca have been examples of the complexities involved in creating a new nation. Gender relationships and the role of women have been brought to the fore. A great deal of literature has been produced on topics such as autonomy and the significance of zapatismo in Chiapas; nevertheless, women's participation needs further consideration. The creation of a new nation entails taking into account indigenous groups rights and a fairer gender system. Views on cultures supposedly stable, timeless and lacking in internal conflicts have been challenged from a transdisciplinary approach, not merely from the standpoint of Anthropology. Similarly, ideas from a feminism viewpoint on multiculturalism and minority groups' rights need to be reviewed

Pollit (1999, p. 27) takes a critical look at the latter and argues that in its demand for equality for women, feminism sets itself in opposition to virtually every culture on earth. In her view 'feminism interrogates and challenges all cultural traditions'.

This article contains the following segments: the first part contains a discussion on the status of the concept/ideology of multiculturalism and the association of woman concepts with nation in general terms. Multiculturalism is revisited in the second part, along with the notion of citizenship and its implications for a fairer gender model. The third part offers several ethnographic examples on the notions of power involved in peasant and indigenous women's political participation. Besides, an analysis on the significance of motherhood (being this consciously assumed either as a political strategy or not) in political participation. Finally we introduce a preliminary debate on power and women leading to our conclusions.

Nation and Multiculturalism

Approaching an Alternative Multiculturalism

Multiculturalism implies the idea, or ideal, of harmonious coexistence among different cultural or ethnic groups within a pluralist society. However, the main uses of the term –multiculturalism – have covered a range of meanings including multiculturalism as an ideology, a discourse, and as a cluster of policies and practices. At the ideological level, multiculturalism has included loosely related themes incorporating acceptance of different ethnic groups, religions, cultural practices and linguistic diversity within a pluralistic society. When applied to policies, multiculturalism has covered a range of formal state policies with two main purposes: maintaining harmony among

---

2   See also Nash (2001) critique on this particular issue.

diverse ethnic groups, and to build a relationship between state and ethnic minorities (Cashmore, 1994, p. 216).

There is, in my opinion, a controversy concerning the meaning of multiculturalism. One position attempts a delineation of the phenomenon in terms of global and hegemonic discourse. This is exemplified by the transformation of the old nation-states into a new form of post-national or multicultural states. As Carl-Ulrik Schierup claims: multiculturalism is an ideological base for transatlantic alignment aimed at the transformation of the welfare state. This alignment aspires to be the hegemonic credo in the contemporary era of postmodern modernity (quoted in Yuval-Davis, 1997, p. 197). This argument could be substantiated by the cases of *Australian* and the incipient multiculturalisms of Mexican states. Besides, the minimalist-state promoted by the neo-liberal discourse – Gledhill asserts – might be seen as a mask for expanded state domination, and its accompanying programmes of deregulation. Therefore, he warns that the current interest of the liberal state in giving space to 'indigenous rights' movements and other forms of 'identity politics' fits into a broader picture of the liberal state as a regulatory agency under late capitalist conditions, whose 'language of recognition of difference as no difference... becomes a vehicle of subordination through individualization, normalization and regulation, even as it strives to produce visibility and acceptance' (Brown, 1995, p. 66 quoted in Gledhill, 1994, p. 102).

Following this line of argument, Rouse (1995) points out that state-sponsored 'ethnic pluralism' could be seen as an aspect of a reworked hegemonic project of bourgeoisie dominated ruling blocs in the era of 'flexible accumulation'.

The second is the subaltern argument on multiculturalism. Thus, we have a multiculturalism movement, involving a grass roots movement coming from the bottom-up as opposed to the post-nationalist bourgeoisie project. In this respect, multiculturalism itself is a matter of debate and confrontation. Trin Minh ha (quoted in Yuval-Davis, 1997, p. 197) has stated that there are two types of social and cultural differences: those that threaten and those that do not. In a wider sense, multiculturalism is aimed at nourishing and perpetuating the latter, which pose no threat.

The debate centres on the limits of multiculturalism

> between those who want a continued construction of the national collectivity as homogeneous and assimilatory, and those who have been calling for the institutionalization of ethnic pluralism and the preservation of the ethnic minorities' cultures of origin as legitimate parts of national project. A controversial related question is the extent to which the conservation of collective identities and cultures is important in itself, or only because of the collective will that promotes this preservation, and whether projects aimed at the conservation of cultures can avoid the reification and essentialization of these cultures.
> (Yuval-Davis, 1997, pp. 197–198).

An important contributor to this discussion is Taylor, who focuses on the discourse of recognition, a main topic for the issue of multiculturalism. He claims that the refusal of equal recognition will lead to the projection of an inferior or demeaning image on another, and in fact may be used to distort and oppress, 'not only contemporary feminism but also race relations and discussions of multiculturalism are under girded by the premise that the withholding of recognition can be a form of oppression' (Taylor, 1994, p. 36). In seeking to construct an alternative to a blind universalism and avoid the existence of 'first-class' and 'second-class' citizens, he draws on the move from honour to dignity, with an emphasis on the equal dignity of all citizens. Even though the principle of equal citizenship has become universally accepted, there has been another important change: the development of the modern notion of identity, which has given rise to a politics of difference. This policy implies recognition of the unique identity of individuals or groups; acknowledgement of their distinctness from all others.

As we have seen, Charles Taylor attempts to reconcile two liberal traditions, a difficult task, as Kuper states, 'is an intractable task (…) not only because cultural politics actually demands positive discrimination (…) but it also requires conformity' (1999, p. 236).

Yet, other authors such as Goldberg (1994) challenge Taylor's view, being of the opinion that despite the importance of the struggle for due recognition, this does not in itself guarantee the economic and social resources needed to provide the basic necessities for a good life. Another critique is that of Bauman (2001) who discusses Taylor's drawing on Kant and Rousseau philosophical premises, containing some specific ideas on justice and value. Therefore, the idea of recognition acquires various meanings depending on the case.

In the wider debate, the case of Mexico could shed light on this point. During the nineties, an article was incorporated into the Mexican Constitution recognizing that Mexico is indeed a multicultural nation. But, in spite of this formal acknowledgement, the Mexican state recognizes rights but does not invest in resources. Thus, rights exist formally within the letter of the law, but in reality, there are no positive, or even negative rights in existence.

This seems to be also the case of *Australian* multiculturalism, in which not all cultural identities have the same legitimacy, as is referred to by Yuval-Davis (1997). The 1989 official government's document on multiculturalism emphasizes 'the limits of multiculturalism'. These limits are referred to in cultural custom (such as polygamy, using drugs, and so on) which is considered illegal as well as illegitimate.

Gunew (1995, p. 104) has discussed some central issues on *Australian* multiculturalism, arguing that multiculturalism is useful for the Anglo-Celtic group which 'continue[s] to man the institutions which orchestrate national affairs' because among other reasons: the multicultural banner obscures the battle for land rights currently being waged by the Aborigines together with a campaign for rescuing what they can of their own cultural history, and in practice, multiculturalism celebrates white, professional, European migration and considers Asian migration less acceptable. Additionally, the emphasis on cultural pluralism has often worked towards obscuring class.

Women and Nation

In France, it was La Patrie, a figure of a woman giving birth, that personified the revolution; in Ireland, Mother Ireland; in Russia, Mother Russia; and in India, Mother India. Women often come to symbolize the national collectivity, its roots, its spirit, its national project (Yuval-Davis and Anthias, 1989; Yuval-Davis, 1993; quoted in Yuval-Davis, 1997, p. 196).

Some authors (Yuval-Davis, Pollit) have emphasized the relationship between women, culture and subjugation. The central link between the place of women as national reproducers and women's subjugation can be found in the different regulations – customary, religious or legal – which determine the family units within the boundaries of the collectivity and how they come into existence (marriage), or reach their end (divorce and widowhood). Women and nation are associated closely, they produce the babies for the fatherland, but punished for sleeping with strangers. Gender plays a significant role on other processes of public conduct, creativity, language and cultural codes.

Natividad Gutiérrez examines this process from a critical perspective in her book *Nationalist Myths and Ethnic Identities, Indigenous Intellectuals and the Mexican State* (1999):

> Indian women attach great importance to the community and the household, because they believe that abandoning these traditional arenas would constitute rejecting the only means they possess of confronting a hostile society dominated by an alien set of values disdaining and fearing the complexity of Indian ways of life (see Arizpe, 1987). Their wishes and political aspirations are not bound by concerns with individualism or politics of gender, which they consider divisive; instead, they seek to reconstruct their culture and language as well as the traditions of the locality to which they belong. (Gutiérrez, 1999, p. 189)

Statements reflecting an emerging type of consciousness involving ethnic and gender factors are becoming accessible: 'Among us – women – there exists more awareness to preserve our culture, because of the discrimination we suffer as poor, as indigenous and as women. Thus, we have to speak Castilian (Spanish), abandon our [usual] dress and all that identifies us with our Maya *pueblos*' (Organización de Mujeres, 1996). Other pronouncements of women involved in militant activities explicitly reject gender divisions and emphasize a joint search to alleviate marginality and poverty: 'Our struggle is not against men, and we have only one path, a common destiny, and the same struggle to carry out'. In this last statement a discourse on ethnicity is used to inform on class politics, they are clear on their subordinated class position within the larger society.

Womanhood is the signifier of the collectivity, women symbolize national and collective honour. Yuval-Davies exemplifies insistence on particular styles of dress and behaviour with compulsory veiling. Ways of dressing and behaviour symbolize the group's cultural identity and its boundaries, as shown later by the case of *Mazahua* women in Mexico. Warfare constitutes another example. Rape has long been a part of warfare as the situation in Bosnia or Chiapas clearly shows. Rape is defined by the Geneva Convention not as a war crime or a form of torture, but as a 'crime against honour'. The honour referred to is not woman's honour but that of her family and her collectivity.

This point deserves more attention; the concept of honour needs to be traced back and related to other notions such as purity of blood and race. The ideology of honour coming from the Mediterranean shaped the political conquest in Mexico as well as in other countries. Virginity, chastity and loyalty of women are linked to honour and purity of blood. Men of 'clean blood' should have the capacity to control their women. Spanish notions of status honour and purity of blood in the specific context of mestizaje thus underpinned a particularly strong process downgrading women. Racism towards indigenous New World populations combined with sexism produced in a situation in which women were seen as sexually and socially inferior (Chant, 1989; Lomnitz, 1992; Zárate, 1996). Discourse of honour and reputation has an outstanding prevalence among rural women (though not only among them) in Mexico, as I shall show later.

Sex and 'race' differences continue to be ideologically marked as socially significant biological 'facts' in class societies as a way of naturalizing and thereby perpetuating class and, in a related way, gender inequality (Stolcke, 1994, p. 30). Moore (1994) adds that violence is strongly sexualized. Gender and race give rise to differences in power and/or prestige, and consequently, power is represented in many contexts as sexualized and racialized. Moore offers two illuminating examples, first, the use of the words 'Arab' and 'Muslim' in Europe as terms of abuse and categories of discrimination. The second example is the treatment of Iraq by the West, which not only includes domination, but 'feminizing and pacifying that which is dominated'. This issue is further complicated because of the recent events (the terrorist attacks on New York and Washington and the invasion of Irak). Even though it is supposed not to be an attack to Islam, for 'civilization' read 'western civilization', and fundamentalist religious discourses used by both sides make analysis even more complex.

Multiculturalism, Citizenship and Gender

The Mexican Nation and its Others

Multiculturalism has a very detrimental effect on women in particular, as 'different' cultural traditions are often defined in terms of culturally specific gender relations, and the control of women's behaviour (in which women themselves, especially older women, also participate and collude) is often used to reproduce ethnic boundaries (Yuval-Davies, 1997, p. 201).

Kymlicka (1999, p. 31) argues that justice within ethno cultural groups is as important as justice among ethno cultural groups. Group rights are permissible if they help promote justice among ethno cultural groups, but are impermissible if they create or exacerbate gender inequalities within the group. According to Kymlicka there are two kinds of group rights, one called 'internal restrictions,' because they restrict the ability of individuals within the group (particularly women) to question, revise, or abandon traditional cultural roles and practices. The second group of rights is called 'external protections'. These are rights that a minority group claims against the larger society in order to reduce its vulnerability to the larger society's economic or political power. Among these rights there are: language rights, guaranteed political representation, funding of ethnic media, land claims, compensation for historical injustice, or the regional devolution of power. Internal restrictions imply the right of a group against their own members, designed to protect the group from the destabilizing impact of internal dissent. The second kind, external protections are designed to protect the group from the impact of external pressures.

As we can realize, a liberal theory of minority groups' rights cannot accept internal restrictions since they constitute violations to the autonomy of individuals and create injustice within the group.

This point leads to the discussion on citizenship as a universal ideal, 'whatever the social or group differences among citizens, whatever their inequalities of wealth, status, and power in the everyday activities of civil society, citizenship gives everyone the same status as peers in the political public' (Young, 1998, p. 263). Young rightly claims that during the political struggles of the nineteenth and twentieth centuries, the excluded and the underprivileged thought that attaining full citizenship status would give them freedom and equality. However, some groups soon realized that they were being treated as second class citizens. Her opinion stems from the recognition that equal citizenship has not eliminated oppression. In her essay she argues that the classic idea of universality of citizenship stands in tension with the other two meanings of universality embedded in modern political ideas: universality as generality, and universality as equal treatment. This difference deserves more attention, universality defined as general as opposed to particular:

> The ideal of the public realm of citizenship as expressing a general will, a point of view and interest that citizens have in common that transcends their differences, has operated in fact as a demand for homogeneity among citizens, citizenship is an expression of the universality of human life; it is a realm of rationality and freedom as opposed to the heteronomous realm of particular need, interest, and desire (…); and referred to equal treatment, universality in the sense of laws and rules that say the same for all and apply to all in the same way, they are blind to individual and group differences. (Young, 1998, pp. 265–266)

Marion Young asserts that universality of citizenship conceived as generality operated to exclude not only women, but other groups.

Therefore, her proposal addresses two main issues: first, group representation in order to include everyone's participation in public discussion, and second, strict adherence to a principle of equal treatment is neither fair nor useful when differences in capacities, culture, values, and behavioural styles exist among groups. If this is the case, adherence to an equal treatment principle tends to perpetuate oppression or disadvantage. Throughout her work, Young argues that inclusion and participation of everyone in social and political institutions therefore sometimes requires the articulation of special rights that attend to group differences in order to undermine oppression and disadvantage.

Eriksen sustains that culture is not a legitimating basis for political claims and that cultural singularities among minorities and majorities in modern societies can only be defended where not interfering with individual human rights. He draws on Turner's 'critical multiculturalism', or viewing multiculturalism as a set of doctrines 'which argue the importance and equivalence of cultural heritage *and* the decentralization of defining power as to what is to count as one, may in practice be a strong form of individualistic thinking about personhood – the world seen as smorgasbord of identity options' (1997, p. 53). This position warns against allowing institutionalized differences form the core of multiculturalism. If this were case, it would produce nihilism, apartheid and/or the enforced ascription of cultural identities.

A central aspect concerns not only the possibilities of differential treatment in terms of access to employment or welfare, but the different cultural needs of different ethnicities. In some cases – as in Australia and Mexico – there have been demands to enable indigenous groups to operate according to their own customary and religious legal systems.

An example of the latter is Mexico. Since its foundation, Mexico has had a pluri ethnic and pluri cultural composition. Despite this fact, its constitutional law has not reflected this reality until very recently. The *indigenismo* (official government policy addressing ethnic groups), has produced different views on the indigenous,[3] most of them carrying the preoccupation of assimilating what is Indian, therefore, having homogenization as a goal. In 1992, Constitutional Article number four was changed in order to establish the existence of the Indian peoples. It acknowledged their cultural rights, yet, it did not specify the principles, relationships and institutions in which those rights should have materialized. Neither did this reform include claims such as autonomy as an exercise of free determination.

Nonetheless, it is important to mention that in 1998 the Mexican state, Oaxaca, partially acknowledged the indigenous systems of law and justice *usos y costumbres*.[4] This reform was influenced by the national discussion following the uprising of the *Ejército Zapatista de Liberación Nacional* (EZLN), the participation of *oaxaqueños* in the *San Andrés Larráinzar* process of negotiation between EZLN and the federal government, the consultation called for by both, the federal government and that of the state of Oaxaca and the consolidation of an ethnic discourse within the indigenous movement in Oaxaca. The approval of *usos y costumbres* (the indigenous system of law and justice) as an instrument for nominating municipal authorities in 412 municipalities presented additional problems. One of them was the political parties' right to propose candidates and the *pueblos* rights to elect its authorities. *Usos y costumbres* allowed election of authorities and not candidates. This was one of the problems posed by the controversial involvement of political parties in some *pueblos*. Some regulations (State's Constitution Article 25) related to political organization state law will protect the indigenous communities' democratic traditions and practices which have been used for the election their *ayuntamientos*. This norm is complemented by the article 29 that states that the *Ayuntamientos* election will be made by way of a free, secret and direct vote, and within the *municipios* which are regulated by *usos y costumbres* the Article 25 will be observed. Consequently, Oaxaca has two forms of election: one by political parties where individuals are

---

3   I use the words indigenous and Indian recognizing their controversial meanings. It is worth to mention that the word *indio* acquired a positive meaning (a symbolic inversion) by the end of the seventies decade when Indian members within indigenous movements began to use it, challenging its racist and pejorative meaning. Also, I recognize the symbolic significance of the term *pueblos originarios*.

4   Other states are discussing their own reforms: Tlaxcala, San Luis Potosí – among others –. It must be also mentioned the most recent form of autonomy experience in Chiapas: las Juntas de Gobierno (2003).

organized, and the election system by usos y costumbres for indigenous pueblos and communities. (López Bárcenas, 1998, p. 139).

Moreover, during 2001, events had changed the Mexican political scene, after a warm welcome to the *Marcha Zapatista* at the beginning of the year and the participation of some of its members, a woman among them, in the debates in the Senate. The so called *Ley Indígena* was approved rapidly *al vapor* with modifications and no respecting the original agreements of *San Andrés Lárrainzar*. There is currently a constitutional controversy among state constitutions and the Federal government, concerning the case of Oaxaca – above mentioned – arguing that the reform approved is not the one approved in San Andrés.

Another point of contention is what is happening to the state's appropriation of multiculturalists discourse in a country which the transnational migration has taken its toll, small towns almost without young population, an increasing abandonment and depopulating process of the country side, along with an ageing population nationwide.

Women Who Know How to Talk: Women and Political Participation

Carlsen (1999) examines discrimination against the political participation of indigenous women as reflected in *the usos y costumbres* of the state of Oaxaca. Some indigenous organizations began to build consensus on the necessity of changing some *usos y costumbres*. *La Ley de Mujeres* of the Zapatistas has encouraged this process.[5] However, this author remarks that modifying *usos y costumbres* is not the only problem. There are other facts to take into consideration, for example, literacy and education. In order to participate in some community positions, women need to fulfil certain requirements. As an example, in answering a question about whether women in their community have held positions in *The Coordinadora Estatal de Productores de Café Oaxaqueños* (State Coordinating Instance of Oaxaqueño Coffee Producers), many women answered yes, but in reality their husbands were the ones who held the *post*. Carlsen adds 'their answers reflected that work and cargo (a series of ranked religious or civil-religious offices through which individuals pass as temporary office holders) responsibility were shared as a couple' (1999, p. 68). Oehmichen (2000, p. 95) offers a similar account on this particular theme. She draws on the political experience of *Mazahua* women. Her investigation illustrates the difficulties of a migrant *woman* presenting her candidacy to a position as *delegada* (municipal officer; *municipio*, political-administrative division) in her town. This woman had to emphasize her ethnic belongingness. She had to wear the traditional dress of *Mazahua* women and had to show her proficiency in understanding and speaking *Mazahua*. This leader confronted the stereotypes of the feminine: 'ya estuvo bueno de que los hombres piensen que sólo servimos para tener hijos' (it's about time men stop thinking we're only fit to bear children). Once she took over the position, both,

---

5   Some recent developments have promoted the discussion on indigenous women's rights. The most striking example was the participation of a woman, Esther, pronouncing a speech on behalf of the zapatistas in the Congress during the *Marcha Zapatista* in April 2001 in Mexico City.

she and her husband were stigmatized: him, because he was not enough of a man and did not control his wife. She was considered to be a public woman.

In my own fieldwork in Michoacan (Zárate, 1996, 1998), the general absence of women in leadership roles seems to be an outstanding feature shared by other organizations as well (see Craske, 1993, on organizations of *priista* and independent affiliation in Guadalajara). My research addressed the issue of the construction and recreation of identities and community among people belonging to an Indigenous-peasant movement, *The Unión of Comuneros Emiliano Zapata* (UCEZ) in the western state of *Michoacan*, Mexico. The UCEZ was created as a formal organization in Tingambato, Michoacan in 1979. Its creation could be characterized first of all as a 'reactive' response to great repression and the unanswered land demands of some communities in Michoacan. Four years after its foundation, the UCEZ was the second most important peasant organization within Michoacan, after the Central Nacional Campesina (CNC), the official peasant central, voicing the demands of near to 150 communities and *ejidos*, albeit with very different levels of intensity. It is a founding member of the Coordinadora Nacional del Plan de Ayala (CNPA), a national umbrella organization for 'independent' peasant movements, with a strong agrarian orientation and predominately 'indigenous' membership. It was also the peasant organization with the greatest capacity for resolving agrarian disputes, and represented the 'most important independent movement in Michoacan'.

Three main topics were discussed in my work on the UCEZ: ethnic identity, gender and the construction of community and communal sentiment of belonging. The interrelation between people's identities and their membership in the organization is examined through investigating how they adopt particular identities and the degree and nature of their participation in the movement. Reasons and motives for participating in such organization are explored, and the statements given by the members of this organization are shown to elucidate how they conceive their participation, appealing not only to instrumental interests as motivation for action, but also alluding to sentiments of ethnic belonging, ancestry, national heroes, and historic memory.[6]

Graciela and doña Pilar from Zirahuén were remarkable within the UCEZ, although there were other women, such as Modesta from Ixtaro or Josefa in the Colonia, whose level of participation and activism was also very significant, even if they did not hold any formal leadership role. Nevertheless, despite these limitations and difficulties thoroughly described elsewhere (Zárate, 1996, 1998). I would stress that the content of inter-personal relationships was challenged in various degrees in the 'communities' which I studied. In Mummert's view 'the challenge in the content

---

6   I decided to choose different types of 'communities'. One of them possessing a history of combative behaviour vis-à-vis the 'outside' – the State and other agents belonging to the larger region or National Society –, with an emphasis on both the past and present in its specific 'ethnic' identity, this is the case of Zirahuén, The second, Ixtaro is a mestizo *pueblo* which does not now have and have never has had the legal status of *comunidad indígena* (as an agrarian and/or an Indian village). The third is an urban community with the social characteristics of the urban *colonias populares* the Colonia communal Emiliano Zapata. All the communities are located in the south-eastern municipality of *Salvador Escalante* in Michoacan.

of inter-personal relationships is reflected in the ambiguity of cultural messages, that is, a discourse that experiments with and at the same time criticizes alternative or even openly deviant roles with respect to the norm' (1994, 1).

The women I studied also challenged the norm in varying degrees. Some openly defied the role that was culturally sanctioned for them. Comments of approval, admiration, or, on the contrary, criticisms were sometimes explicit in other women, whereas disapproval was more frequently shown by their partners and family. Many of them certainly had to confront open opposition to their political participation by partners or husbands (see also Stephen, 1991).[7] We can discuss further the declining interest of women on participation, and it was due certainly a combination of factors: a correct perception of a prolongation of authoritarian and abusive attitudes such as those of their husbands in leadership management, in the most of the cases the economic burden that travelling to many places implied for them. Furthermore, some of these women preferred not to break the norm of being a housewife and continue to assume this role.

Women's participation in the organization of the *Colonia Comunal* and both *comunidades indígenas* revealed rather ambiguous conceptions of womanhood and participation, but these were deeply embedded in the fabric of everyday life. A *comunera* of Zirahuén, Ma. Piedad, defended her right to participate in the struggle for land arguing she liked it, despite the widespread criticism. '¿Hasta cuándo se van a sentar estas mujeres?' (When are these women going to stop making problems and stay at home?). The adjectives used to label women who participate intensely reveal the conflictive nature of discourses and practices within the communities. Again, honour and honesty are at the forefront. The extreme case was that recounted by Modesta (a very participative woman in Ixtaro). Due to her deep involvement within UCEZ, and in the organization of the comunidad indígena her honra (honour) as a

---

7   Juana, a woman from the Colonia, who had previous political experience, described the way in which, at the beginning, when she attended PRD meetings she quarrelled with her husband. But now he accepted his wife's activities in the Colonia. Nevertheless, she still has to confront the critiques made of her militancy by other people: "I continue to go to marches. People say I am a loud mouth (argüendera), a trouble-maker, but it is the only way we can have something. Doña Pilar (from Zirahuén) told me: 'my husband got angry, but he let me continue'. Her husband was president of the local land council. An interesting continuity is that her daughter, Salud P, played an important role at the peak of the community's struggle, and she is married to Marcos P, the de facto leader of Zirahuén's indigenous community. She was disappointed because it was difficult to keep the level of participation going. She complained about her own husband's frequent absences, and thought she was the one Salud was a key figure in the struggle for the community, but she became somewhat left in charge of the family (she also ran a restaurant on the lake shore) because he was always busy with UCEZ. Even the most militant women from the most militant families, are therefore forced to conform to male expectations about their 'proper responsibilities'. Many eventually succumb to the pressure placed on them. Aurelia from Ixtaro took advantage of the absence of her husband: 'I joined the community without my husband's permission; he was in the U.S.A.' Eventually, however, her participation ended because of the community's internal conflicts coupled with her husband's continuing disapproval of her participation. Confrontations with partners or husbands over male respect of women's decisions to participate in demonstrations, meetings, sit-ins and commissions were certainly widespread within the three UCEZ communities.

widow with a daughter was challenged: 'I was called Luis's [the leader's] mistress'. Evidently her situation as a widow, with only one daughter and some reputed economic independence, helped her to become involved in the UCEZ's struggle. She stressed that fact: 'I stand on my own feet, I have no man.' Furthermore, her life history points to diverse experiences that make her unusual in comparison with most other women. In a similar way to some other UCEZ members, but mainly male leaders, she had migrated to Mexico City (Cuajimalpa) and worked for nine years in a restaurant. Her fame as a woman who does not keep quiet (que no se deja) and who actually stood up to the abusive male leader was widespread. A frequent pejorative adjective used against her was *hocicona* (someone who talks a lot). She was also called a rebel. Those adjectives were used to label women who dared to speak up for themselves in their own defense. Similarly, a woman who talks a lot is equated to a *callejera*, a prostitute.

The account presented by Concepción illustrates the meaning of those adjectives in another related context, a dispute over boundaries with a neighbour: 'one neighbour put down boundary markers, *linderos*, and in this way, he was taking over my land. I told him, "look, do not fence there" (no *cerques* ahí), but because he is a man (un señor), they start to shout: "you shut up, you are *hocicona*, *callejera*."' Those insults implied that Concepción should not have opened her mouth and defended her property, because the one who had the right and responsibility to talk was her man (who might therefore be shamed by her action). In transgressing this norm she was behaving as a *callejera*. Such stereotyping was powerful, because it reinforced the abusive behaviour of her neighbour and secured his interests. He went on and planted some trees, although Concepción remained determined to cut them down. Moore (1994) provides an explanation on this matter: concepts such as reputation are connected not only to self-representations and social evaluations of self, but to the potential for power and agency which a good reputation proffers.

Other testimonies given to me did, however, differ and move away from the stereotypes discussed above. Similarly to the way in which Modesta is seen in Ixtaro, women in Zirahuén described some of their companions with obvious admiration, as women 'who know how to talk'[8]. For instance, Timo said: 'Women are always in the forefront, such as Salud or the late Pilar'. Timo held that 'women are better at talking, and wittier. Also we are more courageous.' That comparisons between men and women made by these women enlarged on this idea in various directions, subverting or even inverting male stereotypical ideology. For example, Ma. De la Paz from Zirahuén held that: 'women participate more because we are more talkative (habladoras); a woman is more assertive, a woman always defends her family, and women participate more than men. A woman is in less danger. The father never defends the family.' Though this statement argues, in effect, that women can manipulate male attitudes to their advantage ('a woman is in less danger'), it also clearly subverts male claims to having a 'protector's role'.

---

8   A profound preoccupation on the possibility of taking is clear on these testimonies, and it resonates with the discussion brought by Spivak when she asks, adding to can the subaltern talk?, can women talk? .

This description fits nicely with Moore's statement that: 'there is no single femininity or masculinity for individual women and men to identify with in their social settings, but a variety of possible femininities and masculinities which are provided by the contradictory and competing discourses which exist, and which produce and are reproduced by social practices and institutions' (1994, p. 63).

Recent contributions call attention to the transformation of gender concept in a metaphor (Lamas, 2002) which does not solve the tension among the universal and the particular and specific contexts. Moore summarized this point: '...They reduce sexual difference to a construct of historically variable discursive practices, and reject the idea that there is anything constant about sexual difference. This rejection is an absolute one because the terms of the sex/gender debate in all its various forms revolve around the question of nature versus culture, essentialism versus construction, substance versus signification' (Moore, 1999, pp. 167–168).

Another testimony offers a contrasting opinion:

Women participate more because it is more dangerous for men. Women give the face when something dangerous is going on. Men get angry more easily. They do not curb their anger. We women are calmer, we easily cope more. Here in Zirahuen we have stopped violence erupting. One woman can pull another's hair or scratch, but they generally do no attack with guns.

In opposition to many stereotypes used against women, it appears, in these discourses, that women see themselves as having more control over their emotions than men, that is, that they are more rational, calm and furthermore, more courageous. Besides, there are considerations on the nature of violence. Another important area where women could see their 'superiority' was in issues related to working in the fields. This reflects the enormous, if often unrecognized importance of female labour in the countryside. In my view, rural women from the type of community I studied have never been restricted solely to their homes (the so-called 'private' sphere); they go out and about collecting firewood, sowing, herding animals, and helping their husbands, fathers or sons in the fields. There is also a long-standing tradition of women trading in the Meseta Tarasca, going both, to towns some distance away, and around *mestizo* peasant communities. A proof of this is the willingness of women in Ixtaro to join in the exhausting work in the fields or in the process of migration to engage in wage labour within the state and in the US.

The cases above summarized reveal the complexities of informal participation within communities. Debate increases on this particular issue, and a comparative view of different experiences could help establish the main concerns.

The argument that citizens share the same language and national culture and never ask what sort of institutions would be chosen by ethno cultural minorities has produced grave injustices. Nonetheless, it is worth to understand, as other author says, 'Culture is something rather more complicated than patriarchal permission for powerful men to subordinate vulnerable women. There are brutal men (and women) everywhere. Is it their Jewish, Christian, or Muslim identity that makes them brutal... or is it their brutality?' (Honing, 1999, p. 36).

Another example drawn from South India illustrates the difficulties entangled in the relationships among gender, body and violence. Busby shows us how, even though husband and wife consider themselves as 'one body,' the differences are marked because of gender distinctions. Women and men are different yet equal, complementary and essential to each other. To complicate the picture further, Busby found:

> such notions of men and women as equal and complementary are contradicted by other representations of men as heads of households, as the ultimate decision-makers. This is turn often fits uneasily with the actual control that women are acknowledged to have over the household's money, and over decisions as to what to do with it. More strikingly, the idea that husbands and wives are together 'one body', each nothing without the other, is, for an outsider especially, difficult to reconcile with the widespread fact of domestic violence, and the very real hurt that women sustain from their husbands.
>
> (Busby, 1999, p. 231)

Women's Political Participation and the Politicization of Motherhood (A Strategic Essentialism?)

Women's political participation in Latin America has been reviewed from the perspective of organized movements. In many of these analyses the issue of contention is the role of women and their demands. There is, I would argue, a main concern on women's concept of power. Many of the women's movements analysed have shown an interesting feature: the politicization of motherhood. Logan's analysis on a political urban organization illustrates this point:

> The key to poor women's motivation to mobilize lies in their self-definition as mothers and their commitment to fulfilling the responsibilities attendant in the social practice of motherhood. Low-income Mexican women are socialized to assume motherhood as their primary adult role and identity. In Mexico, as throughout Latin America, motherhood is culturally idealized -if not necessarily always venerated in practice – (Logan, 1990, p. 152). The women who are involved in urban popular mobilizations possess a 'female consciousness' that 'centers upon the rights of gender, on social concerns, on survival'. Such a consciousness arises from a culturally framed division of labour that assigns women the responsibility for preserving life. Under these conditions, women accept rather than rebel against the prescribed gender roles of their societies.
>
> (Kaplan, 1982, p. 545; quoted in Logan, 1990, p. 152)

I found the same in my own research. My fieldwork (1996, 1998) on rural women participating in a peasant organization offered two broad lines of discussion on motherhood. On the one hand, we have the practical difficulties of doing politics and caring for children at the same time and, on the other, the politicization that being a mother can bring about. The first point was illustrated by the difficulties women had when they seized land in the *Colonia* (one of the 'communities' I researched in), especially if they had small children or babies. For instance, Guadalupe had just delivered a baby girl, so she did not participate in the land seizure. Others, whose children got ill when they remained in the lot during the first weeks after the seizure, left it because of that. Some even left the *Colonia* for good. It was a cold month, March, and they were living in makeshift shacks, covered only with sacks and blankets. Once living there, the demands of continuous participation in commissions, outings, meeting, demonstrations, and so on, proved to be difficult for many young women who had small children. The women themselves admitted they had great difficulties adapting to the demands of their new situation. The 'domestic' role certainly constrained and defined the activities of these women, but, the fact of having several children is not in itself problematic and may indeed be regarded as a resource:

> indeed, Arizpe (1982, p. 80) suggests that Latin American women often gain a social centrality and an emotional power through motherhood which Western women lack. However, the status trappings of motherhood are problematic for those who are unable or unwilling to conceive. Unmarried or childless women tend to be seen as 'deviant' and are often subjected to pressures from kin to validate their 'true' gender role by fostering a sister's or a cousin's child. (Chant, 1989, p. 18 quoted in Zárate, 1996, p. 229)

Furthermore, having children (and needing a home for them) was a principal reason for fighting to own land, as we can learn from Reyna's words and those of others such as Concepción or Catalina in Ixtaro: 'It is very good to struggle, because one did not know how, to fight for the children, so that they have something'. Throughout all the interviews there was a pervasive insistence that 'women defend the family'.

In this respect, Westwood and Radcliffe make the following observation about 'the motherist groups' such as the *Madres of Argentina*:

> Generally, the above mentioned, groups present themselves as "apolitical," emphasizing their familiar roles as mothers and wives, and presenting their lives as totally disrupted by their losses which they are trying to recover. By so doing the women reassert the importance of family life and their roles within this in a putatively apolitical manner. The Madres explained that "we don't defend ideologies: we defend life" (quoted in Jelin, 1990: 204). Nevertheless, they asked the men to leave their group, using the image of mothers in need of protection against the state. This, in effect, politicized the family in ways which shifted it from the realm of the "private" to that of the "public". Women involved have often been dismissed and discredited as "crazy". The power of such motherist groups also arises from their ability to draw upon the feminine imagery of Catholicism against the state, by evoking the image of a suffering mother and her sacrifice. (Westwood and Radcliffe, 1993, pp. 17–18)

Women and Power: A Contentious Issue

Gender difference, like other forms of difference, is not merely an effect of significance or language. If we accept the view that the concept of the individual or person is only intelligible with reference to a culturally and historically specific set of categories, discourses and practices, then we have to acknowledge the different ways in which the categories 'woman' and 'man', are involved in the production and reproduction of notions of personhood and agency (Moore, 1994, p. 51).

From an anthropological definition of power:

Power is invoked as an explanation of many different types of event and phenomenon, ranging from the power of a politician to that of a shaman or to a concept such as manna. Adams (1977) defines power in anthropological terms as the 'ability of a person or social unit to influence the conduct and decision-making of another through the control over energetic forms in the latter's environment (in the broadest sense of that term)'. Weber on the other hand had defined power as 'the probability that one actor within a social relationship will be in a position to carry out his will despite resistance, regardless of the basis on which this probability rests'. (Seymour-Smith, 1986, p. 230)

In dealing with women, we are dealing with gender relations, and as Joan W. Scott has put it, gender is a primary source of power relationships. In this sense, gender is an important part of the organization of equality and inequality.

The naturalization of social inequality through sex and race differences 'have been and continue to be ideologically marked as socially significant biological facts in class society as a way of naturalizing and thereby perpetuating class and, in a related way, gender inequality' (Stolcke, 1994, p. 30).

Taking into consideration that gender relationships involve power, we can add other dimensions as well. Women are not the same because of the fact of being women. Generally, people mobilize as Indians, teachers, women and peasants, students and socialists, and so on. I would argue, we own multiple social identities. This consideration has further implications. Nonetheless, the goal of gender theory is no longer to become as alike as possible to men, but to radically transform gender relationships, a political project which, in turn, requires overcoming all forms of social inequality.

In seeking to understand power and gender, I first want to explore the issue of power and values. Virginia Woolf said: 'It is obvious women's values are often different from the values created by the other sex.' In this sense, there is a 'feminine' WorldView Publications and a 'feminine way' of creating relationships with others. We need a positive valorization of the difference. I am not arguing that there is, somewhere, an essential core of something such as the 'feminine'.

Given the fact that feminine has been associated with the private, the domestic and so on, I share Escobar's critique on this point: 'As Ruth Behar has said in her study of a poor market woman from Mexico, we must resist seeing Latin American poor women in terms already fixed in much of the academic and media discourse as "beasts of burden", mothers and wives, staunch traditionalists, or heroic guerrilla fighters.' 'If I looked from a cultural perspective,' Behar continues, 'Latin American women could emerge as thinkers, cosmologists, creators of worlds' (1990, p. 225). Household survival strategies are part of this creativity. However, as Rao (1991) cautions, the focus on the household should be accompanied by an interpretive account, similar to Behar's, of what household means to women. 'Household' must be located within local and transnational paradigms of gender, people and nature. Similarly, 'survival strategies' must not be discussed at the cost of ignoring changes in the subjective dimensions of women's lives. The language of 'coping mechanisms' and 'survival strategies' although an important step in making women's agency *visible*, may still contribute to maintain the image of women as victims, as their dynamism is reduced to short-term defences of their life conditions within the economic domain (Rao, 1991). The second temptation we must resist is the conclusion that what poor women need is development (modernized *patriarchy*), which has been exactly the answer given by the international development establishment (Escobar, 1995, p. 177). Yuval-Davis adds another concern on notions of 'strategic essentialism'. While it is acknowledged that such categories involve 'arbitrary closures' for the sake of political mobilization, these categories become reified via social movements and state policy practices.

A feminist, Amorós (1987) discusses the topic of the absence of women in political life. She argues that the masculine space is the 'space of the equals', while the space of women is the space of the identical. Then, which is the difference? Men can be considered equals among themselves because they share a same tradition and have the same history. Instead, women are simply the negation of that fact: they lack tradition, history, own values, identity. Thus, – she continueswomen's is not a space of equals yet. From this perspective, women do not deserve to be included in political life because they are not equals, nor comparable to those who have always been in it. Victoria Camps criticizes Amoros' proposal: 'she does not defend encouragement of differences, on the contrary: we must fight in order to conquer that space of equals which we lack, and that provides us with entrance to the masculinized world' (Camps, 1990, p. 150).

Camps affirms, 'we won't have a space of equals if we follow the "masculine" model'. But the inequality – she goes on – is not because we lack tradition, history, culture and values. Women own history and tradition, even though they do not like it because the 'masculine model' is more attractive in every way (1990, 150–151).

Hence, this philosopher concludes, if we opt for joining the discourse of difference it would not necessarily mean leaving aside equality of rights. On the contrary, if we share the discourse of equality, it would not imply a proposal of simple imitation and repetition of the masculine. It is true that our thought and language have been made by men following their own images and necessities. It is not possible to throw it away, it is our language too. Nonetheless, it is worth to question it, to criticize it from a different history. In this last respect, defending the feminine difference is arguable.

> Our history – the history of women – has been another, different from men's history. This history has produced some attitudes and a way of being, a psychology, which do not coincide with theirs [men's]. (Camps (1990, p. 159)

Ecuador's women from *Confederación de Nacionalidades Indígenas del Ecuador* (CONAIE) sustained the following in a meeting that took place in Mexico City in December of 1998: 'Women actively participate in all aspects [of life] in Ecuador, but this participation has not been valued. We, women ourselves, first have to assume our own value.'

The anthropologist Moore (1994) expands on this point drawing on the notion of the multiple and contradictory nature of subjectivity. The individuals take up multiple subject positions. Moreover, we have to realize the important part that emotional and subconscious motivations play in the various subject positions. Fantasy, understood as ideas about the kind of person one would like to be and the sort of person one would like to be seen by others.

Harvey (1998) discusses women's rights in his book *The Chiapas Rebellion*, where although he acknowledges that the peasant movements discussed tended to restrict women's participation to 'supportive roles', there was a reappraisal of gender relations. He summarizes, as an example, the case of the colonization of parts of the forest (researched by Leyva and Ascencio, 1996), which required women to adopt nontraditional roles in the new lowland ejidos. The process described by Harvey shares many similarities with the other processes referred to above, of creation of 'communities' in its first stages:

> Due to the lack of government assistance in providing adequate infrastructure, the migrants were left to clear the forest on their own. Women carried out as much of this work as the men, as well as caring for children and the elderly. The second process Harvey describes is the incorporation of women into grassroots agricultural cooperatives and health and education programs by the diocese of San Cristóbal, a number of NGOs, and some craft cooperatives located in San Cristóbal. The third process reported is the creation of the EZLN itself. Male-dominated communities assemblies were transformed by women's demands for equal participation in the struggle. This was reflected in the Zapatistas' Revolutionary women's Law, which states that all women should have the right to a life free of sexual and domestic violence, the right to choose one's partner and number of children, and the right to political participation on an equal footing with men.
>
> (Harvey, 1998, p. 225)

In the words of Rosalva Hernández, zapatismo has brought about new hope for building a different Mexico to a wide sector of the Mexican civil society. After issuing the *Ley Revolucionaria de Mujeres* (Revolutionary Women's Law), meetings and workshops began to take place to discuss women's political participation in the resistance movement of the Chiapanec civil society. This new women's movement is the creation of a longstanding organizational and reflexive process in which both, indigenous Zapatista and non Zapatista women have been involved. Through liberation theology, indigenous and peasant organizations, productive projects, health workshops, indigenous women of the rainforest, the highlands and the sierra have questioned their historical exclusion from the political spaces of decision, and have claimed the need to build democracy beginning at the space of the family. This author shows us the differences between the mestiza advisers coming from the country's centre, who participated in different meetings on rights and culture of the indigenous woman, and indigenous women themselves. Mestiza advisers criticized neoliberalism, while indigenous women described the difficulties of their everyday life because of their economic necessities, violence and discrimination. Despite these different viewpoints, both have challenged not only the State but 'custom' as well.

Indigenous organized women have discussed constitutional changes. As an example, Hernández showed how they, during a workshop on *the rights of women in our customs and traditions* (1994, 133) questioned the dichotomy that both indigenism and to a certain extent the indigenous independent movement share: there are only two options: to remain within the traditions, or to change through modernity. Indigenous women vindicated their right to cultural difference, and asserted the right to change those traditions which oppress and exclude them.

We have to think what to do within our customs, the law should only protect and promote the customary law and traditions that women, communities and organizations have analyzed and agree they are good. Our customs must not do any damage to anyone.

(Hernández, 1994, p. 133)

In their words, customs should be reinvented more than rejected. They did not reject Mexican nationalism nor the autonomistic indigenous discourse; Chiapanec women have not only been mere victims of patriarchal ideologies that attempted to appropriate their bodies to build the mestiza nation, or to perpetuate the Indian tradition. They consider themselves simultaneously Mexican and indigenous. In this respect they are proposing to modify the features of the 'imagined communities' to which they belong.

One of the striking features of this discourse is the enhancement of the discourse on autonomy. Indigenous women are claiming economic autonomy; that is, to have equal access and control over the means of production; political autonomy in order to support their basic political rights; physical autonomy to decide about their bodies and the possibility of living without violence and, finally, sociocultural autonomy defining the right to vindicate their specific identities as indigenous women. Lastly, these women were responsible for reminding all participants in different discussions on autonomy that the indigenous people are not essentially democratic as was held by some indigenous leaders. Democracy has to be built at home first.

Harvey considers the use of ethnocentric models for analysing women in other contexts. These models, as Moore rightly asserts 'have been advanced as a universal model for the explanation of women's subordination' (Moore quoted in Zárate, 1996).

The fact that family, home and the 'domestic' are defined in juxtaposition to the 'public' sphere of work, business and politics in certain cultures, hardly constitutes an ethnographic universal as Moore shows, but it is what follows from accepting the construction at face value in terms of understanding women's participation in politics, which is the key issue here.

According to Marion Young, the bourgeois instituted a moral division of labour between reason and sentiment, identifying masculinity with reason and femininity with sentiment.

In this regard, I would support the critique that Westwood and Radcliffe have made of the public/private dichotomy. That distinction suggests that there is a simple dichotomy between 'practical' and 'strategic' gender interests which can be aligned with notions of the public and the private as spheres of interest for women; this, as I suggest, may be helpful for organizing common sense, but it does not provide a theoretical base for understanding women as political subjects and actors. I would also want to suggest that it, too, has a universalizing quality with a linear view of progress founded upon the post-Enlightenment account of movement towards a goal as part of the grand narrative of rational progress towards a better world. Such a metanarrative suggests a hierarchical relationship between practical and strategic gender interests such that women, in order to progress, must move from one to the other. In addition, by reinforcing this sense of hierarchy it ignores the feminist critique of the ideological basis of the distinction between public and private lives, and it does not take into account the understanding promoted by feminism that the 'personal is political,' the deconstruction of which has always been so central to feminist politics (Westwood and Radcliffe, 1993, pp. 19–20.

In Conger's view, the distinction between 'practical gender interests' and 'strategic gender interests' misrepresents struggles of poor women, who in fact do question or attempt to change the social (gender) order. Furthermore, it tends to separate the struggles of poor women and their social superiors in a way which is again evolutionist in tone and equally empirically questionable. Implying or, in some cases, explicitly stating that poor women's movements are based on 'practical interests' (that is on their practical needs such as income and access to food, water, housing, and health care) and that feminist (typically middle-class) movements are more often based on 'strategic interests' (that is, redefining gender roles and meanings) (Molyneux, 1986; Barrig, 1989b quoted in Conger, 1992, p. 146).

On the basis of her data on Ecuador, Conger challenges this approach in the following terms: It is often assumed that most poor women are only concerned with their daily survival and therefore do not have a strategic agenda beyond their economic welfare. Hence such women are not really challenging the sexual division of labour. Again, the plight of organized poor women is based on a notion of gender/class struggle, in which women fight on behalf of their household because of their particular reproductive roles. This type of analyses overlooks the critical contributions and challenges that organized poor women conceivably represent to the social order. Rarely, if ever, is discussion focused, for example, on how poor women negotiate power, construct collective identities, and develop critical perspectives of the world in which they live

> all elements that challenge dominant gender representations. The politicization of '"basic needs' demonstrates the ways in which such 'needs' are actually more than just the desire for bread and water. As poor women base their politics on their reproductive roles, they challenge the meaning of ascribed gender roles as well as the implication these roles have in the reproduction of society.   (Conger quoted in Zárate, 1996, p. 209)

Craske, working in the Mexican urban context, also argues for the need to find an alternative to those dichotomies:

> the use of a continuum rather than a dichotomy allows for different degrees of participation between the two extremes and the fact that many activities sit between them. Further, it indicates the unlikelihood that a woman is completely immersed in the private with no participation in the public (or that the opposite holds true for men); women have moved between the two as needs have dictated.   (1993, p. 114)

Harvey rightly recognizes that actions of women in Chiapas are, simultaneously, practical and strategic in that 'they sought solutions to material problems and, in so doing, they challenged the gendered power relations that had traditionally subordinated women to men' (Stephen 1996 quoted in Harvey, 1998, p. 225).

In this respect, indigenous women showed the validity of their own particular struggles as women within a patriarchal society.

Conclusion

Understanding women's political participation and the issue of multiculturalism necessitated understanding something about local and national ideas of gender, nation, power and agency.

The alternative discourses on feminism and multiculturalism necessitated also be critically reviewed as the cases of Michoacan, Mazahua and Chiapas indigenous women highlighted. Multiple cultural identities, and moreover multiple gender identities which challenge the idea of monoculture nation and problematize a top-down multiculturalism are shown.

In this regard, multiculturalism had to reviewed as a concept and as a public policy program. Culture as a core concept appears as implying change within the notion of multiculturalism. Instead, the concept of culture in anthropology has not a consensual meaning and not necessarily related to some type of social change. Thus, culture in itself is not a goal in itself but a means for a goal within both the discourse and practice of multiculturalism.

Besides, we must bear in mind that if we do not add the concept of inequality side by side to the concept of multiculturalism, we will have, as Rosaldo once has put it, a multiculturalists concept such as we have in Disneyland.

Closely linked is the urgency of transcending analytical dichotomies such as the public-private, which difuminate in many of the cases presented in this paper. I found interesting Conger's proposal of using a continuum as an alternative to a dichotomy emphasis. Also, I have suggested the possible use of the analytical category of essentialist strategy of motherhood. It is relevant to recognize that essentialism is a part of the realities which the social scientists analyse, because people use them to achieve their goals.

I would like also to highlight that the same situation is applied to culture as a concept, that is to say, there is an essentialist discourse on culture used by people and for those who study social realities and there is a discourse useful for 'the methodical commentary on culture' (Baumann, 1999) used by leaders and social scientists.

Even though there are options in terms of public policies as the discussions of Eriksen and Marion Young illustrated, Mexico is far away of constructing even an official-state policy on gender and multiculturalism. The issue is further complicated with the transition we experimented with the present conservative presidency, that despite ending the 71 years PRI government, now coming to the end of the *sexenio*, presidential term we realize the disastrous state of the country, no growth, no employment, high rates of violence and insecurity, with violence against women at a peak (this violence, is not only patrimony of this *panista* presidential term).

A pending issue is the redefinition of women and gender in a transnational agenda, if we take into account the growing tendency for female international migration and its paradoxical consequences. Fernández Kelly and Sassen (quoted in Chant, 2003, p. 246) argue that: 'in the age of internationalization, gender dynamics permeate the reorganization of production within and across borders'. Their conclusion is that women's subordination forms part of wider systems of domination involving class and ethnicity.

Chant affirms that the continued gender selectivity of most population movements within and from Latin America is in many respects a resounding confirmation of the fact that men's and women's lives remain marked by difference.

'In some cases, the benefits to individuals are perceived to outweigh the drawbacks, whereas in other, the process has divided families and caused major difficulties and vulnerabilities' (Chant, 2003, p. 253). As we discover in this contribution, a transnational agenda taking into account gender and family(ies) issues need to be defined.

Finally, an important element to consider, referring to indigenous rights, is the warning made by Gledhill (1997) in the sense that they should be located within a critical discussion on the social relations of property in this late capitalism. Notions of individualism shape the social movements demands on different type of rights. Thus, it is worth to think how to raise the issue of special rights, including the right to economic resources.

References

Amorós, C (1987), 'Espacio de los iguales, espacio de las idénticas. Notas sobre poder y principio de individuación' in *Arbor* (Madrid), 113–127.

Baumann, G. (2001), *El Enigma Multicultural. Un Replanteamiento de las Identidades Nacionales, Étnicas y Religiosas* (Barcelona, Buenos Aires, México: Paidós).

Brown, W. (1995), States of Injury: Power and Freedom in Late Modernity (Princeton, NJ: Princton University Press).

Brydon, L. and Chant, S. (1989), *Women in the Third World. Gender Issues in Rural and Urban Areas* (England: Edward Elgar Publishing Limited).

Busby, C. (1999),'Agency, Power and Personhood: Discourses of Gender and Violence in a Fishing Community in South India', *Critique of Anthropology*, **19**(3), 227–248.

Camps, V. (1990), *Virtudes Públicas* (Madrid: Espasa Calpe).

Carlsen, L.(1999), 'Autonomía indígena y usos y costumbres: La innovación de la tradición', *Chiapas 7* (México: Ediciones ERA), 45–70.

Cashmore, E. (1994), *Dictionary of Race and Ethnic Relations* (London and New York: Routledge).

Chant, S. (2003), 'Gender and Migration' in *Gender in Latin America*. Chant, S. with Craske, N. (New Brunswick, N.J.: Rutgers University Press), 228–253.

Chant, S. with Brydon, L. (1989), 'Introduction: Women in the Third World: An Overview', in *Women in the Third World: Gender Issues in Rural and Urban Areas*. Brydon, L. and Chant, S. (eds) (England: Edward Elgar), 1–46.

Conger, A. (1992), 'Power, Gender and Development: Popular Women's Organizations and the Politics of Needs in Ecuador', in *The Making of Social Movements in Latin America: Identity, Strategy and Democracy*. Escobar, A. and Alvarez, S.E. (eds) (Boulder, Colorado: Westview Press), 134–149.

Craske, N. (1993), 'Women's Political Participation in Colonias Populares in Guadalajara, México', in *'Viva': Women and Popular Protest in Latin America*. Radcliffe, S.A. and Westwood, S. (eds) (London and New York: Routledge), 112–135.

Eriksen, T. (1997), 'Multiculturalism, Individualism and Human Rights: Romanticism, the Enlightenment and Lessons from Mauritius', in *Human Rights,*

Culture & Context: Anthropological Perspectives. Wilson, R.A. (ed.) (London/ Sterling, Virginia: Pluto Press), 49–69.

Escobar, A. (1995), *Encountering Development: The Making and Unmaking of the Third World* (Princeton, N.J.: Princeton University Press).

Foweraker, J. (1995), *Theorizing Social Movements* (London/Boulder, Colorado: Pluto Press).

Gledhill, John (1997), 'Liberalism, Socio-Economic Rights and the Politics of Identity: From Moral Economy to Indigenous Rights', in *Human Rights, Culture & Context. Anthropological Perspectives*. Richard, A.W. (ed.) (London/Sterling, Virginia: Pluto Press), 70–110.

Goldberg, D. (1994) 'Introduction: Multicultural Conditions', in *Multiculturalism: A Critical Reader*. Goldberg, D.T. ed. (Cambridge, Mass.: Blackwell Publishers), 1–41.

Gunew, S. (1990), 'Denaturalizing Cultural Nationalisms: Multicultural Reading of Australia', in *Nation and Narration*. Bhabha, H.K. (ed.) (London/New York: Routledge), 99–120.

Gutiérrez, N. (1999), *Nationalist Myths and Ethnic Identities: Indigenous Intellectuals and the Mexican State* (Lincoln/London: University of Nebraska Press).

Gutman, A. (1994), 'Introduction', in *Multiculturalism: Examining the Politics of Recognition*. Gutman, A. (ed.) (Princeton, N.J.: Princeton University Press), 3–24.

Harvey, N. (1998), *The Chiapas Rebellion: The Struggle for Land and Democracy* (Durham/London: Duke University Press).

Hernández, A. (1994), 'Reinventing Tradition: The Revolutionary Women's Law', *Akwe: Kon A Journal of Indigenous Issues* (Summer).

Hernández, R. (1998), 'Construyendo la utopía: Esperanzas y Desafíos de las Mujeres Chiapanecas De Frente Al Siglo XXI', in *La Otra Palabra. Mujeres y violencia en Chiapas, Antes y Después De Acteal*. Hernández Castillo, R.A. (ed.) (México: CIESAS-COLEM-CIAM), 125–142.

Honing, B. (1999), 'My Culture Made Me Do It', in *Is Multiculturalism Bad for Women?* Cohen, J., Howard, M. and Nussbaum, M.C. (eds) (Princeton, N.J.: Princeton University Press), 35–40.

Kymlicka, W. (1999), 'Liberal Complacencies', in *Is Multiculturalism Bad for Women?* Cohen, J., Howard, M. and Nussbaum, M.C. (eds.) (Princeton, N.J.: Princeton University Press), 31–34.

Kymlicka, W. (2001), *Politics in the Vernacular. Nationalism, Multiculturalism and Citizenship* (Oxford: Oxford University Press).

Lamas, M. (2002), *Cuerpo: Diferencia Sexual y Género* (México: Taurus).

Logan, K. (1990), 'Women's Participation in Urban Protest', in *Popular Movements and Political Change in Mexico*. Foweraker, J. and Craig, A.L. (eds) (Boulder/ London: Lynne Rienner Publishers), 150–159.

Leyva, X. and Ascencio, G. (1996), *Lacandonia al filo del agua* (México: FCE).

Lomnitz, C. (1992), *Exits from the Labyrinth: Culture and Ideology in the Mexican National Space* (Berkeley/Los Angeles/Oxford: University of California Press).

López Bárcenas, F.(1998), 'Constitución y derechos indígenas en Oaxaca?', *Cuadernos Agrarios*, **16**, 128–146.

Moore, H. (1988), *Feminism and Anthropology* (Cambridge: Polity Press).

Moore, H. (1994), *A Passion for Difference* (Cambridge: Polity Press).

Moore, H. (1999), 'Whatever Happened to Women and Men? Gender and Other Crises in Anthropology', in *Anthropological Theory Today*, Moore, H.(ed.) (Cambridge, Oxford, Malden: Polity Press).

Mummert, G. (1994) 'Cambio sociocultural y género: Internalizando y cuestionando. Relaciones conyugales e intergeneracionales'. Paper Presented in VII Mesa de Trabajo, Centro de Estudios Antropológicos, *La Dinámica cultrual De Cambio Social: Procesos Locales En Michoacán, 1988–1993* (México: Zamora, Centro de Estudios Antropológicos De El Colegio De Michoacán).

Nash, J. (2001) *The Quest for Autonomy in an Age of Globalization* (New York/London: Routledge).

Oehmichen, C. (2000) 'Relaciones de Etnia y Género: Una Aproximación a la multidimensionalidad De Los Procesos identitarios' in *Alteridades 19*. Zárate, M. (ed.) (México: Departamento de Antropología-UAM-Iztapalapa), 89–98.

Pollit, K. (1999), 'Whose Culture', in *Is Multiculturalism Bad for Women?* Cohen, J., Howard, M. and Nussbaum, M.C. (eds.) (Princeton, N.J.: Princeton University Press), 27–30.

Rao, B. (1991) 'Dominant Constructions of Women and Nature' in *Social Sciences Literature* (Santa Cruz:CES/CNS) Pamphlet 2.

Rouse, R. (1995), 'Questions of Identity: Personhood and Collectivity in Transnational Migration to the United States', *Critique of Anthropology*, **15**(4), 351–380.

Scott, J. (1986), 'Gender: A Useful Category of Historical Analysis', *American Historical Review*, **91**, 1053–1075.

Seymour-Smith, C. (1986), *Macmillan Dictionary of Anthropology* (London/Basingstoke: Macmillan).

Stephen, L. (1991), *Zapotec Women* (Austin: University of Texas Press).

Stolcke, V. (1994), 'Is Sex to Gender as Race is to Ethnicity?', in *Gendered Anthropology*. Del Valle, T. (ed.) (London/New York: Routledge), 17–37.

Taylor, C. (1994), 'The Politics of Recognition', in *Multiculturalism. Examining the Politics of Recognition*. Gutman, A. (ed.) (Princeton, N.J.: Princeton University Press), 25–73.

Westwood, S. and Radcliffe, S.A. (1993), 'Gender, Racism and the Politics of Identities in Latin America', in *'Viva': Women and Popular Protest in Latin America*. Radcliffe, S.A. and Westwood, S. (eds) (London/New York: Routledge), 1–29.

Young, M. (1998), 'Polity and Group Difference: A Critique of the Ideal of Universal Citizenship', in *The Citizenship Debates. A Reader*. Shafir, G. (ed.) (Minneapolis/London: University of Minnesota Press), 263–290.

Yuval-Davis, N. and Floya, A. (eds.) (1989), *Woman, Nation,State* (London: Macmillan).

Yuval-Davis, N. 'Gender and Nation', in *Ethnic and Racial Studies* **16**(4), 621–32.

Yuval-Davis, N. (1997), 'Ethnicity, Gender Relations and Multiculturalism', in *Debating Cultural Hybridity. Multi-cultural Identities and the Politics of Anti-Racism*. Werbner, N. and Modood, T. (eds) (London/New Jersey: Zed Books), 193–208.

Zárate, M. (1996) 'The Creation of Community and Identity in a Rural Social Movement: The Union of Comuneros "Emiliano Zapata" of Michoacán. México'. PhD thesis in Anthropology,. University College London.

Zárate, M. (1998) *En Busca de la Comunidad* (México: UAM-I-El Colegio de Michoacán).

Chapter 9

Indigenous Women, Transnationality and Re/narrativized Social Memory[1]

María Eugenia Choque and Guillermo Delgado-P.

'Qhari sapa ma' atinmanchu.'
(Could it be that males on their own are capable?)
(Andean Oral History Workshop, 1990, p. 6)

Introduction

Indigenous women *re/narrativize* oral 'traditions' as they struggle to attain political agency. Both, in fast-changing traditional rural as well as densely inhabited cities of the Americas, indigenous women restore narratives seeking to exercise their rights in the domestic and public spheres. According to them, with the arrival of Western forms of social organization, indigenous women suffered systematic exclusion and ignominy as human beings. Whereas non-Western traditions of social organization allowed indigenous women to exercise different forms of direct and indirect political power in the past, such agency was subverted by the positioning of colonial patriarchy then, and later. Newly *re/narrativized* social memory as oral 'tradition' assist indigenous women to achieve and practice own political authority undermined by colonialism.

In her essay 'Cartographies of Struggle' Chandra Talpade Mohanty clearly states,

> Unlike the history of Western (white, middle-class) feminisms, which has been explored in great detail over the last few decades, histories of third world women's engagement with feminism are in short supply. There is a large body of work on 'women in developing countries,' but this does not necessarily engage feminist questions. There is now a substantial corpus of scholarship among women in liberation movements, or on the role and status of women in individual cultures. However, this scholarship does not necessarily engage questions of feminist historiography. (1991, p. 4)

In this chapter, we shall consider indigenous Peoples (hereafter 'IPs') transnational political actors. Following Mohanty's criticism and focusing on 'ethnic' feminisms

---

1   The chapter is based on interviews conducted by the collective of SAIIC that published Abya *Yala News*. Delgado, along with Nilo Cayuqueo, Gina Pacaldo, Xihuanel Huerta and Wara Alderete, was an active board member, translator and contributing editor. Unfortunately, SAIIC and Journal Abya Yala had folded by 1998 in Oakland, California.

that are invigorating indigenous women's (hereafter 'IW') leadership roles, reflections on current debates waged by women within the indigenous movement of the Americas will be offered. While the theoretical debate on feminism brought up by Mohante aims at understanding historicized social agency and the public space, in recent cases of IW public participation in social movements, ethnicity, gender and sex continue to prompt a rich discussion on the public sphere, the rights of women and feminism itself. In the Andean area, IW overwhelming public presence and agency within the social movements propelled the ousting of two Bolivian governments in 2003 and 2005 (Delgado-P., 2005).

The aim of this essay is to sketch a chronicle based on the political repositioning of IW as we enter a new millennium. IW wage multifaceted battles on private/public, rural/urban, national, and transnational g/local fronts. With the introduction of feminist theory, sexuality, gender, and ethnicity, class theory that permeated dominant Latin America's historiography throughout the twentieth century is further problematized. It is this intersection that continues to 'decentre' and disrupt homogenizing winds prompted by globalization and neo-liberalism in the Americas. Race theory and sexuality/gender analyses locate IW at the very center of persistent discriminatory practices from the part of the nation-state and the society at large. This legacy of exclusion of IPs has deepened at the outset of the twenty-first century global capitalism. Specifically, neo-liberalism has directly contributed to accrue social tensions by shrinking the state's responsibility, affecting marginalized sectors in the Americas as they continue to grapple with the issue of belonging to the nation. The article is subdivided into seven parts, each contextualizing different contesting angles of IW struggles.

Some Historical References

The Quincentennial trans-indigenous mobilization triggered profound changes in the leadership of indigenous social movements that achieved transnational visibility after the unexpected breakdown of the East-West divide in 1989. The indigenous movements of the Americas called for a self-reflexive and revisionist dis/centering of history, stressing the need for political sovereignty, local autonomy and identity since the 1960s. Several of these entered the political arena rejecting the vertical control established, or dominated, by nation-state 'indigenista' institutes and bureaus, political parties, dictatorships, and churches of never ending denominations. Through patronizing and party-sponsored co-optative strategies, state institutions manipulated the emergence of an autonomous indigenous voice, drowning early struggles for cultural sovereignty all over the Americas. This crisis, deepened by the introduction of neo-liberalism, was accompanied by nominal multi-culturalism, forwarding a mixed message for indigenous demands on autonomy. Modern nation-states have been unable to further implement the process of citizenship and would not grant, nor implement, IPs's full rights. In the 1980s and 1990s, contestant indigenous movements took an autonomous stand under the direction of younger leaderships rejecting previous 'caciquista' and prebendal practices, proposing to decolonize politics and to re-invent the state.

The IPs hemispheric campaign to challenge Spain's call for a 'celebration' of the 500 years, changing it to 'commemoration', galvanized IPs mobilizations throughout the Americas in 1992. Indigenous historical revisionism challenged an often triumphal, apologetic yet dominant narrative of the Conquest. Such revisionism re-inscribed IPs' *decolonizing* proposals, native languages and texts, and deconstructed previous colonial *grand récits*. This process provided a new kind of historicism based on IPs multilingual narrative. Above all, it demanded recognition of *collective* human rights, dignity and sovereignty (RedBird, 1995, pp. 121–142).

Despite indigenous Peoples' vastly dissimilar linguistic traditions (yet, belonging to traceable common phylum), new transnational alliances forged *indigeneity*, consolidating an energetic and complex IPs social movement in the Americas. IPs put forth a coherent counter-hegemonic project as they continue to experience the persistent wrath of colonialism's remnants expressed via indefatigable state policies or global capitalism. Particular to the contesting indigenous transnational approach is the assertive agency and militancy of politicized IW leaders who, taking the public space after the 1990s, regained political influence by challenging male leaderships in their communities. They retrieved and re/interpreted their own 'ancient' native mythologies. The re-narrativization of such 'collective mythologies' invested IW with authority, granting them public power and providing them a space in the struggle against persistent colonial behaviours that drown their contestant voices. This change encouraged the active presence of IW as leaders not clearly recognized by earlier forms of national or regional indigenous movements, nor by non-indigenous political institutions (Rivera Zea, 1999; Canaviri Mallku, 2000, Maldonado and Artía, 2004, Potiguara, 2006, Muñoz Ramírez, 2006).

Latin America's non-indigenous, mostly urban leftist-feminism often dismissed pressures from the part of organized IW. Their 'gender/ethnic' positionality made them a faceless 'poor class' linkable to party politicking. In Norma Chinchilla's comprehensive article on women's movements, mostly in Central America, there is a brief passage informing us that: 'Indian women conducted a workshop comparing and contrasting Indian and *mestiza* identities and relations' (Chinchilla 1993, p. 17). While 3 years earlier, an article written by Helen Safa makes no specific mention of IW at all, presumably clustered under the notion of 'poor women, who focus their demands on the state in their struggle for basic survival and against repression' (Safa 1990, p. 354). We are afraid that Geraldine Lievesley repeats this approach in her recent work on *Democracy in Latin America* (1999, pp. 101–30). We should add here that an element of 'invisibility' has historically accompanied the Indian, and IW have not been an exception.

Researchers of social movements have moved beyond the generic 'Indian' or 'Indigenous' and have identified specific indigenous movements such as the Mayas, the Quichua, the Mapuche, the Aymara, and so on only as we enter this first decade of the twenty-first century. And, in this context the social, economic and political life of Andean women, similar to other indigenous peoples in other parts of the Americas, constitute an absent history from official history. Refusing to be represented, IW proceeded to open 'alterNative' paths, forwarding new participatory proposals that re-define and enhance the issue of women as leaders within indigenous social movements today.

According to Maori intellectual Linda Tuhiwai Smith 'The problems of "voice" and "visibility", "silence and invisibility" became important concerns at a concrete level as women began to attend international conferences and attempted to develop international policies related to women's rights, population control, development and justice' (1999, p. 166). In the process of political re-composition, the roads newly opened by IW self-criticize a stagnant cultural practice that has presumably placed IW to subordinately following their men. Likewise, rather than allocating emphasis on the infamous *social class triangle* of exclusion, IW continue to stress gender and ethnicity as ways of contesting one-directional nation-state assimilative models or other non-indigenous social forces, such as political parties that continue to ignore IW's culture-specific demands. In a way, following anthropologist Scott (1998, pp. 11–52), IW have kept 'hidden transcripts' of resistance for a long time, and their recent public militancy can be interpreted as challenging hegemonic forces. 'Hidden transcripts' have been, precisely, retrieved by younger generations of IW who searched for wisdom from their elders. The Aymara of the Andean region of Bolivia gathered around the Oral History Andean Workshop,[2] for example, and were clear about the need to retrieve valuable teachings so as to trigger the debate on IW. The Quechua message '*Qhari sapa ma' atinmanchu*' ('Could males on their own are capable?' (¿acaso los hombres van a poder solos?) is an example of how IW frame their search for power (THOA, 1990, p. 6).

Recent debates concerning gender and ethno-genesis in Americas' indigenous movements have strengthened IW, encouraging new generations to find their voice within the multiple struggles sustained by IPs. Indigenous movements in Latin America largely lead by indigenous men, have begun to acknowledge and encourage new alliances supporting women's proposals by working to implement them as part of a larger strategy that can no longer be dismissive of IW's platforms since the 1990s. The nature of IW's struggles is diverse and entails multiple sites. They include challenges to male-only indigenous leaderships by challenging (or reinventing) 'tradition', and claiming: territorial sovereignty, disputes over autonomy, collective human rights, control over natural resources, health and body, formal education, housing, linguistic rights, full elimination of racial discrimination, the right to practise native religions, indigenous property rights and, naturally, IW rights that parallel each and every one of these demands.

Searching for commonalities, non-indigenous women influenced by early feminism implemented a new sense of agency that, in the end, triumphed over dictatorships and military patriarchies during the hardest moments of the 'internal security wars' led by Latin American dictatorships during the 1960s–1970s. Prominent roles played by non-indigenous intellectuals during these years, timely documented by Ximena Bunster (1986) and Gloria Ardaya (1986), prompted Latin

---

2   The ideas developed in this essay are based on several dialogues between the authors conducted during the Winter and Spring quarters of 1999 when María Eugenia Choque, an Aymara activist and historian, was a Rockefeller Grantee at the Native American Studies Department, University of California, Davis. We would like to thank: Norma Klahn, Sonia Alvarez, Mónica X. Delgado, Marcia Stephenson, and Renya Ramírez who offered suggestions and conceptual criticism. Maylei Blackwell shared with us the work of activist Nellys Palomo. Student Angelica Piz served as researcher assistant on this project.

American civil society to gain a gender perspective. At the height of militarization and dictatorship violence in Latin America in the late 1960s, 1970s and early 1980s mostly urban women, entered the 'personal is political' realm (Navarro, 1989, p. 241). Early awareness of the militant indigenous public awakening, during the 1960s, however, was concealed. It took the 'lost decade' of the 1980s to recognize the presence of earlier forms of the indigenous movements inspired by the notion of ethno-autonomy since: 'Culture is the generative base for adapting to and redefining basic relations in production and reproduction' (Nash, 1986, p. 15). But culture: 'Is located neither in texts, nor as the outcome of its production, nor only in the cultural resources, appropriations, and innovations of lived everyday worlds, but in different forms of sense making, within various settings, in societies incessantly marked by change and conflict. Culture is neither institutions nor genres nor behavior but complex interactions between all of these' (Bhabha, 1994).

Today, among other implemented strategies, we could affirm that organized IW are re-searching their own cultures and *re-narrativizing* traditions, seeking to strengthen their positions of leadership, complementing them with strategies introduced by urban middle class Latin American feminists decades ago. Yet, as Mohanty demonstrates, 'While questions of identity are crucially important, they can never be reduced to automatic self-referential, individualist ideas of the political (or feminist) subject' (1991, p. 33). Re-narrativizing induced IW to look at their *oral histories*, their 'hidden transcripts' and to foreground them. Feminist anthropologists provided strong evidences regarding IW political assertiveness. In several areas of the indigenous world, notions of *matrilocality* have presumably helped IW's movements in their retrieval of traditions and oral histories that galvanize agency.

Within the mode of production debates of the époque, the 1974 ethnography entitled *Women of the Forest* stresses that: 'women's work among the Mundurucú is largely directed and initiated by women, and the men do not intrude upon their area of responsibility and authority' (Murphy and Murphy, 1974, p. 211). These authors go on to describe,

> ...that female status is generally higher in matrilineal societies than in those having patrilineal descent. This pattern is so, however, not as a matter of female dominance, which somehow perpetuates itself in matrilineal descent, but as a result of the fact that many matrilineal societies are also matrilocal. Descent through females may indeed have some effect upon the woman's public prestige, but far more critical is its association with a residence rule that holds together a core of related women. The Mundurucú are a remarkable illustration of this as they have one of the very few societies that combines patrilineality with matrilocality.
>
> (Ibid., p. 216)

Bringing Native American women writers' perspectives from the North and other areas such as the Pacific Islands, help articulate similar trends occurring among IW in the rest of the Americas, proposing, in this way, a productive circulation of the struggle. Paula Gunn Allen, advocating an indigenous humanism, has stated, 'American Indians are not merely doomed victims of western imperialism or progress; they are also the carriers of the dream that most activist movements in the Americas claim to be seeking. The major difference between most activist movements and tribal societies is that millennia American-Indians have based their social systems, however diverse, on ritual, spirit-centered, woman-focused world views' (1986, p. 2). Current constraints, however, such as prioritizing encompassing territorial struggles within the indigenous movement led mostly by men, tend to defer IW's agendas. The inspiration rooted in indigenous cosmologies of equality (based on its *gynocratic* tradition) has opened paths for women to question the constraining patriarchal authority within such movements, as well as in society in general. Their demands are about regaining equal rights for IW in all aspects of public and private life.

Another contribution regarding this issue is offered by Justice Coordinator of the Native Women's Association of Canada, Sharon Donna McIvor in her statement,

> In many aboriginal languages, there is no distinguishing between 'he' and 'she'. Both are seen as being the same (to the extend that they are equal)...The inherent right brings forward the participatory rights of Aboriginal women in traditional matriarchies, and indeed brings forward matriarchal governments. Women's right to participate politically, socially and militarily is part of the custom and tradition brought forward within the existing right to Aboriginal self-government. This balance between men and women to participate in government-making is inherent and brought forward in time... This includes restoring the gender relations that existed between First Nations men and women since time immemorial. Restoring this balance will require throwing aside women's obedience and men's sexual powers over women, getting rid of patriarchy and bringing harmony back into human relations in the home and the community.   (1995, p. 284)

Referring to the past, seen as foundational and now inspirational in its re-narrativization, Paola Gunn Allen asserts,

> The colonizers saw (and rightly) that as long as women held unquestioned power of such magnitude, attempts at total conquest of the continents were bound to fail. In the centuries since the first attempts at colonization in the early 1500s, the invaders have exerted every effort to remove Indian women from every position of authority, to obliterate all records pertaining to gynocratic social systems, and to ensure that no American and few American Indians would remember that *gynocracy* was the primary social order of Indian America prior to 1800.
> (1986, p. 3, italics ours)

The specific references by native women writers have IW always clearly and persistently assertive, direct in their actions, and relentless in pressing for their rights. Within indigenous communities, Scott's notion of 'the hidden transcript' to sustain resistance deals with retrieving the past, or re-narrativizing it accordingly, as ways of reinforcing power IW have. These 'hidden transcripts' can be interpreted as viable strategy of resistance utilized by IW to contest colonial heritages, or rather to de-colonize practices and imaginaries that bestowed indigenous People with notions of Western power, authority, and privilege which often led them to establish dependent linkages within social structures (Delgado-P. 1994, p. 189; Delagado-P. 2003, pp. 71–91).

Indigenous Women: Retrieving 'Hidden Transcripts'

Archival research – in the Andean context – demonstrates that there was active female agency in '*cacical*' movements during 1920s. IW exercised power as equal as *caciques* who, in searching for legitimate recognition from the part of the Bolivian State, protected themselves by including Mama Mallkus or Mama Kuraka. Legitimacy was granted by Creole society on March 4, 1929 in La Paz, as priest Tomás de Los Lagos Molina, of the Parish of San Pedro, celebrated mass welcoming such leaders into office. This process in which women are present to exercise power is erased in the *machista* ideology of Bolivian 'escribientes' (county registers) who often deleted women from official records, erasing IW's effective power.

In another case, on May 18, 1927, 14,000 IW from seven Colombian states drafted and published a document in the Quintin Lame indigenous movement's newspaper of which they were the backbone. The document constitutes probably the earliest printed and circulated IW's avowal. It begins by proclaiming:

> It is time that the daughters of the countryside and abandoned forests raise the cry for social justice, as 435 years passed by, an instant for the Creator of the Universe...Today, women with our courage and strength will cry for protection and justice, as we have always done, because we have lost our voice and our rights, but not our faith. This faith helps us poor women who, beneath sun and rain, facing hunger and thirst, help Indigenous men in our roles as wives, sisters, daughters, and mothers to cultivate the lands... Before the Indigenous peoples of Colombia, we shall cry for death to the elections and that we Indigenous women completely separate Indigenous men from those two established parties which have falsely betrayed us. In our position as wives, girlfriends, mothers, sisters, daughters, and so on, we will allow no one to vote, because the representatives and senators that go to Congress up until now have left Indigenous legislation in obscurity...We direct ourselves to all female religious societies... to the women directors of secondary schools and universities who are aware of injustices and know that today the Indigenous female sex in Colombia has raised its voice to actively defend its material and moral property which has been snatched away from our men, and, so as not to exclude by error, we direct ourselves to all feminine groups in the land, and let them tell us whether or not this is right.[3]

The document above reveals that roads have been opened by women ever since. Not only this, but with recent processes of ethno-genesis and revisionism, the retrieval of IW's *her* stories in writing are newly 'emploting' historical accounts which rendered them invisible. The consistent questioning of nationalism and 'assimilative' policies imposed by the nation-state on indigenous Peoples paralleled the crisis of national-revolutionary models in Latin America. In the North, persistent results of the 1960s Civil Rights movements reinforced the inscribing of indigenous intellectual production to the English language cultural 'canon', along contributions of other 'minority' intellectuals. In Latin America, and during similar periods, indigenous movements, lead mostly by indigenous men, suffered harsh rebuttals from the part of entrenched 1960s authoritarian regimes. Historically speaking, the term 'national security' belongs to the height of the Cold War, in which civilian populations became

---

3   Excerpts from a longer document, translated by Peoples Translation Service, Berkeley, 1975 (mimeo).

internal enemies and targets of military regimes in Latin America; surveillance on indigenous peoples was not an exception, often they were main targets (Zárate Vidal and Rosemberg Seifer, 1989, pp. 27–49).

The legal structure of 1990s neo-liberal democracies collide over specific IPs claims such as the use and ownership of land, demarcation of territories, and/or recognition of recent forms of autonomy within nation-states. Such demands focus on the weakly and nominally granted, much less implemented, *citizenship* rights for indigenous peoples, considered assimilative rather than respectful of difference, despite claims of multi-culturalism. As these demands are constantly negotiated, visible weariness from the part of entrenched male leadership is notable. The emergence of new generations of younger IW leaders with renewed vision, several of which constitute and lead the current internationalized IW's movement, should be considered a strategic, healthy and welcomed new development at the beginning of a new millennium.

Today, gains are visible at a more sophisticated level of coordination and organization of IPs. Researchers and interpreters of such movements have not hesitated to label them a matter of 'national security' as IPs are, indeed, 'defiant again'. As IPs assert themselves against neo-liberal administrations and transnational corporations today, states reduced in the process of economic globalization intend, once more, to resort on repressive strategies to discourage indigenous claims over territories (natural resources), autonomies, demands for sovereignty or human rights. Needless to say, despite some progress, evident in recent legislation (ILO Art. 169) in favour of IPs, daily confrontations of IPs against governments, the military, the judiciary, transnational corporations, and DNA bioprospectors escalate unceasingly. Against this background of a multifaceted, insistent criminalization of indigenous social movements, IW speak up with authority, warning once more against the devastating effect of a violent wave that has been identified as the 'second Conquest' or 'biocolonialism'.

Decentralized Coordination: Indigenous Women Restore Power

As we accompany the mobilization of the indigenous movements of the Americas, gains as well as setbacks constitute part of this socio-political process. Like the previously quoted 1927 text, signed in mass by IW in Colombia – an example of IW agency indicating their historical assertiveness – the current status of indigenous movements seems to privilege a *gynocratic* perspective. Assertive IW are securing open spaces and voicing an alleged tradition where there is an equal place for women to actively and publicly participate. Silvia Rivera Cusicanqui, in her article 'Indigenous Women and Community Resistance' provides sharp treatment on the relationship between oral history, memory and IWs' political agency (1990, 1995).

The debates held over the meaning of feminism based upon contributions by Latin American, European, and US feminist scholars and activists, reached *la crème* of new leaderships of IW. Several rejected it at first and, indeed, were challenged by (white) feminist tenets that incensed IW thinking, shaping 'ethnic feminisms' inspired by indigenous cultures. For many years, IW considered feminism to be another imported, outside contribution, but it challenged them to search for and articulate their own agency, inspired by the need to work on full political autonomy of the indigenous movement, and to restore their active place within it. Dialogue and negotiation promoted the rethinking of an indigenous sense of 'gender complementarity' as indigenous men and women experience forms of exclusion from non-indigenous societies.

The notion of 'gender complementarity' was inspired by an ancient mythology in which women as *numena* played powerful roles. It managed to survive through the oral tradition, which is often thought as *tabula rasa*, but, indeed, oral history is another form through which knowledge is passed on from generation to generation, a method largely privileged in alter-writing cultures (textiles, plants, feathers) of which IPs continue to be an example. Women's participation shows that re-narratizing mythologies legitimize the exercise of political power. Calixta Gabriel, a Kaqchiquel Maya inspired in the teaching of the Popul Vuh regarding women's equality recalls:

> When human beings were created originally, there were four men and four women. Two were the rising suns, two were the sunsets, two were the living air spirits and two were the living water spirits. At no point in our own history were we told that women were lesser beings.
>
> When Ixmakanek took the corn, Ixmakanek formed humans and that is why we are children of the corn... corn is the spirit of life and it represents the nine months of pregnancy. In no instance is there reference to woman being created from man.
>
> (SAIIC, 1992)

The conceptual difference between the *feminine* and the *feminist* trickled down from urban areas to the personal experience of IW. However, IW were rarely seen participating in non-indigenous women's debates that tended to reproduce class and racial tensions, matronage, and manipulation of the indigenous voice from the part of non-indigenous women throughout the 1990s. Assertive IW, both young as well as traditional female elder leaders who exercise the *power to* organize and the *power over* out-of-balance situations in their own communities, came to understand the logics of Euro-American and Latin American feminisms. IW continued to search for 'gender parity' situations that granted them control over the exercise of women's rights within the indigenous communities, evident at home, some say, but often not publicly. Non-Indigenous women have criticized the overemphasis of a gender parity utopia IW privilege, as an unreachable ideal. Although multiple attacks against indigenous peoples have worked to unify them in their multi-layered struggles (of which women's liberation is one), Marcela Lagarde points out that there is a need to pay close attention to the process itself. In reference to women and the 1994 Zapatista Rebellion, she writes:

> As in all processes of women's emancipation in the world, in the conflict of the Chiapas insurrection and in Mexican gender democracy, it is necessary to eliminate the expropriation of women's bodies, gender division and specialization, the relation of dominion of men over women and engendered poverty.
>
> (1996, p. 95)

As indigenous peoples become recognized social actors in the global village, there are clear divisions between IW who remain or retain community affiliations in the

'True Land' (a term coined by Lakota artist Diane Way), and those dis/placed due to multiple reasons, now inhabiting cities. This is a reality the outside world needs to understand: not all indigenous peoples inhabit own territories and not all of them are the same. Indigenous nations have a non-synchronic experience with non-indigenous society, one of the reasons we still think that the Conquest continues to be carried out, a 'second conquest.' Today, several indigenous people live in urban areas and, naturally, others continue to be historically rooted for extensive periods of time (the Mapuche, the Aymara, the Quechua, the Maya, the Lakota, the Hopi, the Maori).

Divisions are created among them, mediated by foreign institutions such as the nation-state, the military, churches, NGOs (Non-governmental organizations) or other aid agencies. In the most persistently inhabited rural communities IW continue to follow cultural rules, several of which are not necessarily favourable to women, where women's rights, or women's agency, need to be legitimized by female elders, some continued to value a sense of communality inspired by re-narrativized mythologies, a site where gender solidarity is enacted. The Darien Kuna activist Gloridalia González, offering a clear testimony of gender awareness and economic marginality, explains:

> Women took care of seeds, watered and tended plants, and harvested them. They were the ones who have maintained our culture. Women have been responsible for household income, for culture, handicrafts, plant knowledge, and family unity within Kuna communities. While recognizing women's participation in resistance and survival, we see that we remain marginalized and discriminated against, both outside as well as within our own culture. (SAIIC, 1992)

IW living in cities enter several daily transactions in which economic survival, within traditional open markets, has granted them control over resources and more responsibility attributed to women-led households of indigenous origin. In this process, IW become economically independent, a sign of assertiveness, but as their economic status increases (consumerism) they may tend to reproduce exploitative relations, thus separating themselves from participating in indigenous movements altogether. The case of domestic workers of indigenous origin constitutes the other side of this coin. As they seek waged employment in urban households they are exposed to systematic abuse, both economically as well as sexually. Needless to say, poverty within an urban context has doubled for indigenous cohorts as seen in the cases of Mexico City and Colombia, Perú, Bolivia, Guatemala, where considerable numbers of indigenous peoples live below the poverty line. As is the case of women living in poverty, pressures increase regarding IW.

Although poverty has had a dominant impact on the lives of IW, as has been the case of indigenous men interacting with diverse forms of capitalist articulations, small percentages of IW surpassing such difficulties, entered Latin American universities in the 1990s. Such young leadership forged the organizing of politicized IW's groups. These changes affected the world of foreign aid assistance to developing countries, and gave way to the creation of NGOs. Several of these new female indigenous leaders have learned to co-work with women-led NGOs, answering directly to negotiated women's agendas. Although still mediated by economic control, the know-how of proposal writings, vertical relations established by non-indigenous urban women, as well as newly formed indigenous professional women tend to re-establish rural indigenous *clientelism*. As indigenous leaderships deal with governments, they continuously run into the dangerous possibility of being co-opted. Old patronage systems, political *clientelism* and factionalism remain strong challenges to the notion of the autonomy of indigenous movements. IW's movements in particular face the challenge, for the first time, of changing entrenched systems that do not seem to offer alternatives to IPs platforms.

In the remote countryside, where traditionalism does not allow IW to openly challenge rigid divisions of labour arrangements, one could say that indigenous movements have failed altogether, or have only been partially successful at addressing IW's rights. For example, at the First Meeting of Native and Colonist Women (where Luzmila Chirisente Mahuanca was elected at Satipo in Amazonia, Peru), did Ashaninka, Nomatsiguengas and Campa women organized themselves to analyse their situation. Likewise, organized IW have attracted international aid in order to carry out their own projects since the early 1990s. Some of these projects deal with creating a visible space for women to discuss their rights as women, and to exercise them, as has been the case of Clelia Mezua, President of the Ngobe (a.k.a. Emberá) General Congress, Panama. Some of these women's spaces previously touched on ignored issues such as abortion, rape, or domestic violence, as these issues were considered too personal or familial. But as they become gender conscious, IW move faster from the private to the public, speaking up, becoming stronger and critical of oppressive situations. Silvia Rivera Cusicanqui believes that feminism and '*Indianism*' (not to be confused with anachronic forms of *indigenismo* – state sponsored ideology GD-P.) can produce an edifying reflection establishing a dialogue from which shared utopia can emerge (1995, 25).

International Politics

The earliest programs of legal literacy during the late 1970s, triggered by the 1975 UN Women's Conference in Mexico City and followed with the July 1985 Nairobi Conference – part of the non-governmental activities connected with the UN Decade for Women – transformed themselves to promote legal instruments to advance human rights for women and further educational programs. Although this seems like a positive advance for IW, note that a very small number of women identified themselves as 'Native' or 'Indigenous' in the first meetings of Mexico City and Nairobi, nor was there an IW's Rights agenda. Despite the isolated, non-organized presence of Latin American IW, several noticed that other women delegates presented themselves *qua* ethnic feminists rather than using class ascription. The rough confrontation between Israeli and Palestinian women during the Nairobi conference became an eye opener for several IW of Latin America attending the non-governmental women's conference as issues pertaining gender, nationalisms, language, territory and ethnicity cropped up. A different confrontation between Domitila Barrios de Chungara, a Bolivian mining camp leader, and Betty Friedan marked a classic watershed 'classic' as in class.

Twenty years later, a delegation of IW forced its way to the Beijing conference (4–15 September 1995) that, initially, rejected their presence. Such a delegation attended the parallel NGOs conference and was not heard at all by the official UN Women's Conference itself, which learned about IW denouncing their exclusion. The following statement, written by an indigenous collective circulated by *Abya Yala News*, illustrates the case:

> From the beginning there was a limited flow of information between Indigenous and non-Indigenous women. The former had little access to contact information, and financial resources...The location of the conference made it hard for IW to attend. Only 30 IW arrived, an abysmal number (considering the number of Indigenous nations in the Americas)... After a preparatory continental meeting of IW in Ecuador (July 31–Aug 4, 1995) attended by about 150 women from 24 Indigenous nationalities, a final document entitled "The Declaration of Indigenous Women in Beijing" forwarded the following proposals and demands:
>
> 1. Recognize and respect our right to self-determination
> 2. Recognize and respect our right to our territories and development, education, and health;
> 3. Stop human rights violations and all forms of violence against indigenous women;
> 4. Recognize and respect our cultural and intellectual inheritance and our right to control the biological diversity in our territories;
> 5. Assure the political participation of indigenous women and amplify their access to resources. (*AbyaYala News*, 1996, p. 13)

According to Wara Alderete, an indigenous Calchaki activist from Northern Argentina who attended the Beijing Conference, and helped co-organize the Ecuador IW preparatory meeting, 'Indigenous women's lack of participation was a significant weakness in Beijing. We need to devise new strategies so that our vision can become an integral component of the broader women's movement, a presence to be recognized especially during watershed encounters such as Beijing' (personal communication).

The next step for IW has been that of learning the know-how in the world of NGOs, and to become active members in their own indigenous movements. Carmen Gualán, a Quichua (Ecuador) emphasizes the idea of full participation of IW. She writes, 'As women and as communities we want to participate in Congress, where we can express and shape what we want and feel.' Marcela Lagarde reflecting on Mexico agrees:

> Ramona, Susana, Ana María, Silvia and their guerrilla companions want the same human rights specific to their gender. But to materialize such society's demands under patriarchal conditions, means to revolutionize the whole of society and State, to transform women as founding co-participants of history in daily life... this requires us to modify the nation. (1998, p. 94)

If means of communication are successfully implemented by IW in urban areas, such as the video project lead by Carmen Ruíz with urban Aymara women (Bolivia), as well as the recent IW Chiapas video experience, in the country-side, some continue to struggle for native language programming and broadcasting. IW in rural areas tend to be highly illiterate in dominant languages, which makes it hard for them to enter into equal relations of a political nature with non-indigenous peasants who may continue to take advantage of their situation.

In 1993, the Center for Education and Communication of Puno (Peru) invited for the first time, Aymara women from community radio stations, who worked to produce radio programs for and by women dealing with the problems faced by IW everywhere. Some of the issues they discussed were domestic violence, racial discrimination, and economic marginalization. Rosa Palomino who acted as an organizer at the end of the session noted, 'The radio programs provide a system of mutual support, a form of development. If we do not include women, we will not develop.' These programs for the first time addressed themes in native languages closely related to the needs of women. Several of these programs continue to inform listeners about a woman's rights to have control over her own body, and the right to be informed about unwanted pregnancies, highly contagious venereal diseases, and AIDS, which is spreading fast in Latin America. The case of AIDS transmission by *garimpeiros* (gold miners) to women of a Yanomami tribe is known, but there has been ineffective assistance from the non-indigenous society to halt such aggression. Women's 'triple struggle' coined by Bronstein (1983), is now a 'quadruple struggle': 'woman, poor, Indian, and uninformed'. Yet, as demonstrated in the examples, fast IW mobilizations are happening in order to solve the challenge posed by the 'quadruple struggle.'

Trickle Down Effects and Indigenous Women Militancy

The distinction between non-indigenous peasants and indigenous Peoples is often still hard to understand for outsiders, and even for political activists who tend to clump non-indigenous peasantries with indigenous peoples. The issue at stake is a different understanding of land and territory, so important for IPs. However, indigenous peoples in rural areas, continue to be neglected by the nation-state, and/or abused by transnational corporations who prey on IPs' territorial notions. Organized IPs have been successful at attracting international media attention to voice their demands. But more often these debates remain restricted to the 'Pueblos Indígenas and State' issue. For example, a recent book published in Ecuador on the proceedings of a colloquium on IPs and the State barely mentions women as part of the debate. Women's issues tend to be swallowed by the dynamics of political strife, territorial and/or environmental struggles. Recent cases such as the women and children's protest marches from the coca producing Chapare to La Paz, Bolivia, and lately from oil areas of Pastaza to Quito, Ecuador are situations in which women's demands merged along with environmental struggles that tend to obfuscate the specificity of ethnic feminist demands.

Recent examples of insurgent ethnic feminisms raised by Zapatista women known as the 'Indigenous women's Petition,' in 1994, are the 'Twelve Points'. The first of such demands reads: 'Childbirth clinics with gynecologists'. This openly denounces high mortality rates of both mother and child in indigenous communities throughout Latin American rural areas. 'Captain Silvia', writes Marcela Lagarde, said 'she learned to read and write in Spanish when she joined the guerrilla, and that she has married a captain like herself, and that she takes the pill ...' Such a statement is then complemented by the subsequent tenet: 'The right to marry whoever we want. The right to have as many kids as we want and take care. The right to be whatever we wish to be, including becoming truck drivers, the right to hold positions in the community' (Lagarde,1996, p. 89). Likewise, Guiomar Rovira collected testimonies of armed insurgent IW who have achieved positions of power in the already extended and unsolved Chiapas Uprising.

The Zapatista women have pushed IW's agenda very far, inspiring other IW to voice daily life problems of teenage pregnancy, divorce, machismo, abortion, as well as opening debates over homo-sexuality, and sexism. Several of these latter issues are still, in less informed indigenous rural communities or communities, overtly influenced by fundamentalist missionaries, and continued to be seen as taboo. In these cases, IW are working first at liberating the language by talking, printing and circulating it. *La Correa Feminista* in Mexico acknowledges that the EZLN has opened strategic doors.

> The EZLN had reopened doors to validate rebellion and more, revalidated the right to press for a realization of your difference, the right to not submit yourself to oppressing legalities... another important aspect has been (especially for us feminists) the explicit discourse... A comparable communication [strategy] has been one of the feminist utopias of communication, lost in the erroneous belief that we can only be heard if we speak the language of the Other.   (1999, p. 133)

A clear example of this is *Mujer Pública* the all-women's newspaper of national circulation whose members constitute a young generation of interethnic Bolivian feminists, published by Florentina Alegre, a journalist, who points out:

> Governments are not mothers nor fathers, they have not been born of poor Quechua or Aymara women. For us pregnant women, pre- or post- childbirth, attention is not available at the 'free' health care centers the government talks about. Instead, because we are Indigenous, there is discrimination at such places. We know that women who die from childbirth are mostly Indigenous. Also, in our communities there are no medical doctors, no health centers, no medicines, no hospitals, and no labs. So, what kind of free attention are governments talking about?   (Personal communication from Kantuta Isabel Lara)

Other women leaders such as Marta Vitor Guaraní, of the Guaraní-Kiowa people, who inhabit at least in four countries (Argentina, Brazil, Bolivia, and Paraguay), articulates an upper limit situation when she denounces the mistreatment of hundreds of Guaraní, both men and women. She states,

> Over seven thousand Indians are working in the charcoal factories and in the sugar cane processing plants. They live in a state of slavery. This is the integration that white society offers us... Poste Indigena Dourados has seen the greatest concentration of Indigenous suicides in the country... and in the Summer of 1994 one hundred and six Guaraní-Kiowa families from Jaguapire (Mato Grosso do Sul, Brazil) threatened with collective suicide as Federal Court's ordered to expel them from their lands.   (SAIIC, interview)

Although Marta Vitor Guaraní has been outspoken, she does not attempt to separate a whole people's fate as they struggle through colonized conditions, giving us an indication of non-indigenous societies complexities.

IW leaders living in urban areas have maintained relations with *Originary* (First Nations) communities today. They re/present voices that sometimes are hard to re/present. There have been situations where IW accomplished representatives reproduced discriminatory relations among their own kin. This is understandable because leadership, in several cases, needs to play the funding game of foreign aid agencies, which in turn contribute to further decimate indigenous organizations in intra-competition for meagre resources. Pro-Indigenous Rights activist Silvia Rivera Cusicanqui called this process the 'NGOization' of Latin American societies. Certainly, rather than looking at indigenous movements as value-free, we must consider them as forming part of the world system, for it is precisely their territories that may become the last resource of capitalistic takeover: biodiversity and genetic resources are found in such places, extensively targeted today by TNCs. Only 12 nation-states are signatories of ILO's Article 169 (since 1989) that, if implemented in other countries with high percentages of IPs, guarantees the rights of IPs, but hardly offers specific rights for IW. ILO's concern reflects the economic situation indigenous peoples face worldwide.

The Indigenous Fe/male as a Gender Issue

As gender issues provoke the consciousness of indigenous America, IW are making their voices heard. Sharper debates are now waged with entrenched patriarchies as IW see the nation-state and its institutions (the military, the church, the judiciary, the police, class-inspired political parties, unions, educational and health systems) as relentlessly discriminatory. Indigenous solidarities between males and females tend to reinforce a gender equality utopia often referred to in indigenous cosmologies, against systematic discrimination. This, in turn, has reestablished women's ceremonialism that works as a healing strategy, legitimating their leadership within indigenous communities. Resignified religious ceremonialism, based on the retrieval of 'ancient practices,' endows women with moral authority over the community with the power of political leadership that is consensual and anti-hierarchical.

It has been through the resignification/renarrativizing of these religious and 'ancient' healing practices that women can reestablish control of the human body. Alicia Canaviri, a founder of CDIMA. the Aymara Women's Development Centre in La Paz, Bolivia has dedicated herself to training 40 Aymara women selected from eight communities. At the end of her workshops she successfully says, 'These first forty women are now liberated, empowered, and organized to defend and fight for the rights of the Aymara woman. It is fundamental that the women are trained to occupy important positions' (SAIIC interview). Among the Wayuu, several of which live in Maracaibo, Venezuela, girls born and raised in the Wayuu neighbourhoods are offered a traditional rite of initiation as they carry on with their Guajira territory culture. Wayuu women have successfully organized the *Network of Indigenous Women* which serves as a hub for multiple activities to defend Wayuu women's rights and IW living in cities, among those, the Warao of Tucupita, the Piaroa and Guajibo of Puerto Ayacucho. However, the concern over assertiveness has left behind other problems such as programming on teen-age pregnancy, venereal diseases, AIDS, alcoholism, domestic violence, and economic hardships which would require stronger implementation from the part of indigenous organizations. Nation-state ministries and recent juridical innovations regarding indigenous areas within nation-states tend to co-opt male leaderships. In such areas, women are still distant from exercising their rights and/or the nation state has been unable to grant and honour notions of citizenship.

The collective indigenous self-definition challenges the concept of nuclear family, but it has also helped raise other questions over women's rights within families and communities. Several indigenous matrilocal societies, such as in some of the Miskitu of the Rio Platano Biosphere (Honduras), women are granted the right to inherit land, to own it, and to be able to pass it on to future generations. To value complementarity over gender separation of males and females, several indigenous languages posses only one term to describe the third person singular = human, she/he. This is because the working domestic unit is based upon a process of participation entailing couples, children, and above the collective survival of all. Among the several policies that have worked against such conditions of reciprocity, lay tremendous pressures similar to the ones experienced by the Guaraní-Kaiowa who considered collective suicide as a last resort. Note that in this case, the idea of collectivity is beyond the notion of individual men and women, young and old.

Trial marriages or '*sirwiñaku*' are often practiced by Andean Quechua, because kinship ties and collective need ensures a high level of couple viability, which is related to the reproduction of the domestic unit, kin, and access to arable land. There have been cases, observes anthropologist Alison Spedding (1997, pp. 325–344), where female adultery is not seen as punishable, but male laziness or drunkenness is. If marriages fall apart, or widows/widowers enter new arrangements, it is more likely that females can carry on 'male' duties, and less often that 'males' can carry on 'female' duties, although it happens. Likewise, there are women who seek potential suitors depending on their land accessibility, and are able to reject men by judging their ability to subsist economically. One could say that the economics of survival have a priority over emotional relations. Mauricia Castro, a Xicaque (Honduras) illustrates this point:

> Women participate in decision making, whether the men like it or not. In FETRIXI (Federation of Xicaque Tribes, Yoro) there are women who have a man as a secretary and they tell him what to do. But we do not wish to make a parallel organization of women because we believe that, and this is a custom of the Xicaques, women without men can do nothing, but likewise men without women are stuck. Even though 'machismo' always existed, we resist it by saying: 'Do not walk in front of me, do not fall behind, let's walk together.'

Due to her leadership Mauricia had her life threatened by security forces, she recalls this: 'They were going to kill five of us and that is what they did. They said it would be those board members. They said that we were going to be dead. But the five, two women and three men, belonged to different councils' (SAIIC, interview).

An extraordinary case has recently been documented by a small tribe made up of 1,349 individuals, of them 712 are Ebêrawera (native women) of Alto Sinú, Colombia. In this case, these Ebêrawera got together as '*Werara bia zhebudaka aba yi udukabadape bed ea abarika oda ita*' (Welcome Ebêra women so that we will talk with one voice) at the community of Dosá, on the region of Iwagadó, Resguardo Ébêra Katío on 22–26 November 1999. According to their final report they stated:

> In this encounter we dealt with several subjects that have to do with our lives, our problems, our children, our elders, our struggles and our people. We also talk about taking care of nature and territory, of our food and especially our culture and our Organization. We *Nokowera*(women mayors, gubernatorial leaders, *jaibanaweras* [healers] and women shamaness, regular women, elders and young girls, got together to think about ourselves, as well as about children and elders…Several [of us] do not know how to read or write, however, we know how to think and to love our culture, our children, our communities and our territory. (Werara Bia, 1999, pp. 1–2)

And this is exactly what they did, retrieved their strength, re/narrativized their own power and re-established it in clear statement that illustrates their force and unity qua women. In this case, the Nokowera, that is women that have authority to control river rights of entry, a role given to community mayors, repositioned their territorial authority vis-à-vis the non-indigenous Colombian society.

Migration of Indigenous Mesoamerican Women to the US

Population displacement and migration of IW has had important repercussions regarding human rights and specifically rights for women. After several years of organizing, IW that belong to the 'Frente Mixteco Zapoteco Binacional,' composed of migrants from Mexico that work in the agricultural fields and service sector of California, have constituted teams to provide direct economic assistance known as 'remesas' (remittances) to their base communities. IW exposed to other women's struggles in the US and Mexico often acquire their political agency although encountering entrenched racisms from the part of non-indigenous society, racism in Spanish and English. However, as a transnational indigenous movement, they have asserted themselves on both sides of the border. Their secret is to assist each other, to reconstitute their cultural collective identity, which adopts the best from home. Women's rights are one. Their community changes slowly. Laura Velasco Ortíz conducted research among Mixtecas in the border city of Tijuana and found that Mixtecas 'have been forced to develop a great capacity for survival, they combine their experience of resistance as IW but also as women. This "habit of surviving" is manifested in several multisites' (1998, p. 19). Calchaki scholar and activist Alderete (1999), while co-working with the Mixtec and Zapotec migrants in California agricultural areas, has found that some suffer from depression, and have considered suicide as a way of dealing with cultural transitions and the stresses of discrimination.[4]

---

4   Former director of CIESAS-Oaxaca, Dr Margarita Dalton, observed the exercise of political power by Zapotec women and found that, despite their acknowledged agency as matriarchs, once elected to public office they do not receive, as men do, the same governmental

The bi-national Mixtec and Zapotec are probably one of the first indigenous groups to have received direct assistance in learning about health risks such as depression and sexually transmitted diseases including AIDS in their own language (Personal communication from Gaspar Rivera). Winnebago scholar Renya Ramírez, arguing for 'transnational citizenship' has documented the emergence of indigenous identity of individuals 'living a transnational existence, outside... Chicano/a and Native American reality in the context of California.... Sense of Indian culture, community, and identity are not based solely on a geographical homeland...' (2002, pp. 78–79).

IW continue to be depositories of languages, implement domestic and public organizing strategies and reproduce cultural practices in general. IW consciously reject assimilative aims proposed by nation-states. By stressing on their own forms of resistance, IW consciously act against the forgotten category of colonialism, which persists in relation to indigenous Peoples. Although, it is thought that indigenous movements need to be politically visible to be taken into consideration, forms of cultural resistance in the hands of women have been as effective if not more than politicized indigenous movements. The articulation of anticolonial policies and indigenous movements' proposals to *decolonize* human relations and histories and to deal with the recognition of women's contributions to such movements constitute lessons gained. The same process of *decolonization* is touched by an editorial of *Mujer Pública*, which poses a question: 'Does feminism have allies? We definitely think so, we have experienced sisterhood and solidarity from the part of males toward feminists, but it is as complex as feminism itself' (personal communication from Kantuta Isabel Lara).

Finally, as globalization is now looking at biodiversity found mostly on indigenous territories, women are being exposed to unwanted side effects brought in by bioprospecting, unconsented DNA collection and biotechnology. The defense of Indigenous Property Rights (patenting of indigenous genes, medicinal plants, and genetic resources) continue to inspire new transnational mobilizations. Several of these aspects are, indeed, in the hands of women, in their accurate knowledge of concrete environmental repositories which make us think about the uphill battle not just for rights, but longer and sustained struggles against transnational entities (Zurita Vargas, 2003) and intermediaries that, in the best of circumstances, will be waged by women as they regain shared authority within the indigenous movement.

Conclusion

Documenting recent developments of IW organizing creates evident challenges for researchers of social movements in the Americas. Naturally, we acknowledge the fact that 'not all feminist struggles can be understood within the frame-work of "organized" movements. Questions of political consciousness and self-identity are crucial aspects of defining third world women's engagement with feminism' (Mohanty Talpade, 1991, p. 33; Schutte, 2004, p. 197). More than 350 Peoples (about

---

assistance to succeed in their administrations. (Personal communication. Oaxaca, México, August 2003).

50 million in the Americas) descendants of 'Originary or First Peoples' have now closed a full circle of demographic recuperation that is comparable, in all probability, to the initial colonial 'dis/encounter' 500 years ago in the Americas. As we contrast its social movements, indigenous militancy can be described as having reached a stronger level of continental coordination both in the North and the South; territories of the People of the Condor, Peoples of the Eagle and Peoples of the Quetzal and the Jaguar. It seems that the twentieth century's persistent defense of indigenous identity was strongly refurbished and galvanized by the Civil Rights movements of the 1960s in the North, having its equivalent in the renaissance of growing ethnic identity and gender consciousness in the Americas (Varese, 1996, pp. 122–142) which argue for full *decolonization* and full recognition of indigenous 'Immemorial Rights', rights that have been denied.[5] *Decolonization*, according to Maori intellectual Linda Tuhiwai Smith: 'is now recognized as a long term process involving the bureaucratic cultural, linguistic, and psychological divesting of colonial power'. For Satya Mohanty it is: 'the process of unlearning historically determined habits of privilege and privation, of ruling and dependency, such a difficult intellectual matter that we cannot acknowledge our past or present location and simply get on with the business' (Mohanty, 1995, p. 108; Smith, 1999, p. 98).

A crucial period of shift was prompted in the 1960s by US Native American intellectuals's refined contestant histories against entrenched 'official histories' little disputed until then. In the Latin American case, however, indigenous intellectual movements were overshadowed by a predominant presence of 'Indigenista' ideology sponsored by the nation-state. 'Indigenismo' put forward feeble and mistaken projects of full assimilation of indigenous Peoples to homogenous nation-states. 'Engaged anthropology' a proposal of several scholars-activists gathered around *The Barbados Declaration* (1971) worked as the only voice to criticize new forms of colonialism in the Latin American context. Recent indigenous notions of autonomous stands and insistence on sovereignty, however, propose to redefine the current version of the nation-state, forcing it implement notions of multi-culturalism and diversity. In their words, IWs state:

> The organization we are seeking as indigenous women implies and confronts power, both within the boundaries of the State and the prevailing legal system, and within our own indigenous communities because it demands our own specificity and it questions certain ways and customs which violate our human rights.   (IWGIA, 1999, p. 328)

Organized IW benefited from the dynamics of the 'circulation of struggles', in that IW pondered the influence of feminist thinking but also because it assists IW in understanding the crossroads of gender and ethnicity:

> The resulting tensions and conflicts illustrate an innovative change that transforms women into their own agents, agents who can accept, reject or negotiate different situations at the

---

5   Marcia Stephenson in her afterword 'AlterNative Institutions' offers a comprehensive summary regarding debates concerning decolonization, gender and Indigenous Aymara women's influential leadership paying attention to this article by Choque and Delgado.

same time that they question homogeneous and essentialist visions of indigenous customs and normative systems.   (Maldonado and Artía, 2004, p. 507)

Mapuche activist Isolde Reuque Paillalef states that: '*Kumin* in the Mapuche language can be understood as "knowledge", and it (Kumin) has been destroyed' (1998, p. 238; Millet, 1987, p. 427). Despite the fact that IW argued with Anglo-European feminism, de-homogenizing it, to these authors such a debate helped in the *repositioning* and *re-narrativizing* of 'decentred' feminisms, as the opus of Sonia Alvarez indicates. In a sense, such indigenous feminisms de-historicized myths and brought in a process in which IW *re-historicized the mythical* to strengthen their oral histories, languages, memory, knowledge and political power.[6] All help revive what IW think can restore strong notions of gynocratic power.

References

Alderete, W. (1999), *The Health of Indigenous Peoples* (Washington, DC; World Health Organization).
Allen, P.G. (1986), *The Sacred Hoop: Recovering the Feminine in American Indian Traditions* (Boston: Beacon Press).
Ardaya Salinas, G. (1986) 'The Barzolas and the Housewives Committee', in *Women and Change in Latin America*. Nash, J. and Safa, H. and contributors (Massachussetts: Bergin & Garvey), 326–345.
Bhabha, O. (1994), *The Location of Culture* (New York: Routledge).
Bronstein, A. (1983), The Triple Struggle: Latin American Peasant Woman (Boston: South End).
Bunster, B.X. (1986), 'Surviving Beyond Fear: Women and Torture in Latin America.' *Women and Change in Latin America*. Nash, J. and Safa, H. and contributors (Massachussetts: Bergin & Garvey), 297–325.
Canaviri Mallku, A. (2000), 'La Mujer Aymara en el Proceso de Reconstitución de Ayllus y Markas', in *Aruskipasipxañasataki. El Siglo XXI y el Futuro Del Pueblo Aymara*. Ari, W. (ed.) (La Paz: Amuyañataki), 67–71.
Castillo Cárdenas, G. (1973), 'El Derecho de la Mujer Indígena' in *Las Luchas Del Indio Que Baja de la Montaña Al valle de la Civilización* (Bogota: Comité de Defensa del Indio).
Chinchilla, N. (1993), 'Women's Movements in the Americas: Feminist's Second Wave', *NACLA Report on the Americas*, **28**(1), 17–23.
Choque-Quispe, M.E. (1998), 'La identidad y liderazgo de la mujer indígena en la lucha por el territorio' Informe de Trabajo Para Native American Studies, University of California Davis. Programa Rockefeller para Becarios Indígenas de las Américas (ms).

6   Two major historical events covered by the international press acknowledged the dominant organized presence of Indigenous women (IW) in Bolivia during the so-called 'Water Wars' (April 2000), and during the uprising that ousted President Sánchez de Lozada, known as 'The Gas War,' (October 2003). This is clearly, the result of IW political assertiveness.

Congreso Nacional Indígena with Beatríz Avila Encuentro Nacional de Mujeres Indígenas (1996) *Construyendo Nuestra Historia* (Mexico: Kinal Antsetik).

Costa, C. de Lima (2000), 'As teorias feministas nas Américas e a política transnacional de Tradução', *Estudios Feministas (Florianópolis)*, **18**(2), 43–48.

Delgado-P., G. (1985), 'Industrial Stagnation and Women's Strategies for Survival at the Siglo XX and Uncía Mines,' in *Miners and Mining in the Americas*. Greaves, T. and Culver, W. (eds) (Manchester: Manchester University Press), 162–170.

Delgado-P., G. [2000] (1992), 'L'organizzazione continentale India: Dopo cinquento anni, per cominciarne altri cinquento', *Supplemento Tepee*, **21**, 107–113.

Delgado-P., G. (1994), 'Ethnic Politics and the Popular Movements' in *Latin America Faces the 21ˢᵗ Century*. Jonas, S. and McCaughan, E. (eds) (Boulder: Westview).

Delgado-P., G.(2002) 'Makings of a Transnational Movement', *NACLA Report on the Americas*, **25**(6), 36–38.

Delgado-P., G. (2003), 'El Espacio de las Epistemologías Indígenas', in *Renacerá la Palabra: Identidades y Diálogo Intercultural*. Valenzuela, J.M. (ed.) (Tijuana: COLEF), 71–91.

Delgado-P., G. (2005), 'Bolivian Social Movements in the First Lustrum of the 21st Century' http://isla.igc.org/Features/Globalization/BSM2k.html (see Special Features).

DePalma, A. (1998), 'Throughout the Americas, Natives Invoke the Law of Land', *The New York Times*, August 30.

Espina, Y. (1999), '¿Hasta dónde nos sirven las identidades? Una propuesta de repensar la identidad y nuestras políticas de identidad en los movimientos feministas étnico-racial' http://creatividadfeminista.org/fr_articulos.htm.

EZLN/Zapatista Army of National Liberation (1994), 'Chiapas: El Alzamiento de las Mujeres Indígenas: Ley sobre las Mujeres', *Debate Feminista*, **9**(95), 14–16.

Falquet, J. (2001), 'La costumbre cuestionada por sus fieles celadoras: reinvindicaciones de las mujeres indígenas', *Debate Feminista*, **24**, 163–190.

Gabriel, C. (1992), 'We are each Half of this World, Indigenous Women Before and After Colonization', in *Daughters of Abya Yala*. SAIIC (ed.) (Oakland: SAIIC), 11–13.

Gutiérrez, M. and Palomo, N. (1999) 'Autonomía con Mirada de Mujer' in *México: Experiencias De Autonomía Indígena.*, Burguette, A Cal y Mayor (eds) (Guatemala: Nawal Wuj/IWGIA), **28**, 54–86.

Indígenas de la Conaie, M. (1994), *Jornadas del Foro de la Mujer Indígena del Ecuador* (Quito: CONAIE, UNFPA).

International Working Group for Indigenous Affairs (IWGIA) (1999), 'The Presence of Indigenous Women on the American Continent', *The Indigenous World 1998–99* (Copenhagen: IWGIA), 323–333.

Kinal Antsetik, A.C. (Avila, B., Mata, M.E. and Palomo, N.) (1998), *Il Encuentro Continental de Mujeres Indígenas De las Primeras Naciones de Abya-Yala* (México: D.F.).

La Correa Feminista (1999), 'Chiapas, Reflexiones Desde Nuestro Feminismo', in *Las Alzadas*. Lovera, S. and Palomo, N. (eds) (México: CIMAC, Convergencia Socialista), 129–139.

Lagarde, M. (1996),'Identidad Femenina e Insurrección en México: Las Zapatistas del EZLN, 1994', in *Reflexiones sobre la identidad de los pueblos*. Ruíz, E.R. and Ruíz, O.T. (eds) (Tijuana: COLEF), 89.

León, R. (1990), 'Bartolina Sisa: The Peasant Women's Organization in Bolivia', in *Women and Social Change in Latin America*. Jelin, E. (ed.), Zammit, J.A., and Thomson, M. (trans) (London: Zed Books), 134–150.

Lievesley, G. (1999), *Democracy in Latin America: Mobilization, Power and the Search for a New Politics* (Manchester: Manchester University Press).

Maier, E. (1990), 'Aplicaciones y limitaciones de la categoría de género', *Revista Frontera Norte*, **10**, 39–52.

Maldonado, C. and Patricia Artía, R. (2004), '"Now We Are Awake":, Women's Political Participation in the Oaxacan Indigenous Binational Front' in *Indigenous Mexican Migrants in the United States*. Fox, J. and Rivera Salgado, G. (eds) (La Jolla, California: Center for US/Mexican Studies), 495–510.

Martínez García, M. (1995), *La Historia de Cómo la Niña Sawachi Nunca Encontró la Frontera* (Maracaibo, Venezuela: Astro Data).

McIvor, S.D. (1995), 'Native Women's Rights as Aboriginal Rights', in *From Basic Needs to Basic Rights: Women's Claim to Human Rights*. Schuler, M.A. (ed.) (Washington, D.C.: Women, Law and Development International, PressXpress), 267–288.

Mignolo, W. (2000), 'Letter to Forum', *PMLA*, **112**(5), 1140–1141.

Millet, K. (1987), 'Framing the Narrative: The Dreams of Lucinda Nahuelhual', in *Poética de la Población Marginal*. Romano, J.V. (ed.) (Minneapolis: The Prisma Institute), 395–428.

Mohanty, S.P. (1995), 'Colonial Legacies, Multicultural Futures: Relativism, Objectivity and the Challenge of Otherness', *PMLA*, **110**(1), 108–118.

Mohanty Talpade, C. (1991), 'Introduction: Cartographies of Struggle Third World Women and the Politics of Feminism', in *Third World Women and the Politics of Feminism*. Mohanty Talpade, C., Russo, A. and Torres, L. (eds) (Bloomington: Indiana University Press), 1–50.

Mujeres Ebera (1999), *Werara Bia Zhebudaka Aba Yi Udukabadape Bedea Abarika Odaita Bienvenidas para Que Hablemos una Sola Lengua* (Bogotá: Editorial Códice).

Muñoz Ramírez, G. (2006), 'Ramona, comandanta' *Ojarasca*, **105** (Enero). http://www.jornada.unam.mx/2006/01/16/oja105-gloria/html.

Murphy, Y. and Murphy, R. (1974), *Women of the Forest* (New York: Columbia University Press).

Nash, J. (1986), 'Research Guidelines: How to Study Women in Latin America', in *Women and Change in Latin America*. Nash, J., Safa, H. and contributors (Massachussetts: Bergin & Garvey), 22–34.

Navarro, M. (1989), 'The Personal is Political: Las Madres de la Plaza de Mayo', in *Power and Popular Protest*. Eckstein, S. (ed.) (Berkeley: UC Press), 241–258.

Pallares, L. (1996), 'Los Cautiverios de las Mujeres', *La República de las Mujeres* (Uruguay), 6–7.

Palomo, N., Avila, B. and Mata, M.E. (eds) (1999), *II Encuentro Continental De Mujeres Indígenas de las Primera Naciones De Abya Yala* (Mexico: Kinal Antsetik A.C.).

Potiguara, E. (2006), 'Manifesto da Mulher Indígena' http://www.elianepotiguara. org.br/textos1.html.

Prada, A.R., Ayllón, V. and Contreras, P. (eds) (1999), *Diálogo Sobre Escritura y Mujeres* (Memoria La Paz: Sierpe).

Ramírez, R. (2002), 'Julia Sanchez's Story: An Indigenous Woman between Nations', *Frontiers*, **23**(2), 65–83.

RedBird, E.B. (1995), 'Honouring Native Women: The Backbone of Native Sovereignty', in *Popular Justice and Community Regeneration: Pathways of Indigenous Reform*. Hazlehurst, K.M. (ed.) (Westport/London: Praeger), 121– 142.

Reuque Paillalef, I. (1998), 'La Identidad es un Asunto de Afirmación de Uno[a] Mismo[a]', in *Pueblos Indígenas y Estado En América Latina*. Alta, V., Iturralde, D., and López-B., M.A. (eds) (Quito: Abya Yala), 221–238.

Rivera Cusicanqui, S. (1990) 'Indigenous Women and Community Resistance: History and Memory', in *Women and Social Change in Latin America*. Jelin, E. (ed.) (London: Zed Books), 151–180.

Rivera Cusicanqui, S. (1995), 'Mujeres y estructuras de poder en los Andes: de la etnohistoria a la política', *Escarmenar, Revista Boliviana de Estudios Culturales*, **2**, 16–25.

Rivera Zea, T. (1999), *The Roads of Indigenous Women* (Lima: Chirapaq).

Robbins, J. (1999), 'An Old Rite Is Invoked to Protect Park's Bison', *The New York Times*, March 2, A17.

Rovira, G. (1997), *Mujeres de Maíz* (México: Era).

Safa, H. (1990), 'Women's Social Movements in Latin America', *Gender and Society*, **4**(3), 354–369.

SAIIC (South and Mesoamerican Indian Information Center) (1996), 'Indigenous Women Organizing', *Abya Yala News*, **10**(1), 6–15.

SAIIC (South and Mesoamerican Indian Information Center) (1992), *Daughters of Abya Yala: Testimonies of Indian Women Organizing Throughout the Continent* (Oakland: SAIIC).

Schuler, M.A. (1987), *Poder y Derecho. Estrategias de Mujeres del Tercer Mundo* (Traducción de G. Delgado P.) (Washington, D.C.: OEF).

Schutte, O. (2004), 'Feminism and Globalization, Processes in Latin America', In Latin American Perspectives on Globalization. Sáenz, M. (ed.) (Oxford: Rowman & Littlefield), 185–199.

Scott, J.C. (1998), *Seeing Like a State* (New Haven: Yale Press).

Smith, A. (1994), 'For All Those Who Were Indian in a Former Life', *Cultural Survival Quarterly*, Winter, 70–72.

Smith, L.T. (1999), *Decolonizing Methodologies: Research and Indigenous Peoples* (London: Zed Books).

Spedding, A. (1997), '"Esa mujer no necesita hombre": En Contra de la "Dualidad Andina": Imágenes de género en los Yungas', in *Más allá del Silencio: Las*

Fronteras De Género En Los Andes. Arnold, D. (ed.) (La Paz: ILCA/Stampa), 325–344.

Sponsel, L.E. (1995), 'Relationship Among the World System: Indigenous Peoples, and Ecological Anthropology in the Endangered Amazon', in *Indigenous Peoples and the Future of Amazonia: An Ecological Anthropology of an Endangered World*. Sponsel, L.E. (ed.) (Tucson: TUAP), 263–294.

Stephenson, M. (1999) 'Afterword: Alternative Institutions', in *Gender and Modernity in Andean Bolivia*. Stephenson, M. (ed.) (Austin: University of Texas Press), 203–206.

Stephenson, M. (2002), 'Forging an Indigenous Counterpublic Sphere: The Taller de Historia Oral Andina in Bolivia', *Latin American Research Review*, **37**(2), 99–118.

THOA (Tallter de Historia Oral Andina) (1990), *La Mujer Andina en la Historia* (Chuquiyawu: THOA).

THOA and Rivera Cusicanqui, S. (1990), 'Indigenous Women and Community Resistance: History and Memory', in *Women and Social Change in Latin America*. Jelin, E. (ed.) Zammit, J.A. and Thomson, M. (trans) (London: Zed Books), 151–183.

Varese, S. (1996), 'The New Environmentalist Movement of Latin American Indigenous People', in *Valuing Local Knowledge: Indigenous People and Intellectual Property Right*. Brush, S.B. and Stabinsky, D. (eds) (Washington, D.C.: Island Press), 122–142.

Velasco Ortíz, L. (1998), 'A través de las fronteras etnicas y de género: Vendedoras Ambulantes Indígenas En Tijuana', *Chicano Latino Research Center, UCSC, Working Papers*, 19.

Werara Bia/Mujeres Ebera (1999), Werara Bia Zhebudhaka Aba Yi Udukabadape Bedea Abarika Odaita. Bienvenidas para que hablamos una sola lengua. (Bogotá. Ed. Códice

Zárate Vidal, M. and Rosemberg Seifer, F. (1989), *Los Indios De Brasil: Su Proceso De Lucha* (México: UAM).

Zurita Vargas, L. with Caballero, M.C. (2003), 'Coca Culture', *The New York Times*, October 15, A23.

Chapter 10

Engendering the 'Right to have Rights': The Indigenous Women's Movement in Mexico and the Practice of Autonomy[1]

Maylei Blackwell

Mujeres de ayer, Mujeres de hoy, Mujeres de siempre
Tejeremos el amanecer de nuestros pueblos....
(Women's Weavers Collective, La Realidad, Chiapas)

As a force for social transformation in Mexico, the emergence of indigenous women as new social subjects during the 1990s represents a sector of women's organizing whose political, cultural, economic, and social claims are both new and old. While the indigenous women's movement draws on local and regional histories and organizational roots that stem back 20 years, the genealogy of indigenous women's resistance has been tied to the re-emergence of indigenous organizing in Mexico since the Chiapas uprising in 1994. Engendering the indigenous movement's demands for the 'right to have rights', indigenous women's organizing is characterized by the right to 'difference' as indigenous people as well as new claims to rights as gendered citizen subjects that push the limits of state-defined citizenship. Women have played a vital role in the indigenous movement and have supported the juridical, territorial, and cultural claims to autonomy. They have also expanded the meaning of these claims to include women's bodily, political, cultural, and economic autonomy. Expanding the framework of autonomy beyond rights discourse, the indigenous women's movement has situated their own demands in a practice of autonomy within the embedded gendered structures that govern the conditions of their lives.

This essay examines how indigenous women have not only become important new actors in the indigenous movement, but how they have effectively shifted indigenous political demands by adding their own analyses of how political and cultural power is organized through the intersections of gender, indigeneity, and

---

1 '(Re)ordenando el discurso de la nación: El Movimiento de Mujeres Indígenas en México y la Práctica de la Autonomía,' in *Mujeres y nacionalismo: De la independencia a la nación del nuevo milenio*, edited by Natividad Gutiérrez Chong, Universidad Nacional Autonoma de Mexico, 2004.

class. The participation of indigenous women in Mexico's growing civil society mobilization, their demands against the state and economic order, and their insistence on women's autonomy within their own communities dismantles the notion that others could speak for them. The emergence of the indigenous women's movement in Mexico and its reverberations rock the foundations of the order of discourse of the nation shifting the dialogue on political representation, violence, cultural practices, and the ordering of power.

Whereas media and scholarly attention has been largely isolated to the Zapatista uprising in Chiapas, this article examines the historical and political context that gave rise to the first independent national indigenous women's organization in Mexico's history, the *Coordinadora Nacional de Mujeres Indígenas* (CONAMI) (National Coordinating Body of Indigenous Women).[2] Representing the majority of Mexico's 56 distinct indigenous pueblos, the organization focuses on indigenous women's human rights, reproductive health, family and military violence, and collective self-education on international and national treaties, pacts, accords, and conventions concerning the rights of indigenous peoples, specifically indigenous women. The Coordinadora examines how gender and women's rights fit into indigenous juridical frameworks focusing on the cultural discourses deployed in a call for indigenous autonomy and they have done innovative work expanding the boundaries of what indigenous autonomy means for women. As indigenous women, they have begun to decolonize knowledge by moving within their own indigenous epistemologies and forms of knowing while engaging and reworking official state discourses as exemplified in the demand for the right to 'difference', their call for autonomy, and the rearticulation of themselves as citizen/subjects of the nation.[3] They have called for indigenous autonomy based on traditional *usos y costumbres* (practices and customs), indigenous jurisprudence and self-governance while at the same time critiquing and transforming those practices in relationship to their own gendered understanding of power.

Indigenous Women in Mexico and the Order of Discourse of the *Nation*

With the largest indigenous population on the continent, Mexico has been affected by the large-scale mobilization of indigenous social movements throughout the hemisphere within the last 15 years.[4] A pan-indigenous consciousness has

---

2   This analysis is based on archival research, fieldwork and oral histories with over a dozen women in the leadership of the indigenous women's movement in Mexico conducting between March 1998 and March 2002. As a secondary source of information, I also conducted interviews with government officials, academics and NGOs and have been attending local, national, regional, continental and international forums organized by the Coordinadora Nacional de Mujeres Indígenas since 1998.

3   For an important piece on native epistemologies, see Joanne Marie Barker and Teresia Teaiwa's article 'Native In/Formation' in *Inscriptions* 7 (Santa Cruz: The Center for Cultural Studies, UCSC, 1994).z

4   For more information on indigenous movements in Latin America, see Roxanne Dunbar Ortiz, *Indians of the Americas: Human Rights and Self-Determination* (New York:

allowed greater cooperation among indigenous peoples to lodge demands at both the international and national levels. Mexico's 56 distinct pueblos make up approximately 12 million inhabitants, about 11 per cent of the national population by official count.[5] There is a historic and persistent connection between indigenous peoples and poverty. The economic crisis of the 1980s spread and deepened poverty in such a manner so profound that models of Western development fell in crisis leading to a renewed critique in the 1990s of the failures of capitalist modernity. The economic crisis caused impoverishment and dislocation to indigenous communities, but particularly impacted indigenous women as many men migrated to search for work and a good number of women moved to urban spaces or out of the country. The deepening poverty has impacted the re-structuring of households, often leaving women alone to etch out daily survival strategies as heads of households and these economic conditions have led to shifts in gendered roles and familial structures. There are several paths that lead indigenous women to organize but many stemmed from efforts to escape dire poverty. Women sought economic alternatives, joined weaving cooperatives, or participated in collective community projects as first steps in larger local and national mobilization.

While the state has historically used the discursive practice of defining the identity of indigenous people in Mexico through the criteria of language in all official matters, indigenous women's organizing does not take the meaning of identity as given. Much of the organizing of indigenous women has revolved around the reflection and analysis of their shared living conditions and political visions and has led to the process of constructing a new gendered, ethnically specific subjectivity of indigenous women. Paloma Bonfil Sánchez and Raúl Marcó del Pont Lalli draw out the connection between cultural survival and the economic crisis produced by the debt crisis and resulting peso devaluations:

Praeger, 1984); Donna Lee Van Cott (ed.), *Indigenous Peoples and Democracy in Latin America* (New York: St. Martin's Press, 1994); Raquel Barceló, María Ana Portal and Martha Judith Sánchez, co., *Diversidad étnica y conflicto en América Latina, Vol. 1: Organizaciones indígenas y políticas estatales* (México: Universidad Nacional Autónoma, 1995); Hector Díaz Palanco, *Indigenous Peoples in Latin America*, Trans. L. Rayas (Boulder, CO: Westview Press, 1997); Alison Brysk, *From Tribal Village to Global Village: Indian Rights and International Relations in Latin America* (Stanford: Stanford University Press, 2000).

5   'Población total y población indígena estimada por entidad federativa, según evento censal', Indicadores Socioeconómicos del los Pueblos Indígenas de México, INI: http://www.sedesol.gob.mx. ini.al3.htm. Throughout this work, I will use the word pueblos or pueblos indios without translation because the term refers simultaneously in Spanish to Indian communities, peoples, and towns. Following Lynn Stephen (1997, 1999), I do not translate them in order to keep these multiple meanings intact, which is crucial for a viable call for Indigenous autonomy. Both the United Nations (UN) and the Mexican Government have tried to undermine their own commitments to the self-determination and autonomy of indigenous peoples through these linguistic contestations. The UN Decade of Indigenous People (s) has been contested in terms of the singularity implicitly imposed by the UN in recognizing the world community of Indigenous people and thereby homogenizing and erasing vast differences between pueblos. The Mexican Government reneged on its own negotiations in the San Andrés Accords by recognizing only 'the' Indian community of Mexico in an attempt to homogenize the diversity of pueblos in Mexico and weaken their legal claim to autonomy.

In the last decade, the economic crisis has hit the lower strata of society much more violently, and it is this [fact] that magnifies both the misery in which the indigenous pueblos live, as well as the vigour and force of their cultures which, by adapting themselves, have managed to preserve the crux where they construct their identity. The recent political mobilizations of the indigenous pueblos have constructed, precisely, an especially important stage for the visible and specific participation of women and their demands that have referred to, among other things, the problematics of identity and the right to difference.[6]

This problematic of identity and the right to 'difference' has been used to frame political and economic demands arising from material conditions. The concept of political representation that indigenous women have produced draws upon cultural resources to expand and redefine notions of citizenship and participation. Moreover, it has required the construction of a new political identity of indigenous women as subjects of political, gender, cultural and economic rights for the first time in the nation's history.

The emergence of a new political subjectivity, indigenous women, as the subject of a new rights discourse, is also tied to larger democratization movements that are pushing for a restructuring of the State. They are challenging the traditional, corrupt channels of political representation in Mexico's corporatist political system and local forms of *caciquismo*. The focus on indigenous peoples and indigenous women specifically is historically significant because, as with other 'new' social movements in Mexico, they have forged new forms of political identity in order to avert blockages within channels of formal political representation inherent in the corporatist structure.[7] The work of indigenous women's organizing has been to articulate claims to political rights and means to social change outside of those corrupted channels through both conventional modes of grass-roots political organizing as well as engaging in the cultural work needed to re-orientate state discourses and practices. In addition to challenging social views and ideologies of ethnicity and gender that demean them, they work to displace the ways in which the order of discourse of the nation has circumscribed the symbolic and material conditions of their lives.

Dismantling the state's assimilationist project of indigenismo, a state policy and discourse developed during and after the Mexican Revolution and institutionalized in the 1930s under Cardenas's Autonomous Department of Indian Affairs and later through the founding of the National Indian Institute in 1948, has been a key result

---

6   Paloma Bonfil Sánchez and Raúl Marcó del Pont Lalli, *Las Mujeres Indígenas al Final del Milenio* (México, D.F.: Secretaría de Gobernación y Comisión Nacional de la Mujer, 1999), p. 10.

7   For theories of new social movements, see Ernesto Laclau and Chantal Mouffe, *Hegemony and Socialist Strategy: Towards a Radical Democratic Politics* (London: Verso, 1985); drawing from Laclau and Moufe, David Slater's collection theorized new social movements in the context of Latin America, see *New Social Movements and the State in Latin America* (Amsterdam: CEDLA, 1985); and for an important contribution in how movements are theorized in Mexico, see *Popular Movements and Political Change in Mexico*, Joe Foweraker and Ann Craig (eds.) (Boulder, CO: Lynne Rienner, 1990), specifically Alan Knight's essay in that collection on historical and new identities, 'Historical Continuities in Social Movements'.

in the articulation of indigenous women's political identity in Mexico.[8] As a state policy of 'modernization', this discourse was supposedly pro-Indian and sought to modernize the Indian by means of the state. Produced by leading intellectuals and anthropologists, such as Manuel Gamio, Moisés Sáenz, Alfonso Caso, and Gonzalo Aguirre Beltrán, as well as state actors, indigenismo can be seen 'simultaneously as a theory, an ideology and a state policy'.[9] Key to understanding how the state's project of assimilation and the ideology and policy of indigenismo has endured is to see how it has been rooted in nationalist myths of origin, descent and civic inclusion and how those myths have been founded in racial and gender hierarchies.[10]

By deploying a common symbolic economy of the nation prevalent among populist regimes where the indigenous roots of Mexico are acknowledged, this nationalist imaginary simultaneously celebrates indigenous people while erasing the way indigenous peoples have suffered historic and persistent racism and remain marginalized culturally, socially and economically. The construction of one the most powerful and enduring forms of nationalism not only served to unify Mexico as a nation, it helped to maintain the PRI's hegemony as guardians of that national patrimony for over three-quarters of a century. The racial ideology of this nationalism invokes a process of mestizaje as a cultural and political policy of integration whereby distinct indigenous cultures and languages were meant to disappear through the 'imagined community' of the nation. The institutionalization of the ideology of indigenismo in the Cárdenas populist state was part of the commitment made to popular, rural, and indigenous sectors after the revolution and although there were real gains in the redistribution of land to indigenous communities, it

> ultimately resulted in a sorry situation whereby the peasantry, in particular indigenous peoples, retained their status as the symbolic base of the nation but were excluded from effective participation and were left out in the distribution of resources by the very same state that "represented" them.[11]

So while Mexico has the largest population of indigenous peoples in the hemisphere, mass mobilization of indigenous peoples based on their own rights has been historically

---

8   See Roger Bartra (1974), 'El Problema Indígena y la Ideología Indigenista', *Revista Mexicana de Sociología*, **36**(3) pp. 459–482; Alan Knight', 'Racism, Revolution, and *Indigenismo*: Mexico, 1910–1940' in *The Idea of Race in Latin America, 1870–1940*. Graham, R. (ed.) (Austin: University of Texas Press, 1990); Guillermo Bonfil Batalla, *México Profundo: Una civilización negada* (Mexico City: Editorial Grijalbo, 1987); and Lynn Stephen, *¡Zapata Lives! Histories and Cultural Politics in Southern Mexico* (Los Angeles: University of California Press, 2002).

9   Luis Hernández Navarro, 'Ciudadanos iguales, Ciudadanos Diferentes: La Nueva Lucha India' in *Acuerdos de San Andrés,* Luis Hernández Navarro and Ramón Vera Herrera (eds) (Mexico: Era, 1998), p. 24.

10 For an elaboration of these myths and important study of indigenismo and nationalism see: Guitérrez, N (1999), *Nationalist Myths and Ethnic Identities*: *Indigenous Intellectuals and the Mexican State*.(Lincoln: University of Nebraska Press).

11 George Yúdice (1998), 'The Globalization of Culture and the New Civil Society' in *Cultures of Politics/Politics of Culture: Re-Visioning Latin American Social Movements*. Sonia E. Alvarez, Evelina Dagnino and Arturo Escobar (eds), (Boulder, CO: Westview Press)), p. 360.

undermined by the legacy of unfulfilled promises guaranteed through the Mexican Revolution, state policies of indigenismo, and the racial ideology of mestizaje. The policies of the post-revolutionary state, especially under Cárdenas, were formed and conceived in order to homogenize a diverse citizenship through the ideal of legal equality, with the goal toward integration and assimilation.[12] These policies endured and 'during the 1950s, the indigenous policy goal was to promote the substitution of the indigenous peoples' basic cultural traits for those considered 'national,' and this approach continued with some nuances and variations for almost two decades. This offensive paternalism was justified by the goal of redeeming the indigenous by 'civilizing them'.[13]

This constellation of state discourses *constructs and maintains* the relations of rule in Mexico and governs the daily conditions of indigenous women's lives. More than abstract philosophies, state discourses produce state policies and practices that are inscribed on the lives and bodies of indigenous women and saturate their social and political being through mechanisms that regulate identity, citizenship, health, reproduction, education, nutrition, political representation, labour, agriculture, and environment, to name only a few.

Generated through the power relationships that structure the material conditions of indigenous women's lives, the order of discourse defines the discursive possibilities of political identity formation and regulates the relations of rule and the ordering of power at multiple levels. As Neil Harvey has argued:

> The power exercised through the state is not a commodity that one group possesses and another lacks. Instead, it is constantly affirmed, resisted and transformed (Foucault 1980, 93). The power of state discourses cannot be traced to some rational understanding of social needs but to the precise mechanisms (economic, institutional, and cultural) that allow them to assert a hegemonic position vis a vis other discourses. The power that diagnoses maladies and recommends cures is not a new form of power, but the fact that it is able to conceal itself so well behind apparently objective knowledge of scientific discourse is characteristic to the modern state.[14]

This understanding of power relationships motivates Harvey to suggest that 'consequently, the intelligibility of state strategies is given not by the declared interests they pursue but by the relations of power they set in motion'.[15]

The order of discourse produces the state's hegemony and regulates the relations of rule determining the field of what is politically possible, constituting what I describe

---

12 For a discussion of the formulation of Cárdenas' policy of indigenismo in Michoacán, see Marjorie Becker, *Setting the Virgin on Fire: Lázaro Cárdenas, Michoacán Peasants, and the Redemption of the Mexican Revolution* (Los Angeles: University of California Press, 1995). For a critical understanding of these state ideologies, see Guillermo Bonfil Batalla, 1987.

13 Maria Magdalena Gómez Rivera, 'Indigenous Autonomy and the strengthening of National Sovereignty and Identity', *Cultural Survival Quarterly*, Special Issue edited by Jonathan Fox, Gaspar Rivera, and Lynn Stephen, 'Indigenous Rights and Self-Determination in Mexico', 23(1) (Spring 1999), 41–44.

14 Neil Harvey, *The Chiapas Rebellion: The Struggle for Land and Democracy* (Durham, N.C.: Duke University Press), p. 147.

15 Ibid. p. 148.

as the conditions of enunciability. The symbolic and material context maintained through the order of discourse has been largely signified through narratives of nation and *indigenismo* thereby constituting the indigenous female subject. Following Foucault's notion of archaeology, a statement-event can be known discursively through its archive or *the system of its enunciability*.[16] I am interested in this inasmuch as it can tell me the conditions of enunciation through which indigenous women construct a new political subjectivity. By recasting the gendered *indigenista* narratives, they thus resignify the conditions of enunciation in the symbolic order of the *Nation* and the terms under which citizenship is practiced. Moreover, indigenous women enact a displacement of this archive or system of enunciability by co-opting and re-working discourses of the state which they transform and blend with their own demands based on their gender and indigenous social locations.

Indigenous women, as the most marginalized sector of Mexican society, have effectively moved within the limited social and political spaces allowed them, borrowing forms of identity, social meaning and strategy within the crevices of discourses that exclude them, in order to build new forms of political subjectivity. Out of the most restrictive locations, indigenous women have developed a form of differential consciousness, which, more than a survival strategy, is a political skill through which they have begun to alter the order of discourse.[17] Indigenous women's organizing and how they have begun to rupture the order of discourse is tied to their ability to shift the conditions of enunciability and articulate new possibilities within the field of political action; abilities that require a change in the cultural discourses and representational apparatuses that circumscribe and define them historically as social actors.

Genealogies of Resistance: The Emergence of an Indigenous Women's Movement in Mexico

The First Zapatista Uprising and the Dual Logic of Racism

> La montaña nos habló de tomar las armas para así tener voz, nos habló de cubrirnos las caras para tener rostro, nos habló de olvidar nuestro nombre para así ser nombrados, nos habló de guardar nuestro pasado para así tener mañana. (Major Ana María, del EZLN)

On 1 January 1994, the Ejército Zapatista de Liberación Nacional (EZLN) lodged an armed insurrection in Chiapas, Mexico on the day that the North American Free Trade Agreement (NAFTA) was to go into effect. Amid the armed uprising, a war of ideas and words was also launched. Apart from taking over municipal buildings and destroying places that signified repression like police stations, insurgents distributed a pamphlet call *el Despertador Mexicano* (The Mexican Awakening) which

---

16 Michael Foucault, *The Archaeology of Knowledge and the Discourse on Language*, trans. by A.M. Sheridan Smith (New York: Pantheon Books, 1972).

17 For a theory of differential consciousness, see Chela Sandoval, 'US Third World Feminism: The Theory and Method of Oppositional Consciousness in the Postmodern World', *Genders*, **10** (Spring, 1991), 1–24.

made mention of the EZLN's revolutionary laws, including the Ley de Mujeres (Revolutionary Law for Women). Many commentators mentioned that one of the greatest surprises of the Zapatista Uprising was the presence of so many young women, who comprised about a third of the fighting forces and led several key attacks on January 1st. While little press attention was given to the Ley de Mujeres within the first hours of the revolt, several of the women leaders of the EZLN were among those making statements to the press including Captains Laura and Elisa, Major Ana María and Comandanta Ramona.[18]

Even in this early moment of the uprising, official state reaction embroiled the Chiapas conflict in a struggle over representation. In a first effort to discredit the EZLN, Mexican state officials tried to deny that the insurgency was authentically indigenous by suggesting that Indian revolts are spontaneous and lack organization while the 1 January insurrection was well-planned and executed. Jonathan Fox argues that:

> [t]he government alleges that the many Indigenous people who participated were actually duped by non-Indigenous professional revolutionaries. Indigenous peoples are supposed to have only local, immediate demands; the official view is that they are not concerned with national politics. For this reason, the Zapatista emphasis on political democracy is offered as conclusive evidence that this is not an authentic Indigenous movement.[19]

One of the key modes in which power operates in the order of discourse is through definition or the State's attempt to hold onto the ability to define and pronounce what is and is not legitimately indigenous. In an even more complicated turn of events, this struggle over authenticity and meaning took on a gendered twist. Aída Hernández problematizes the static depiction of gender and indigenous peoples by arguing that:

> For those who have been denying the Indigenous foundation of this movement, the claim to reproductive rights for women and their greater participation in the community is yet more proof that 'outside' forces are an underlying part of this movement. For those who continue to view Chiapaneco Indigenous people as descendants of the Maya who live in… closed communities… it would be difficult to imagine that Indigenous women could demand the right to participate in politics or to marry the partner of their choice.[20]

Racism reveals one of its dual and contradictory logics especially in relation to women's rights within indigenous cultures. On the one hand, the presence of the Women's Law, specifically the claims to reproductive health and the right to decide when and how many children to bear, is given as clear evidence of outside influence on the indigenous uprising. On the other hand, when claims to indigenous autonomy are made, they have been denied by the government because indigenous cultures

---

18 Márgara Millán, 'Las zapatistas de fin del milenio, Hacia políticas de autorrepresentación de las mujeres indígenas', *Chiapas*, **3** (Mexico, 1996), 19.

19 Jonathan Fox (1994), 'The Challenge of Democracy: Rebellion as Catalyst', *Akwekon Journal*, 18.

20 Rosalva Aída Hernández Castillo (1994), 'Reinventing Tradition: The Women's Law', *Akwekon Journal*, 67.

are dismissed as not being advanced (read civilized) enough to protect the rights of women within their cultures. While the legitimacy of the Mexican state's claim to be a defender of women's rights is definitely up for question, what is revealed is how the question of indigenous women's rights has been caught up within an externally imposed, state-defined binary between indigenous tradition and change. Entrapment in this dual logic of racism emerges from an order of discourse that is grounded historically in a symbolic economy of the nation, which has relegated indigenous women as mute figures who labour and bear the burden of history/nation but who do not participate in making it. The conditions of enunciability through which indigenous women articulate themselves as political subjects have been bound and circumscribed through this dual logic of racism.

As Márgara Millán argues, not only did women's presence within the indigenous uprising put the question of women on the agenda, it began to alter the *order of discourse* that has kept indigenous women locked into silence as social and political subjects.[21] The conditions of enunciability for indigenous women to become political and historical subjects have shifted and the ways in which they are inscribed into the order of discourse of the nation have begun to be contested. One of the first sites of contestation has been the local and daily lived experiences from which indigenous women organizers have struggled to become citizen subjects. Indeed, the Women's Revolutionary Law was not a process of feminist infiltration but grounded in the very local processes of resistance and EZLN mobilization. Although 1 January 1994 will always be inscribed into history as the beginning of the Uprising, the first uprising, as historicized by subcommandante Marcos, was not 1 January 1994 but International Women's Day, 8 March 1993 when the women of the EZLN and their base communities passed the Women's Revolutionary Law. The Revolutionary Women's Law is a product of a grass-roots consultation process among indigenous women in Chiapas lead by Comandantas Susana and Ramona.[22]

The meaning of gender, indigenous identity and politics has been shifting in longer histories of organizing and economic restructuring that has caused men and women to leave their communities to settle the jungle, to work in cities and areas of oil industries, and even to migrate as farm workers to other parts of Mexico and across the border to the US. More than rejecting their 'traditional' practices, many indigenous women have reinvented them under these new historical terms, economic conditions and processes of social transformation.[23] Moreover, many of

---

21 Márgara Millán (1996), 19–32.

22 There are several sources that document the process of the Women's Law such as the testimony of Captain Maribel in Guiomar Rovira Sancho's text *Mujeres de Maiz*. She also describes the process in detail in her chapter, 'Mujeres: la lucha dentro de la lucha', in *Zapata Vive. La rebelión indígena de Chiapas contada por sus protagonistas* (Spain: Virus, 1995). The widely circulated communique from Subcomandante Marcos regarding the Women's Revolutionary Law also appeared in *La Jornada*, 26 de enero (1994); see also English translation published as 'The First Zapatista Uprising: An Extract from Subcommandante Marcos', trans. Jonathan Fox, *Akwekon Journal* (Summer, 1994), in Spanish it can be found in *Las Alzadas*.

23 Hernandez Castillo, 'Reinventing Tradition', p. 76.

these changes to gender and cultural identity have organizational histories that stem back before the Uprising:

> The emergence of this new women's movement was the expression of a long process of organization and reflection in which indigenous zapatista and non-zapatista women have been involved. Through liberation theology, indigenous and peasant organizations, productive projects, health workshops, indigenous women in the jungle, in the Altos, and in the mountains have begun to question the ways in which they have been historically excluded from decisive political spaces, and they have established the need to construct a democracy that begins in the sphere of the family.[24]

Like the Chiapas Uprising, the result of a long history of indigenous and *campesino* organizing, the emergence and growth of the indigenous women's movement has roots that span back decades. The women that make up the Coordinadora Nacional de Mujeres Indígenas (CONAMI) have organizational roots that are deeply layered and reflect the multitude of forces that affect their lives and communities. With very few opportunities or access to formal education, their organizing has been rooted within the existing routes and institutions to which they have had access. The oral histories narrated by women active in the CONAMI discuss these prior routes and organizing experiences. The focal points of their early organizing revolve around women's productive projects, rural and peasant organizations, liberation theology and early indigenous organizations at the local and regional level. Before working collectively at a national level, members of the CONAMI travelled along these varying routes of resistance which they expanded to contribute a gendered vision.[25] Despite this deeper, embedded history of survival and resistance, the strength of the women's presence in the EZLN and their call for women's rights is a historic turning point and shift in consciousness which has inspired thousands of other indigenous women to speak out and build a movement.[26]

---

24 Hernandez Castillo, 'Construyendo la utopía: Esperanzas y Desafíos de las Mujeres Chiapanecas De Frente Al Siglo XXI' in *La Otra Palabra* Mexico, pp. 129–130.

25 Despite the fact that there are two distinct generations of activists in the organization, all of the women I interviewed began organizing in the 1980s, suggesting that the younger generation began participating at a very early age. The first generation began their participation through church groups, indigenous community projects and women's community-based productive projects mostly as married women with families who responded to the severe economic crisis, a burden laid especially heavy on those women's shoulders who occupy the most marginalized sectors of the Mexican economy. Others, representing the younger generation of activists, were young girls who began to participate in indigenous and peasant organizing with their parents or through other routes to became organizers in their own right. Many of this younger generation have resisted established community practices to become 'capacitadas' and begin working in the leadership of weaver's cooperatives, indigenous rights organizations, communal structures as well as indigenous women's groups.

26 The impact of the Women's Law in Chiapas spawned many independent women's organizing such as La Organización Independiente de Mujeres Indígenas (OIMI), las Mujeres de Motozintla, Mujeres de Margaritas, Mujeres de Ocosingo, Mujeres de Jiquipilas, and organizations of women artisans of Chiapas such as J'pas Joloviletik in Los Altos. See

The reverberations of the Women's Revolutionary Law not only had an impact on women in the EZLN and the Zapatista base communities, it marked a turning point for women working in mixed organizations to demand their own rights as indigenous women. 'Lorena' (Tzotzil, Chiapas), an active member of the Coordinadora Nacional de Mujeres Indígenas (CONAMI), described how, although she had participated in weaver's cooperatives since 1984, women began to change their strategies within the cooperative based in the Women's Law:

> Then we began to participate in politics in '94, when we began to change the theme because we realized that in the cooperative we were not taken into account and ignored by the men. We had a cooperative but we did not get to manage it. It was the men who decided, the men who gave their opinions on how they wanted the cooperative to function. Now we are beginning to participate since '94, since we have begun to take on more strength and valour. It's not just in the cooperative; it is in different events that we have attended as women. Now we can make the decisions, we can also be in the decision-making process that had only been men that ruled. After '94 various organizations emerged, the women organized, began to work collectively in ways they had not before. We always had had a lot of fear.... We were always dependents of our fathers, or our husbands.... We were not able to speak of things that we felt. Now that we feel a bit more free, because we can think, and it was [organizing] that gave us courage so that we could express our feelings too.[27]

After the 1994 Zapatista uprising, the demands of indigenous women were developed through their participation in larger processes of indigenous mobilization – meetings, marches, conferences, seminars and workshops. Through these organizational and analytical processes indigenous women forged a space for themselves by analysing their lived conditions and by calling into question relations of power. Defining their own identities and political demands (that is their right to difference) and how they

---

Hernández Castillo, 'Las voces de las mujeres en el conflicto chiapanceco: Nuevos espacios organizativos y nuevas demandas de género', diciembre de 1994, mimeo.

27 'Lorena' (pseudonym selected by the narrator), interview conducted by author, 1 April 2000, tape recording, Chilpancingo, Guerrero. She said:

Entonces ya después empezamos a participar así ya en lo político en el 94. Entonces es ahí donde empezamos a cambiar el tema. Es ahí donde nos dimos cuenta también estar en una cooperativa, y ni siquiera te toman en cuenta, ni siquiera te hacen caso los hombres. Según, nosotras tenemos una cooperativa, pero ni siquiera lo manejamos. Son los hombres los que deciden, son los hombres los que dan sus opiniones, o como quieren que funcionara una cooperativa. Ahora, empezamos a participar desde el 94. Es ahí donde empezamos a tomar más fuerza, valor. Digamos éste... no solo en la cooperativa, así como estamos ahorita, en diferentes eventos, hemos asistido también como mujeres. Entonces ya ahorita ya podemos tomar decisiones, podemos decidir también, que ya no solo los hombres que siempre mandan también. En ese tiempo surgieron varias organizaciones y por ejemplo, las mujeres se organizan, empiezan a trabajar así colectivamente y antes no lo hacían así. O sea, siempre le tenemos mucho miedo, será que sí podemos hacer o no lo podemos hacer, ¿no? Siempre estamos éste... dependientes de nuestros papás, o de nuestros papás o de nuestros maridos, como lo dicen allá que no podemos decir cosas a lo que sentimos, siempre le preguntas a alguien si es que lo puedes hacerlo o no. Entonces ahora que ya nos sentimos un poco libres porque ya podemos pensar, ¿no? Es ahí donde nos dio mas valor para que nosotras podamos expresar nuestros sentimientos también.

relate to other sectors, indigenous organizer and leader of the Coordinadora Marta Sánchez (Amuzgo, Guerrero) states that for them, it is collective women's spaces where the indigenous women's movement has been able to build their own political identities and practices.

Women's Participation in the Indigenous Movement

> When we began to organize we did not have our own face because we always base our struggle in that of our people, but to have initiated [this struggle] was fundamental for the space we have today. We began with a voice that hardly was heard by anyone, like a little whisper, but today we speak with a strong voice that organizing has helped us to mature as we walk forward.[28]

In the years since the uprising in Chiapas, the mobilization of indigenous peoples has continued, spread and coalesced on the national level. Women have made themselves much more visible as actors within this movement by constructing a specific space to articulate their own demands, denunciations, hopes and projects.[29] A series of cross winds within civil society mobilization converged to ignite a space for indigenous women's organizing that lead to the emergence of indigenous women as new political, historical and social subjects. This space of enunciation occurred largely in the public spaces of participation that have opened up in the post-1994 period, which gave rise to the formation of the Coordinadora Nacional de Mujeres Indígenas in 1997.

The numerous forums in which women have participated constituted a space of 'encuentro' where new proposals and forms of gendered analysis have been taken up through the eyes of indigenous women. The sites of this convergence and dialogue occurred at the National Democratic Convention (6–9 August 1994), the National Indigenous Forum, the Seminar about Reforms to the Fourth Article of the Constitution, and the national and international processes involved in the 4th World Conference on Women in Beijing. Women also began to gain ground within the growing national independent indigenous movement and specifically through the founding of the *Congreso Indígena Nacional* (CNI) (16–18 December 1994), the *Asamblea Nacional Indígena Plural por la Autonomía* (ANIPA), the National Meeting of Women of ANIPA (December 1995), as well as the women's commission of the National Indigenous Congress which launched the CONAMI. This series of regional events where women of different pueblos have begun to meet facilitated the growth of a indigenous women's movement in Mexico reflected by the first National Encuentro of Indigenous Women held in Oaxaca in 1997. This meeting served as a national preparatory meeting to host the Continental Encuentro of Indigenous Women held in Mexico City later in 1997 and led to the formation of the Coordinadora

---

28 Participant in Indigenous women's organizing, cited in Margarita Gutiérrez and Nellys Palomo, 'Autonomía con Mirada de Mujer', in *México: Experiencias de Autonomía Indígena*, Aracely Burguete Cal y Mayor (ed.) (Copenhague, Dinamarca: Grupo Internacional de Trabajo Sobre Asuntos Indígenas, 1999), p. 62.

29 Bonfil and Marcó del Pont Lalli, *Las Mujeres Indígenas*, p. 239.

Nacional de Mujeres Indígenas (CONAMI). Since then the CONAMI has met for bi-monthly National Workshops to develop community educators and forge a national movement which came together again in Guerrero in 2000 at the Second National Encuentro of Indigenous Women.

Margarita Guitérrez (Ñha-ñhu, Hidalgo) suggests that it is through public participation that indigenous women have forged a new political subjectivity as indigenous women.[30] Women's participation within the post-94 indigenous organizing paralleled the growing power of the indigenous movements as it simultaneously sought to create spaces within it for dialogue about engendering the demand for the 'right to have rights'. As a form of differential consciousness that fuses indigenous women's cultural identities with their new claims as emergent subjects of rights discourse, the struggle for indigenous women's presence at the national level has also been part of their work in shifting the order of discourse.

A political identity as indigenous women has been constructed through women's participation in various events that occurred in a larger civil society mobilization called for by the EZLN.[31] Key to developing and articulating an indigenous women's political agenda was women's participation in this process of the peace negotiations or San Andrés Accords. Initiated in February 1994, the San Andrés Accords were the first in series of negotiations between the EZLN and the federal government in what was supposed to be several rounds of talks addressing different aspects of indigenous demands.[32] The Accords were eventually signed on 16 February 1996 in San Andrés Larráinzar (renamed by the Zapatistas as San Andrés Sacam ch'en, San Andrés of the Poor in Tzotzil) but the government has yet to fulfil its side of the negotiations.[33]

The Accords on Indigenous Rights and Culture are historically important because they recognize *pueblos indios* as legal subjects and legitimate concepts of self determination and autonomy, thus laying the groundwork for cultural autonomy, greater political participation and legal claims to indigenous rights. The accords not only guarantee access to political representation within governing state structures but also guarantee the validity of internal structures of indigenous self-government. 'Situation, Rights and Culture of Indigenous Women' was one of the working sessions in the dialogues between the EZLN and the government in which indigenous women, 19 invited guests and 12 advisers from Indian communities and women's organizations throughout Mexico. In relation to

---

30 Interview with Author, August 2001, Durban, South Africa.

31 A first step in creating space for women within the indigenous mobilization was won in the Zapatista's first Consulta Nacional in 1994. The 'sexta pregunta' asked whether women should have parity in all positions (cargos) of responsibility and participation. It received a resounding yes.

32 The dialogues focused on Indigenous Rights and Culture were sub-divided into six aspects: 1) Autonomy; 2) Justice; 3) Political Representation and Participation 4) Situation, rights and culture of Indigenous Women 5) Means of Communication and 6) promotion and development of Indigenous culture.

33 The San Andres Dialogue documents, communiqués, accords, testimonies and analysis are gathered in *Acuerdos de San Andrés*, Luis Hernández Navarro and Ramón Vera Herra (eds.) (Mexico, D.F.: Era, 1998).

questions of gender within Indigenous Culture and Rights, it was recognized that indigenous women live within the same dire situation as their pueblos, that both men and women are oppressed and discriminated against and that the Mexican State has demonstrated a racist and sexist attitude of extermination. Consensus between the invited advisers of both the government and the EZLN was reached on the triple oppression of indigenous women.

One of the key issues to come out of indigenous women's participation in the dialogues of San Andrés Sacam ch'en was an articulation of a women's demand for autonomy. Women from the Tzotzil, Tzetzal, Tojolabal, Chinanteca, Chol, Mixteca, and Nha-ñhu pueblos deliberated and presented their list demands despite language barriers. 'We women manifest that the autonomy of the pueblos indios is the path toward the initiation of a new relationship amongst ourselves, with the Mexican state, with other Mexicans, and between men and women.... Within this framework of autonomy, we Indigenous women demand our full participation, and that no internal or external condition impede it'.[34] Although the *Comisión de Concordia y Pacificación* (COCOPA) did not ratify the women's document, the call for autonomy reverberated within several other important seminars and women's meetings and there was a reflection of the growing fusion of demands for indigenous autonomy and respect for women's rights. For example, Article E of the San Andrés Accords calls for 'legislation about rights of indigenous pueblos to elect their own authorities and to exercise the authority in accordance to their own norms in the interior of their autonomous environments, guaranteeing the participation of women in conditions of equality'.[35] The EZLN themselves recognized formally that the Accords fall short in the area of women:

> In reference to the theme, Situation, Rights and Culture of Indigenous Women, the EZLN delegation considers insufficient the actual points of the accords. Due to the triple oppression suffered as women, as indigenous, as the poor, they demand the construction of a new national society, with a different economic, political, social, and cultural model that would include all (both women and men) Mexicans. [36]

The work of indigenous women on the question of autonomy addresses the proposal for state reform but also moves beyond engagement with the state in that they have expanded the process by engendering the indigenous movement's call for autonomy to include indigenous women's bodily, political, cultural autonomy.

National Plural Indigenous Assembly for Autonomy (ANIPA)

After women's growing participation in the National Democratic Congress in Aguascalientes, Chiapas and the National Indigenous Convention in Tlapa, Guerrero

---

34 Quoted in Maya Santamaria, 'Two Watershed Encounters for Indigenous Women in Mexico', *Abya Yala News*, **10**(1) (Spring, 1996), 6

35 Nellys Palomo, 'La Ausencia de las Mujeres Indígenas en Las Iniciativas Sobre Derechos y Cultura Indígena', *Cuadernos Feministas*, **5**.

36 Ibid.

of 1994, indigenous women continued to explore and expand the meanings of indigenous autonomy and to create greater spaces for themselves within the growing national indigenous movement. One turning point in forging these new spaces that in themselves helped to constitute indigenous women as new social subjects and new subjects of rights discourse occurred in August of 1995 at the Third Asamblea Nacional Indígena Plural por la Autonomía (ANIPA) held in the city of Oaxaca.[37]

Women meeting within ANIPA's third assembly were critical in demarcating the new levels of women's participation as well as their histories of exclusion. They demanded the right to participate in decision making processes and initiated a national meeting of indigenous women to discuss in-depth new initiatives of autonomous indigenous regions. The Mexican delegates returning from the First Encuentro of Indigenous women of the First Nations of Abya Yala held in Quito, Ecuador, 30 July to August 4th, discussed their commitment to hold the Second Continental in Mexico in 1997. It was at this meeting that ANIPA's initiative to establish autonomous indigenous regions and to reform the constitution was debated. The women protested this initiative because the proposal for autonomous regions had not taken into consideration the voice of women. After the women's session debated the ANIPA's proposal for constitutional reform to establish a *Régimen de Autonomía* and Zoila José Juan, member of UCIZONI, expressed the final rejection of Anipa's autonomy proposal with the following words:

---

37 The Asamblea Nacional Indígena Plural por la Autonomia (ANIPA) is a space of assembly or dialogue which was formally established after the second Convención Nacional Indígenas in Juchitán, Oaxaca and after the dissolution of the Convención Nacional Democrática marked by tensions in its efforts to unite indigenous organizations as a sector. ANIPA is a product of attempts to construct internal consensus among indigenous pueblos in relation to the legislative proposals surrounding autonomy in 1995 was convened by indigenous deputies and senators of the PRD the Commission of Human Rights and indigenous Peoples of the PRD, indigenous organizations and NGOs. They held the first Asamblea Nacional Indígena Plural por la Autonomía (ANIPA) 8–10 April 1995 in Mexico City within the meeting rooms of the Congress of Mexico. Between 1995 and 1998 Anipa has held seven national assemblies and although ANIPA functions as a network among indigenous organizations, it was established as a space of dialogue to forge a unified proposal for autonomy and claims to have broad participation of indigenous pueblos. ANIPA is the organizational heir to the Consejo Mexico 500 Años de Resistencia and has declared itself an agrupación política. Margarito Ruiz Hernández, who has served as a federal deputy in the lower house of the Mexican Congress, began introducing a proposal for indigenous autonomy based on constitutional reforms and the establishment of Regiones Pluriétnicas (RAP) as far back as 1990. A need to clarify and develop the proposal by wider participation of Indigenous organizations lead to the convening of ANIPA by Auldárico Hernández Gerónimo, Chontal senator from the state of Tabasco, and Antonio Hernández Cruz, Maya-Tojolab'al deputy from Chiapas, as well as Las Regiones Autónomas Pluriétnicas de Chiapas (RAP), el Grupo de Apoyo al Autonomía Regional Indígena (GAARI), and la Comisión Mexicana de Defensa y Promoción de los Derechos Humanos. See Ruiz Hernández, 'La Asamblea Nacional Indígena Plural por la Autonomía: Proceso de Construcción de una Propuesta Legistlativa Autónoma Nacional', in *México: Experiencias de Autonomía Indígena*, Aracely Burguete (ed.) (Copenhagen: International Working Group on Indigenous Affairs, 1999), pp. 21–53.

The decreed initiative for the creation of autonomous regions does not incorporate, as part of its explanation of motives, the major problematic and exclusion of women, and because of this, emphatically, we women are protesting because our participation is not always taken into account in meetings in Tlapa, Juchitán, Distrito Federal, and Sonora that ANIPA has made. Women have made written proposals that have not been taken into account in the explanation of motives, nor in the editing of the initiative, and we hope that in this assembly we will be taken into account.[38]

Committed to taking the San Andrés Accords to their own pueblos to generate national discussion, the emergent indigenous women's movement met again to discuss the issues. Two hundred and seventy women from different parts of the country and diverse pueblos came together at the Encuentro Nacional de Mujeres de la ANIPA in December 1995 in San Cristóbal de las Casas, Chiapas, two days before the Third Assembly of ANIPA. The first national Women's Conference of ANIPA helped to shape women's demands within the call for indigenous autonomy. Dialogues around autonomy not only confronted structural and societal factors that contributed to the oppression of indigenous women but also addressed *usos y costumbres*.[39] Indigenous women argued that within the call for autonomy, forms of self-governance and a recognition of cultural and traditional norms are positive but they broke with the acritical celebrations of tradition to identify both positive and negative customs.

There 'are customs that can be counterproductive or contrary to the dignity or liberty of women' remarked Juliana Gómez (Mixteca), representative of the Editorial Center of Indigenous Literature in Oaxaca. She recognized women's role in the practice of autonomy by stating that often it is 'we women... [who] are the ones transmitting bad customs with the education we give our children'.[40] Considering ANIPA's proposal for Autonomous Pluri-ethnic Regions (RAP) at the women's conference, indigenous women organizers demanded a better definition of the legislative initiative of Anipa in terms of guaranteeing women's rights within regional autonomy and the issue of autonomy was debated extensively:

Autonomy for us women, implies the right to autonomy [where] we as women can empower [capacitar] ourselves, to look for spaces and mechanisms to be heard in community assemblies and to have positions of responsibilities [cargos]. Similarly it implies facing our own fears and daring to make decisions and to participate, to seek out economic independence, to have independence in the family, to continue informing

---

38 Cited in Nellys Palomo, 'Tejiendo visibilidad: La presencia de las mujeres indígenas', unpublished paper.

39 See Laura Carlsen, 'Autonomía indígena y usos y costumbres: La inovación de la tradición', *Chiapas* 7 (Mexico City: Instituto de Investigaciones Económicas UNAM/Era, 1999), pp. 21–44.

40 Santamaria, 6–7 and "Mujeres indígenas de Chiapas: Nuestros derechos, costumbres y tradiciones", Folleto published by K'inal Ansetik, A.C. and the Unión Regional de los Altos de Chiapas. NGO pamphlet detailing the information gathered in a series of indigenous women's workshops compiled by Nellys Palomo, Yolanda Castro and Cristina Orci. Republished in *Las Alzadas*, second edition, Nellys Palomo and Sara Lovera (eds.) (Mexico City: CIMAC and Convergencia Socialista, 1999), 65.

ourselves, because knowledge gives us autonomy. To spread women's experiences in order to encourage others to participate, to be able to participate in this type of meeting.[41]

To build continuity to all the advances that indigenous women had gained a Legislative Seminar on the Reforms to Article 4 (*Seminario de Legislación y Mujer, Reformas al Artículo 4o. Constitucional*), organized by K'inal Antsetik and SEDEPAC, was held from May to December of 1996 meeting two days each month. Formulating a legislative reform proposal to Article 4 of the Constitution from the perspective of indigenous women, specialists in gender, jurisprudence and indigenous law analysed the deficiencies in the San Andrés accords in the area of gender and explored strategies for implementation.

The National Indigenous Congress

Amid growing urgency caused by increased government and military harassment of Zapatista base communities in los Altos and la Selva, the National Indigenous Forum, held the 3rd through 8th January 1996, was convened by the EZLN as way to forge dialogue on the San Andrés Accords working session one on 'Indigenous Culture and Rights'. The meeting signalled unprecedented growth of indigenous participation and was seen as the death of state-sponsored policies of indigenismo because it signalled the existence of a broad spectrum of indigenous actors among multiple sectors of indigenous society that began to converge and consolidate through these processes of consultation around the San Andrés Accords.[42]

As regional indigenous meetings spread throughout the country and the government increased its militarization, the organizations within the Permanent National Indigenous Forum convened an urgent meeting in Mexico City in October of 1996 in an effort to bring together all indigenous organizations in the country to dialogue. Due to the stalemate between the EZLN and the government who would not grant the right to free transit, the EZLN selected Comandante Ramona to be their representative at the meeting as she had garnered much respect and admiration at the dialogues. Comandante Ramona, along with a thousand delegates came to the meeting that officially formalized the National Indigenous Congress (CNI).

This was a unifying moment in the indigenous movement and one of the founding leaders of the Coordinadora Nacional de Mujeres Indígenas María de Jesús Patricio read the final declaration. The National Indigenous Congress aimed to become a broad-based and representative national indigenous organization with a wide range

---

41 See *Influencias del zapatismo en las mujeres indígenas*, Nellys Palomo, Compilación (México: Comisión de Seguimiento de Mujeres de la Anipa, K'inal Antsetic. A.C., 1996), which includes the 'Conclusiones de Encuentro Nacional de las Mujeres de ANIPA', 'El Mesa de Mujeres del Foro Nacional Indígena (convocado por los zapatistas y la COCOPA)', and 'la Mesa del Diálogo'. See also, 'Encuentro Nacional de Mujeres de la Asamblea nacional Indígena para la Autonomía (ANIPA)', published in *Las Alzadas*, 1999, p. 363.

42 Ramón Vera Herrera, 'La Construcción del Congreso Nacional Indígena' in *Acuerdos de San Andrés*, Luis Hernández Navarro and Ramón Vera Herrera, Comp (Mexico City: Ediciones Era).

of involvement from diverse communities, peoples and organizations independent of both the government and political parties.[43] During this period the indigenous women's movement was also growing and consolidating in a parallel manner. In the mesa de mujeres of the National Indigenous Forum in January of 1996 the accords that were discussed and approved in San Andrés were further considered from the perspectives of indigenous women.

Yet, when the results of the Legislative Seminar that had been meeting for the better part of 1996 were brought to the Congreso Nacional Indígena (CNI) in Mexico City in October, indigenous women leaders found that in the scheduled working sessions, there was no session dedicated to women's issues. They struggled to institutionalize a woman's session but there was opposition to the women's proposal. The vote on the proposal was lost by 50 votes of the 500 delegates. Working quickly, they came up with an alternative plan and won a resolution to have the document that the women presented be discussed in every working sessions. This 'defeat' of their initial proposal eventuallyl led to their success in guaranteeing that women's concerns were taken up in each of the working sessions. Participants claim that although this was disappointing it was also

> ...where we won our first battle in the debate between men because some leaders supported our proposals and while other opposed. In this way we felt... that we had gained some male allies in favour of our organization as women.... The presence of Comandante Ramona of the EZLN in that event was an initiative to not fall into pessimism and disillusionment and it opened our hearts and nourished us to continue convinced that it was possible that the women organize ourselves.[44]

While the Congreso Nacional Indígena was seen as moment of unity of the national indigenous movement, 1996 was also a year full of events that began to build a cohesion of indigenous women nation-wide. Through the women's commission of the CNI and a national meeting of indigenous women, a first National Encuentro of Indigenous Women was planned.

'Constructing Our History' Primer Encuentro Nacional de Mujeres Indígenas: The Founding of the Coordinadora Nacional de Mujeres Indígenas

The first National Encuentro of Indigenous Women held in August of 1997 in Oaxaca was the largest meeting of indigenous women in the nation's history with the participation of over 700 women from a majority of the 56 Indian pueblos in Mexico. In the context of indigenismo, indigenous women are represented only as mute figures, usually as bearing the burden of their silent labour and mothers of *la raza*. So when indigenous women came together to seek their rights as women and as indigenous peoples for the first time in Mexico's history, it is no coincidence that

---

43 Luis Hernández Navarro (1999), 'The San Andrés Accords: Indians and the Soul', *Cultural Survival Quarterly*, **23**(1), 32.

44 Guitérrez and Palomo, p. 69.

such a watershed event was convened under the title 'Constructing Our History'.[45] Such a broad base of participation and support served as a mandate to create a space of 'encuentro' among indigenous women where they could 'speak their voice' at the national level and this first national encuentro formally established the Coordinadora Nacional de Mujeres Indígenas.[46]

The conference itself was historic in that it brought indigenous women's organizations and women's commissions within mixed indigenous organizations throughout the country together as the convening organizations or '*convocantes*'.[47] Besides the approximately 700 women in attendance, the First *Encuentro Nacional* was also honoured by the presence of a commission of women from the EZLN base communities and with the presence of la Comandanta Ramona. With words of welcome, Comandanta Ramona stated that it was with

> Much resistance that we have had arrived to this point; resistance from the owners of power in Mexico that do want us to be isolated and silent; from the rich of Mexico that want us to be like animals they can exploit; from the foreigners who remain with our best lands and want us like slaves; from the military that comes to our communities, rapes us, threatens our children, and bring drugs, alcohol, prostitution and violence; those who want to act and speak in our name, who don't like that men and women Indians state their word and our rebellion gives them fear.
>
> To arrive here, we have had to overcome all those who see us as something left over, something that they want not to exist. We have arrived here also overcoming the resistance

---

45 Those who participated at the First National Encuentro of Indigenous Women included Zapoteco, Teneek, Totonaco, Otomí, Nahuatl, Chol, Mixe, Tzotzil, Purépecha, Tlapaneco, Popoluca, Triqui, Ñhuu Save, Maya, Mazateco, Chamula, Tzeltal, Chinanteco, Chatino, Mixteco, Cuicateco, Amuzgo, Chocholteca, Zoque, Mam, Tlapaneco, Ñahñu, Tsa Ko Wi, Chat'nio, Ngigua, Bini Za, Ayuuk, Ikoots, Yoreme and Mazahua women from the states of Puebla, Chiapas, Distrito Federal, San Luis Potosí, Guerrero, Michoacán, Estado de México, Hidalgo, Oaxaca, Morelos, Jalisco, Querétaro, Sonora and Verzacruz. See, Memoria del Encuentro Nacional de Mujeres Indígenas, 'Construyendo Nuestra Historia', Oaxaca de Juárez, 29–31 August 1997 and Sylvia Marcos, 'Nunca más una revolución sin nosotras. El Congreso de las Mujeres Indígenas: un despertar', *Double Jornada*, Año 11

46 The objectives of the Encuentro were to forge the process of coordination and organization of indigenous women at the national level, to plan the preparation of the II Encuentro Continental de Mujeres Indígenas, to analyse the scope of the Accords of San Andres Sacamch'em from a gendered perspective, and to search for forms of organization and representation as indigenous women in the different national, regional and community levels. The Final Declaration of the Encuentro stated that 'the Coordinadora Nacional de Mujeres Indígenas de México [be established] in order to articulate ourselves at the national level, to concretize and fortify the project of free (self) determination of our Indian pueblos'.

47 Reflecting the convergence of diverse roots of the CONAMI, the convening organizations included: Servicios de Pueble Mixe 'Ser', Unión de Comunidades Indígenas de la Zona Norte del Itsmo, A.C. (UCIZONI), Mujeres Olividadad del Ricón Mixe, Oaxaca, Asociación Rural de Interés Colectivo (Aric-Democrático), Chiapas, Jolom Mayaetick and J'Pas Lumetik, Chiapas, Central Independiente de Obreros Agrícolas y Campesinos (CIOAC), Chiapas, Maseual Siuamej Mosenyolchicauani, Puebla, Unión de Mujeres Campesinas de Xilitla, San Luis Potosí, Comisión de Mujeres de la ANIPA, Sedac-Covac de Hidalgo, Comisión de Mujeres del Congreso Nacional Indígena.

of some of our compañeros that do not understand the importance of women being here participating the same way as men... ¡ Nunca más un México sin Nosotras! !Nunca más una rebelión sin nosotras! ¡ Nunca más una vida sin nosotras! ¡ Viva el Encuentro Nacional de Mujeres Indígenas![48]

With the attendance of 700 women coming from diverse states, pueblos and organizations, the formation of the CONAMI was seen as a mandate from the gathering that achieved a significant representation of indigenous pueblos of Mexico. The founding documents laid down by the CONAMI defined it as being plural, inclusive and independent space with a direct participation of indigenous women. While they sought recognition and respect from governmental institutions and social organizations, they declared themselves autonomous from political parties.[49]

Since its formal founding at the 1997 Oaxaca Encuentro, the work of the CONAMI has focused on indigenous women's human rights, reproductive health, stopping family and military violence, and collective self-education on international and national treaties, pacts, accords and conventions concerning the rights of indigenous peoples, specifically indigenous women. In order to demand recognition of their rights by the different levels of government, the CONAMI educates other indigenous women on signed governmental accords, the fourth Article of the Constitution, as well as international laws and treaties such as the Convention on the Elimination of All Forms of Discrimination against Women, the work of the International Working Group on Indigenous Peoples, the International Labor Organisation's Convention 169, and the Convention of Biological Diversity among others. The organization engages in dialogue through seminars, workshops and, meetings to delineate demands against the state and cultural demands, discuss women's participation in the UN Decade of Indigenous Peoples and to strategize ways of guaranteeing indigenous women's rights in the movement for the Mexican Constitutional Recognition of the Rights of Indigenous Peoples.[50]

The CONAMI holds bi-monthly national workshops and has been training promotoras in areas ranging from reproductive health, human rights, prevention of violence against, and indigenous women's autonomy. The axes in which CONAMI promotoras are trained and the topics of the national workshops are two-fold in focus, which is characteristic of all of the CONAMI's work to guarantee indigenous women's human rights on both internal and external levels of indigenous pueblos

---

48 Ibid., p. 8.

49 Plenary on the Plan of Action for the CONAMI, II Encuentro Nacional de Mujeres Indígenas.

50 The stated objectives of the CONAMI are: to construct a space of analysis and reflection on the problems confronting indigenous women in Mexico; to sensitize indigenous pueblos and national society about the respect of the human rights of indigenous women, including a vision of gender; to influence in an organized manner the political, social and cultural processes that affect indigenous women; to fortify and consolidate the Coordinadora Nacional de Mujeres Indígenas of Mexico as a site of coordination between all organizations, networks, and projects as a plural and inclusive space of indigenous women throughout the country; and to fortify the processes of autonomy and self determination of indigenous pueblos, with a conscious and true participation of women.

(communities). On the internal community level, indigenous women's organizing has included demands for reproductive health, campaigns against violence against women and interfamilial violence, a call for greater participation of women in the decision making structures of their pueblos, a reconsideration of traditional cultural customs and practices (usos y costumbres) so that they do not violate women's human rights, the right for women to inherit land or access to land in communal structures. Training and discussion of issues external to the pueblos in which indigenous women reside include demands for human, cultural, collective and territorial rights of pueblos indios, the violence against indigenous women carried out by police and military forces as well as state agencies, international conventions on labour, discrimination against women, intellectual property rights and biological diversity.

The Coordinadora Nacional de Mujeres Indígenas operates as a representative coordinating body of the organized indigenous women's movement in Mexico which is comprised of approximately 100 organizations where members participate as representatives of their own pueblo, community or regional-based organizations. While a good number the participants belong to independent indigenous women's groups, the majority belong to mixed gender organizations so the CONAMI functions as a vital space of participation and reflection on how to address their political, economic, cultural and social problems and devise strategies surrounding the specificity of their lived conditions as indigenous peoples, women and members of the most economically marginalized communities in the nation.

The Coordinadora Nacional de Mujeres Indígenas mirrors the diversity of mobilized sectors within the indigenous movement. The CONAMI includes representatives of local and regional organizations that represent a geographical range and broad spectrum of kinds of organizations. Many women come from indigenous councils, unions and assemblies, some with traditional community orientation or regional councils comprising a several indigenous organizations and others more focused on indigenous rights and political mobilization which include organizations like the Unión de Comunidades Indígenas de la Zona Norte del Istmo, A.C. (UCIZONI) and Servicios del Pueblo Mixe, A.C. (SER) from Oaxaca or the Consejo Guerrerense 500 Años de Resistenica Indígena, as well as the Consejo de Pueblos Nahuas del Alto Balsas from Guerrero, Consejo de la Nacionalidad Nauhautl from Estado de México or the Nación Purhéphecha/Zapatista from Michoacán. There are also an impressive number of indigenous women's organizations such as Grupo de Mujeres Indígenas and Masehaulcihuame (meaning women who work together and support one another) from Puebla, Mujeres Indígenas en Lucha and Mujeres Independientes both from Guerrero, Mujeres Olvidadas del Rincón Mixe from Oaxaca, Grupo Erandi (meaning Dawn in Purhépecha) from Michoacán, those who come from women's organizations like the Grupo de Mujeres de San Cristóbal de las Casas Chiapas.

The diversity of organizations represented in the CONAMI is an example of the forms of differential consciousness forged out of a longer history of regional organizing, which effectively expand new social spaces of participation through national organizing. A large cross section come to the CONAMI from peasant organizations, both mixed and women's groups, such as the Consejo Estatal de Organizaciones Indígenas y Campesinas (CEOIC), the Asociación Rural de Interés

Colectivo (ARIC-Democrático), and the Central Independiente de Obreros Agrícolas y Campesinos (CIOAC) all from Chiapas –as well as women's rural and peasant organizations like the Unión de Mujeres Campesinas de Xilitla from San Luis Potosí, the S.S.S. Titekititoketaome Sihuame from Guerrero and the S.S.S. Maseual Siuamej Mosenyolchicauani from Puebla. There are also women participating from groups organized around productive projects such as small coffee producers from Vera Cruz and Puebla, and women's weaving collectives such as J'Pas Lumetik, and Jolom Mayaetik, Organización de Mujeres Artesanas Expulsadas de Chamula (OMAECH). K'inal Antsetik, meaning women's land in Tzetzal, is a feminist NGO that has worked on empowering indigenous women in the areas of commercialization of *artesanía*, women's human rights, indigenous women's rights and reproductive health. Founded in Chiapas with an office in Mexico City, K'inal has had a historically close relationship to the CONAMI training promotoras and sharing office space and resources with them with the goal of the CONAMI operating in an independent manner. Nellys Palomo of K'inal Antsetik has advised and accompanied the birth and growth of the indigenous women's movement through her close role as adviser and facilitator, as well as through her writings. While they participate in women's commissions of the National Indigenous Congress (CNI), the CONAMI has the commitment to remain autonomous of both the CNI and ANIPA in a commitment to working together as women despite any tensions or divisions in the larger movement.

The Coordinadora Nacional de Mujeres Indígenas, as a coordinating body, functions like a network with very little hierarchy or bureaucracy. The network approach is important because it is in alignment with indigenous philosophies about forms of power and representation that the indigenous movement is explicitly constructing. These philosophies are based on a commitment to a plural and open process, decision making based on indigenous practices of consensus building within community councils and assemblies, and a lack of concentration of power where positions of power are seen as a service to community under the philosophy '*mandar obediciendo*'. But as spaces within indigenous traditions where there are uneven traditions regarding women's participation, their mobilization has been critical to making the new forms of power (based on old modes of indigenous practice) truly democratic in terms of gender.

The first act of the CONAMI as organization was to organize the Second Continental Encuentro of Indigenous Women from the First Nations of Abya Yala, 'Advancing in Diversity, Constructing our Identity' in Mexico City in 1997. Other work in forging multi-tiered spaces for women's participation include National workshops held every two months where women come from diverse regions to Mexico City to gain training as community educators in a range of topics. The Segundo Encuentro Nacional de Mujeres Indígenas in Mexico was held 31 March through 2 April, 2000 in Chilpancingo, Guerrero. Organized and convened by the CONAMI, participants from a wide array of indigenous women's groups, as well as mixed indigenous organizations, came from across the country to discuss the theme of the conference, ¡ *Construyendo la Equidad, Democracia y Justicia*! (Constructing Equity, Democracy and Justice.) With participation ranging from 350 to 500 indigenous women from over 12 states, this was a strong showing for the second national encuentro that included delegates representing over 50 different organizations ranging from cooperatives of weavers and artisans, human rights organizations, independent women's organizations, traditional indigenous councils, social solidarity societies, and campesino organizations.[51]

Multiplying the Spaces of Autonomy: Locating the Practice of Autonomy in the Embedded Structures of Indigenous Women's Lives

The call for autonomy forms the larger framework of basic rights for indigenous people that includes the right to be a pueblo, the right to land and protection of territory, the right to self determination and autonomy, the right to their own cultural traditions and forms of political representation and jurisprudence, the right to protect and use the natural resources of the land, among others. Autonomy, asserted as a legal claim of collective group rights, has been intertwined and woven with threads of Mexican nationalism. One of the more subtle and sophisticated discourses of Zapatismo, that has been echoed throughout the indigenous movement, is the way that it poses a challenge to the State while grounded itself historically within the legacy of the Mexican Revolution.[52] As indigenous women began to enunciate themselves as autonomous political subjects, they not only looked to the state to demand their rights as citizen/subjects but they turned to the place where the practice of those rights occur. Thus, indigenous women turned to their homes, communities, and traditional indigenous customs of governance so that they could transform not only discourse of autonomy but the practice of autonomy which is at the very heart of any project of decolonization.

While the demand for autonomy is the framework for basic rights of indigenous peoples in Mexico, women are shifting the way in which this demand has been seen until now as a juridical framework used to contest state power. Autonomy in the eyes of indigenous women has also come to mean – not just something the state can grant a people or a right guaranteed by the state – but a faculty or capacity (*facultad*) built from the ground up. Congress recently passed new legislation on indigenous rights that activists denounce as undermining the San Andrés Accords and the basic guarantee for indigenous self-determination. This change in state strategy from denial to state co-option has sent the indigenous movement to re-gather its political forces and redirect its strategies and organizing efforts. In light of the latest move by the government to renege on the peace talks, indigenous women's effort to put autonomy in to practice in every sphere of life experience has become ever more

---

51 Delegates came from a diverse indigenous pueblos including Mixe, Tzotzil, Tlapaneco, Mixteco, Amuzga, Nahua, Purépecha, Maya, Ña-ñhu, Zapoteco, Mazateco, Totonaco, and Mazahaua from the states of Puebla, Jalisco, Estado de México, Yucatán, Quintana Roo, Guerrero, Oaxaca, Michoacán, Chiapas, Querétaro, Hidalgo, and Veracruz.

52 In an important article that examines how various forms of historical as well as new proposals for autonomy have differed from indigenous region to another, Lynn Stephen offers an analysis of how re-appropriated forms of nationalism provide a shared sense of national belonging while at the same time making specific claims for indigenous autonomy. See her article 'Redefined Nationalism in building a Movement for Indigenous Autonomy in Southern Mexico', *Journal of Latin American Anthropology*, 3(1) (1997), 72–101.

important in implementing and sustaining a struggle for self-determination for the long haul. Their efforts are an important first step in the practice of self-determination because it grounds the call for autonomy into the localized practices and spaces that determine the conditions of indigenous women's lives.

For example, this kind of critical remapping of autonomy occurred at the Taller Nacional (National Workshop) 'Las Mujeres Indígenas en el proceso autonómico' organized by the CONAMI held 20–21 August 1999 in Mexico City. The national workshop included representatives from Querétaro, Guerrero, Oaxaca, Chiapas, Veracruz, Michoacán, Jalisco, and Quintana Roo and focused first on international and national frameworks for indigenous autonomy. Familiarizing participants with the reforms to Article 4 of the Constitution proposed by indigenous women to the National Indigenous Forum and the ILO Convention 169 by distributing copies in multiple indigenous language, the first day focused on reviewing the frameworks for autonomy and examining where indigenous women fit into them. Several speakers drew upon experiences of existing autonomous regions such as the Zapatista regions in Chiapas, Rancho Nuevo a la Democracia in Guerrero, and San Miguel de la Laguna in Michoacán to discuss how women have been participating in these forms of regional autonomy.

At the workshop there was an emphasis on autonomy as a capacity and a practice linked to their lived experience. After the presentations, the participants broke down into working groups where they began to construct a shared understanding of how indigenous women's demand for autonomy multiplies the levels and spaces of the practice of autonomy from the perspective of their daily lives. Complementing the conventional modes of autonomy based on pueblos, municipalities and regions, the participants called for indigenous women's autonomy to include a range of spaces and practices such as the home, their communities, their bodily integrity and self-determination of life decisions. Autonomy has become an important political tool and mode of consciousness in discussing the ways women enact cultural autonomy when practicing their socializing roles in the community, in how they refuse commodification of their cultures and bodies by maintaining traditional dress, and in how they recuperate indigenous forms of medicinal knowledge, nutrition, and agriculture.

While supporting the indigenous movement's demands for autonomy, indigenous women have claimed autonomy as a capacity that is developed and as a political tool used to democratize and empower indigenous women's own autonomy within the embedded gender structures that shape their lives. Indigenous women engage in a decolonizing practice of creating new forms of autonomy in their own social and political worlds as precursory and parallel strategies to state contestation and negotiation.[53] Perhaps the most succinct formulation of the indigenous women's movement expansion of autonomy into the daily lived structures of their lives is

---

53 Subaltern studies historian, Partha Chatterjee, argues that it is not through engagement in conflict with the state but within the cultural realm that prefigures this struggle where a decolonizing political imaginary is constituted creating a domain of sovereignty within colonial society. See his *The Nation and Its Fragments. Colonial and Postcolonial Histories.* (Princeton, NJ: Princeton University Press), 1993.

in the *Indigenous Women's Proposals about the Reforms to the Fourth Article of the Constitution* presented in January 1996 to the National Indigenous Congress. Reaffirming that the place for guaranteeing women's rights is within a larger call for indigenous autonomy, they state '[o]ur rights as indigenous women find the space for resolution in the recognition of Autonomy for the Pueblos Indios, as the most democratic way, beginning with our persons, from our homes, to the community and people and embedded in the State'. Their statement reflects the innovative way indigenous women have expanded the call for autonomy:

> Autonomy in its economic dimension refers to our right as indigenous women to have equal access and control over the means of production. Political autonomy is backed by basic political rights, to have representation. Physical autonomy involves the decisions about our body and the possibility of living without violence, and sociocultural autonomy refers to the right to express our specific and self-determined identities as indigenous women, personally and collectively sustained and enriched by our vital, social and community processes.[54]

Indigenous women's proposals for autonomy have generated controversy because some critics feel that indigenous women's expansion of autonomy is a destabilizing current that can potentially derail what is essentially a legal claim to the state to share power where indigenous pueblos would be in charge of exercising power of self-governance. Yet, at the Second National Encuentro of Indigenous Women held in Chilpancingo, Guerrero in April of 2000, the discussion grounded the indigenous women's call for autonomy as a complementary practice of collective self-determination and liberation within indigenous pueblos.

The discussion of the participation of women in the Processes of Autonomy for Indigenous Peoples was lead by Tomasa Sandoval (Purhépecha, Michoacán), member of the Organización Nación Purhépecha Zapatista, who reflected about the question of autonomy drawing from experiences in Michoacán. She laid out the basic proposal for indigenous autonomy in Mexico noting that the seeming tension between autonomy of indigenous women and the autonomy of indigenous pueblos are 'dos rostros de un mismo problema' (two faces of the same problem). Historicizing the larger national call for autonomy with the EZLN uprising in 1994, she noted that autonomy had two dimensions. First, the individual right of each human being to autonomy in which the call for autonomy for indigenous women fit and second, a corresponding notion of the collective right to autonomy for indigenous peoples. Cutting through the ways that these two questions have been called contradictory, Sandoval stated 'More precisely, we insist that the right to autonomy for indigenous women can not exist unless the autonomy of indigenous pueblos is guaranteed.'[55]

Sandoval argued that it is important to see autonomy as a faculty (*facultad*) that has emerged historically out of relations of domination and inequality. Indigenous

---

54 'Indigenous Women's Proposals to the National Indigenous Congress', trans. Jonathan Fox, *Cultural Survival Quarterly*, 23(1) (Spring, 1999), 52–53.

55 Más bien tratamos de insistir de que el derecho de autonomía de las mujeres indígenas no puede existir sin no se garantiza la autonomía de los pueblos indios. Es decir, el derecho individual y el derecho colectivo no se contraponen sino se complementen.

pueblos have sought out autonomy based on the historic projects and cultures of their peoples and many pueblos have practiced limited forms of community autonomy for centuries with traditional structures operating outside of the purview of the State. Sandoval claimed that whereas autonomy is largely thought of as a juridical question, she noted that the call for various levels of autonomy – the individual, communal, municipal, and regional – were interlinked and vital to one another. In relationship to the indigenous demand for autonomy, she suggested that without a consideration of women, it would not be '...a complete autonomy because women's right to land and to equality with men is not recognized'.[56]

Delegates deliberated the question of autonomy within the working groups and the final declaration of the Encuentro reflected the critical work of indigenous women in multiplying the spaces where autonomy is practiced and inflecting it with gendered demands and considerations:

> We believe that autonomy of our pueblos overlaps [intersects] each area of our lives, the home, the family, the community, the region and that this has to be seen with the respect and recognition of our culture, our territories, our traditional medicines. For us, autonomy means parity, democracy, and equity between men and women, indigenous and non-indigenous, that is to say between all human beings and above all, that our rights as original peoples that we are be recognized.[57]

Women's rights within indigenous cultures and the larger movement's call for autonomy are seen as 'two faces of the same coin,' or complementary because indigenous women's autonomy can not exist without the guarantee of the autonomy of indigenous pueblos. Because autonomy is practiced within the material conditions of indigenous women's lives, it is embedded within the communal structures safeguarded by the proposals for autonomy. For this reason indigenous women have been active to ensure those structures also respect the autonomy of indigenous women.

This sense of complementarity has been the product of a series of dialogues that preceded the Second National Encuentro, but it was reaffirmed and clarified

---

56 Aunque no es una autonomía completa porque no se reconoce el derecho a la tierra de la mujeres indígenas o una igualdad con los varones, sí tienen prácticas autónomas como la de elegir a sus propias autoridades mediante una democracia más directa, organizar las faenas o el trabajo comunitario, cuidar y conservar los bosques, las aguas o las mines y organizar las fiestas en que participa toda la communidad.

57 Nosotras decimos que queremos encontrar eco en nuestra voz y que esta retumbe en cada uno de los rincones de nuestro territorio, que fluya como nuestros rios y mares, que sople como el viento y se enraice en nuestra madre tierra para que las futures generaciones tengan una historias que contar sobre como las mujeres inciamos este largo camino de luchar por una autonomía para los pueblos indios con voz y rostro de mujer donde tenga valor lo que decimos y pensamos y que la libre determinación de nuestros pueblos sea un caminar junto entre hombres y mujeres. Consideramos que la autonomía de nuestros pueblos atraviesa todos los ámbitos de nuestras vidas, el hogar, la familia, la comunidad, la región, y que esta tiene que ver con el respeto y reconocimiento de nuestra cultura, nuestros territorios, nuestra medicina tradicional. Para nosotras la autonomía quiere decir la paridad, democracia y equidad entre hombres y mujeres, entre indígenas y no indígenas, es decir entre todos los seres humanos y sobre todo que sean reconocidos nuestros derechos como pueblos originarios que somos.

at the Encuentro where the legal call for autonomy was grounded into the levels which most directly impact the way indigenous women live. Through this series of meetings where indigenous women have constructed their discourse and philosophy of autonomy they have come to understand autonomy, not just as a collective right that the State grants, but a practice that they have begun to incorporate into each aspect of social organization. The exploration of the meaning of indigenous autonomy for women lead the small working groups at the Encuentro to discuss how autonomy is practiced for indigenous women in areas ranging from the communal control of environmental resources, to the guarding and renewal of indigenous forms of medicinal knowledge, to their own role as mothers who socialize children, to how questions of autonomy affect child rearing practices, health and education. This critical understanding that came out of the working groups amplifies the concept of autonomy into a practice of collective self determination for women encompassing: economic autonomy (the right to access and control over production and the right to land); political autonomy (to have the right to representation as a people and as women within their pueblos); physical autonomy (living without violence, the right to chose a partner, and when and how many children to bear); and social and cultural autonomy (the right to wear their traditional dress and the right to reproduce and contribute to their own identities and indigenous cultures, and the right to collectively sustain collective or communal structures).

Conclusion: Dislodging the Order of Discourse and the Struggle for Self-Representation

The most basic act of autonomy, to speak for oneself, brings us back full circle to the question regarding the order of discourse of the nation. Indigenous women are calling for collective self-representation and the fact that they have come to a national space of articulation and taken up voice destabilizes decades of *indigenista* state discourse. Mapping this convergence of systems of power, Márgara Millán asserts that as indigenous women, 'they are subjects "without voice" and so their capacity to resist resides in discourse, and within that meaning, that which is recuperated in a central manner through Zapatismo and through feminism and that is because both emanated from the experience of being "other". Gender and ethnicity, like class, share in differing ways being vectors of power and subjectivity'.[58]

CONAMI member, Hermelinda Tiburcio from Rancho Nuevo de la Democracia has also spoken of the importance of indigenous women speaking for themselves. In a denunciation of human rights violations at the Second National Encuentro in Chilpancingo she insisted on the need for 'Those [women] with their own voice to state what they are experiencing in the indigenous zones because much of the time it is from the desks [those who have the power to write] who say that nothing is occurring in the indigenous zones'.[59] Speaking against official silence and a

---

58 Millan, p. 24.

59 Las que con su propia voz digan lo que ellas sienten en las zonas indígenas, porque muchas veces los que saben escribir lo hacen por ellas y muchas veces desde los escritorios dicen que no ocurre nada en las zona indígenas.

government generated discourse that denies violence against indigenous women, sterilization abuses and increased rapes by the federal military during the growing militarization of indigenous communities in Mexico, Tiburcio's statement presents a startling and simple truth that speaks against power and a history of silence. Indigenous women have been kept silent through state generated discourses of *indigenismo* that even in its best intentions paternalistically viewed culture as static in their attempt to recognize the 'traditions and communities' of indigenous people. It has failed to take into account that traditions are lived and ever changing and that in this process of social transformation coming from the roots of indigenous communities, indigenous women have seen that a culture that is not changing and whose members do not engage it, is a dead culture. Part of changing the discourse of indigenismo has been to take the right to represent indigenous cultures away from the government, anthropologists or technical bureaucrats – essentially take their culture back – reclaiming it from the dusty, stale air of museums to bring to public light that tradition and culture are lived.

Tiburcio's understanding that the knowledge that is produced at official desks generates a discursive reality is key in how indigenous women are shifting the order of discourse and creating their own. This subtle and complex understanding refuses the romanticized view characteristic of early feminist ethnography that focused on 'giving voice' to its subjects or that indigenous women, as speaking subjects, are the bearers of truth in and of themselves. It reflects an understanding of the constructed nature of discourse and that those who have been the objects of the knowledge/power produced at the desks of state technocrats are challenging the reality that was produced by that discourse. Other political analysts such as Neil Harvey have also recognized what is at stake in this struggle over power, representation and meaning within the Indigenous Movement:

> Officials representing the government in the peace negotiations recognized that adding a fourth level of government (in addition to municipalities, states, and the national government) through formally establishing autonomous indigenous regions (multi-ethnic or mono-ethnic) could severely curb the state's ability to define who was 'indigenous' and could provide the basis for mounting a national political challenge... in some regions of the country.[60]

The order of discourse where the state defines indigenous identity and regulates these identities through a set of relations of rule has been disrupted. The ability to have access to representation, especially self-representation, has been denied to indigenous women. There is a lot at stake in shifting the registers of meaning and signification and being able to build their own collective selves, visions and voice.

Thus, the critical work in changing the order of discourse to dismantle indigenismo – as a state project of assimilation – has required indigenous women to shift conditions of enunciability. They have been successful in shifting these conditions to challenge unequal power relationships within the distinct sites of power that overlap to create a matrix of domination from the home, to community assemblies, to local forms of caciquismo, to state policies and economic programs,

---

60 Harvey (1998, pp. 147–148).

to contesting the identity the state has imposed on them. Often translating these shifts in the conditions of enunciability to the material and subjective conditions that rule their lives (for example from reproductive health to tradition medicine, calls for education to international and national accords on indigenous rights), they have begun a process of cultural and democratic renewal that does not rely solely on the State to make change. Deploying a new form of differential consciousness, indigenous women have created their own counter discourses and practices renewing their cultural identities and claims to citizenship in relationship to the question of autonomy.

Conclusion

This book has explored some of the processes or methodological associations that often crop up in Latin American studies on women and nationalisms. It foregrounds, for example, the exclusive nature implicit in the national phenomenon because of the currency of the idea that nationalism is a doctrine invented in Europe and given its fullest expression in the public sphere, the sphere dominated and controlled by men. When the discussion is put in a Latin American context, we discover that there are many different ways in which this phenomenon may be analysed in theoretical and empirical terms. The broad scope of the subject and multiple creative corollaries has determined the 'typification' of nationalisms, given the impossibility of using one type of nationalism as the starting point. This methodological procedure is inevitable in any academic study of nationalism. Hence, we have based our study on the documentary evidence and discernible existence of three nationalisms. The first type refers to those heroic gestures and independence struggles undertaken expressly to abolish the colonial regime and to set up independent republics. The next type includes the state's instrumental and symbolic construction of the nation in order to unite populations in linguistic and cultural terms, considering the diversity of geographical, regional and ethnic differences. The last type of nationalism concerns the contestation on the part of many different ethnic and gender groups to the nation-state. With varying degrees of creativity, these groups have resisted linguistic and cultural assimilation, considered a global exigency and an ideal for unifying nations which promised to be the chosen land for development and modernization.

These three types of nationalism, which Gutiérrez explains and exemplifies in the first chapter, constitute the methodological starting point for the subsequent case studies. A variety of themes were covered in this book. One way of organizing the results and reaching a congruent conclusion from this diversity and creativity of situations is to invert the main topics running through the three kinds of nationalism and to re-arrange the chapters. The construction of the nation-state (the second type of nationalism) poses one of those paradoxes of the sensitive field of gender and ethnicity, which concerns the processes of exclusion and inclusion. As instrument and institution, the state seeks national unity by including the citizens of a given country, but its lengthy and strategic process eventually excludes indigenous communities, immigrants and women from the symbolic body of the dominant cultural group. This exclusion is rendered visible in the widespread structural poverty and cultural loss of prestige of indigenous people.

Our methodological approach proposes the five intersections vis-à-vis women and nationalisms (See Introduction and Chapter 1, Anthias and Yuval-Davis, 1989) in conjunction with the three types of nationalism; these intersections exert a great influence on the congruent and prospective study of the different cases and themes within this book. For example, one can obviously provide the proof for the argument that women are the 'biological reproducers' of collective movements. However, as Leticia Paredes (Chapter 7) demonstrates in her monograph on the leadership of a Maya woman, it was her sense of unfilled motherhood that made her become a political activist.

The cases studied in this volume reveal, once again, the possibility of linking and/ or comparing examples that challenge the methodological starting points originally proposed. Taking things in order, let us begin with the first instance: women as 'active transmitters and producers of national culture'. The influential theory of nationalism proposed by E. Gellner (See Chapter 1) emphasizes how crucial the official educational system is to the forming of a nation. Undoubtedly, women, as the teachers during that important stage of literacy and the implantation of the values and principles of national unity, play a role of the utmost significance. This aspect of gender has been widely documented, but its discussion within the context of the different theories of nationalism has not received enough attention. While fully recognizing the significance of Gellner's modernist theory, we discover that women have moved, in qualitative terms, from one form of nationalism to another (from independence to the nation-state) in relation to their literacy and access to knowledge. Formerly mostly illiterate or semi-illiterate, they have become, within a century, the campaigners for and teachers in the national educational system. Our recognition of women as the 'transmitters' of national culture returns us to Mimí Derba's cinematographic work (García, Chapter 5), to Anita Brenner's career as a cultural journalist and to Astrid Hadad's performances (Gutiérrez, Chapter 1). The theme common to all these creative women is the conceptualization and transmission of their visions of 'Mexican-ness' which involves arduous and systematic intellectual work. The nations of Latin America have ceased to be that historical masculine sphere; for this reason, the supposed exclusivity of the male public sphere is transferable and may be located in the imaginary of these creative women who take on the task of envisioning, defending and imagining their culture.

Another aspect of women's intellectual creativity with respect to the renewed interest in the culture to which they belong is the (re-) telling of collective mythologies in the Quechua language. Ignored by official history, these narratives are currently being revisited and transmitted by women and indigenous peoples (Choque and Delgado, Chapter 9). An outstanding contribution has been made by Dolores Cacuango, an indigenous woman who bases her ideas of reconciliation and national unity on ethnic pride (Bernal, Chapter 2). Her proposal that the plan for the future should be underpinned by the concept of 'fatherland' or 'nation' has been so successful that it is among those put forward by indigenous movements in modern Ecuador.

We observe that women, whether they be indigenous or not, as 'intellectual creators' (rather than mere 'biological reproducers'), have participated actively in constructing the nation which challenges, under their authorship, the official histories and meta-narratives. The creative women discussed in the pages of this book all play an inspiring role in the construction of national identity and culture.

Women as 'symbolic signifiers of differences' bring to the fore how they are romanticized and idealized in the different languages that attempt to popularize a sense of belonging and collective identity among the masses. A perfect example is

Schneider's study of the photographs in Gaby Herbstein's calendar (Chapter 4). The photographer and the producer of the calendar do, indeed, exploit the archetypal image of a beautiful body in commercial terms (tall, skinny and impassive models), placed in an indigenous, wild and mythological background, in order to transmit to the spectators the Argentinian 'ethnic origin'. In Schneider's opinion, the result is idealized and portrays stereotypes of beauty and aesthetics in Argentinian urban society. It demonstrates how the Indian universe is appropriated by utilizing non-European artefacts and contexts and by refusing to negotiate or transgress the conventional stereotypes of beauty. In Argentinian society, the task of re-fashioning and recuperating indigenous symbols has received little attention, especially when we compare it to the drive and continuity it has in cultural policy in Mexico. There is still room for extreme idealization that meets the demands of non-indigenous consumers. We might remember, for example, that passage in Schneider's analysis in which a lizard is placed on the head of a model, supposedly a *Toba*, since the reptile is related to the cosmogony of this indigenous group. However, the lizard has lost its cultural and symbolic meaning of rain-forest exuberance, because nowadays most *Toba people* are members of the Pentecostal Church.

The representation of the fatherland as a woman is another powerful instance of the debate concerning the 'signifiers' of national differences. Robust 'mestizo' women depicted as protectors symbolizing the 'fatherland' or placed in rural Mexican settings have been the illustrations on cards and calendars since the 1940s, as they have on the covers of free textbooks (1960). In this kind of visual language – the calendar is widely distributed and easy to buy – it is clear that female archetypes are fashioned to emulate and inspire a sense of identification with the value and information system deemed most appropriate for each national identity. Whereas the Argentinian identity seeks western bodies and beauties placed in mythologized and exotic settings, Mexican self-representation prefers happy mestizo women placed in rural scenarios or transformed into exotic figures of the fatherland, such as the case of the indigenous fictitious heroine, Eréndira (Chapter 6).

One theme that crops up in several chapters is that of the defence of natural resources and the symbolic loss of access to the same. Thus, we have read of those women who, in spite of their extreme marginality, look for creative ways to express the collective imperative to control resources, to be in the position to take decisions and to contribute to the planning of their agendas and strategies. For this reason, women are also 'active participants in national struggles'. Lazos's study of the *Nahua* women in the Sierra Santa Marta (Chapter 3) presents a wide spectrum of inequalities, rendered visible by their marginality and lack of resources, which at once reveal a marked loss of prestige in both the family and the community. For these women, access to resources represents their interrelation with the symbolic space, 'the mountain', which makes their collective life meaningful. It is, moreover, the 'area of primary vegetation' that provides the knowledge and creativity they need for the continuity of their rituals, customs and festivities, among others. The reduction of this space means they have lost access to the 'the mountain' and, subsequently, to their cultural symbols; in this situation, women have had to produce alternative strategies for survival and empowerment. This does not mean that they have overcome their harrowing marginal existence; indeed, we observe in other contexts that the structural poverty of women has motivated them to organize themselves politically as much to have access to as to defend the resources.

The growing mobilization of women seeking the opening of spaces which leads to political representation, the power to take decisions and the recognition of their rights is another constant, particularly in the studies of Lazos (Chapter 3) and Blackwell (Chapter 10). In this respect, Blackwell argues that the agenda and policies of the nation-state have led to the three-fold exclusion of indigenous women. To their exclusion by gender, race and poverty, Delgado and Cheque (Chapter 9) add a fourth, due to modernity: the lack of information at the service of indigenous women. Another kind of political participation, following the vertical and corporative lines of the dominant party, is that shown by *Doña Emiliana* in Yucatán. What is particularly worth noting, in this case, is her awareness and use of ethnicity; dressed in the Maya *pupil* and shawl, she plays a key role in the organization of the local constituency groups of the Revolutionary Institutional Party, in exchange for status and remuneration (Paredes, Chapter 7).

The first chapter proposes that access to knowledge is related to the impact and development of modernity. High rates of illiteracy were the norm to pre-nationalist women. For this reason, women did not contribute to the first type of nationalism, through literature and the press. What motivated to defence of and struggle for sovereignty was their awareness of their poverty, exclusion and discrimination. In this way, we may draw a parallel between the women who struggled for the fatherland and those of today who mobilize and organize themselves to defend their patrimony or gain access to resources to improve their conditions, which are not necessarily those set out officially. The difference between the first nationalism and the defence and struggle behind the mobilization of contemporary indigenous women is that now they do not have to act as men in order to overcome the inequalities (Zárate, Chapter 8), nor do they have to write under pseudonyms to communicate new modes of thought to an audience unaccustomed to reading women's ideas or to admiring nationalist aesthetics women propose and implement.

In conclusion, the cases which document the five intersections of gender and nationalism appear to be included in the three historical types of nationalism. This means that these intersections are not particular or exclusive to one period, one change or structural transformation espoused by the state. Every type of nationalism works in contradiction: it strives to create inclusive national unity, but in the process it excludes ethnic groups and women, and, therefore, indigenous women. Far from drawing its last breath, the nationalist phenomenon may be noted in the resurgence of indigenous groups within the consolidated nation-states, in which women play such an active role that they have become political and intellectual leaders. Like those who envisaged and made the fatherland, or rather contributed to nationalist aesthetics on their own terms, these women have made the proposal of focusing on how autonomy and independence can be created so that they have power of decision, equal access to and control of resources, and, above all, enjoy life in a violence-free society in which every human right is guaranteed; their ultimate aim is to express their love and feeling for their culture, for their patrimony or territory and for their history. The theoretical framework of nationalisms demonstrates its limitless elasticity, which can sustain the multiple cases of women struggling to defend and recuperate their cultures. There can be no doubt that nationalisms have long since ceased to be those doctrines fabricated in Europe, which were imported and transmitted by a masculine elite of the nation-states on the new continent.

Index